[redacted]

AF732698

First Glance

Childhood Creations of the Famous

Tuli Kupferberg and Sylvia Topp

HAMMOND INCORPORATED
MAPLEWOOD, NEW JERSEY
New York Chicago Los Angeles

Book design by Dwight Dobbins
Cover illustration by Victor Valla

Library of Congress Cataloging in Publication Data
Main entry under title:
First glance.
1. Biography. I. Kupferberg, Tuli.
II. Topp, Sylvia.
CT105.F47 920'.02 77-17424
ISBN 0-8437-3403-5
ISBN 0-8437-3402-7 pbk.

© COPYRIGHT 1978
BY TULI KUPFERBERG AND SYLVIA TOPP

All rights reserved. No part of this book may be reproduced or utilized in any form or by any means, electronic or mechanical, including photocopying, recording or by any information storage or retrieval system, without permission in writing from the Publisher.

PRINTED IN THE UNITED STATES OF AMERICA

CONTENTS

The creations of all children in whatever forms they choose to express themselves are always interesting.

And how fascinating it is to study the first works of young people who later become well known.

This book allows us a *first glance* into what obscure dreams and experiences help to form the adults we later came to know so well.

H. G. Wells
Age 12

At his companion's request Ebenezer recited the poem.

"Very good," Sayer said when it was done. "Methinks it puts your notion aptly enough, though I'm no critic. Yet 'tis a mystery to me, what ye'll sing of save your innocence. Prithee recite me the other piece."

"Nay, 'tis but a silly quatrain I wrote as a lad—the first I ever rhymed. And I've but three lines of't in my memory."

"Ah, a pity. The Laureate's first song: 'twould fetch a price someday, I'll wager, when thou'rt famous the world o'er. Might ye treat me to the three ye have?"

Ebenezer hesitated. "Thou'rt not baiting me?"

"Nay!" Sayer assured him. "'Tis a mere natural curiosity, is't not, to wonder how flew the mighty eagle as a fledgling? Do we not admire old Plutarch's tales of young Alcibiades flinging himself before the carter, or Demosthenes shaving half his head, or Caesar taunting the Cilician pirates? And would ye not yourself delight in hearing a childish line of Shakespeare's, or mighty Homer's?"

"I would, right enough," Ebenezer admitted.

John Barth, *The Sot-Weed Factor*

This lexicon, compiled by Sholom Aleichem before he was 15, can be considered his first work.

It is a list of all the curse words his new stepmother addressed him with, which he tastefully and alphabetically arranged for the convenience of the reader.

SHOLOM ALEICHEM
born Feb. 18, 1859
Pereyaslavl, Ukraine

Before age 15

STEPMOTHER'S VOCABULARY

A—Annoyance, ape, apostate, apple-thief, ass.
B—Bare-bottom, barker, beast, bedbug, beggar, belly-ache, belly-button, blinker, blockhead, bone-in-the-throat, boor, botcher, bottomless-gullet, brother-in-sorrow, bully, butcher.
C—Cake-and-honey, cap, carcass, cattle, cheat, cheeky, clown, cockroach, convert, cow, crazy, creature, cripple, cry-baby.
D—Dandy, devil, dirty-mouth, dog-catcher, donkey, don't-touch-me.
E—Ear-ache, eel, effigy, egg, empty-barrel.
F—Fiend, fool, foundling, frog.
G—Gambler, garbage, glutton, good-for-nothing, greedy.
H—Half-wit, Haman, hash, hen, heretic, hog, holy-seed, hoodlum, hump.
I—Idiot, image, imp, infidel, ingrate, ink-blot, innocent lamb, insect.
J—Jackal, jackass, jail-bird, Joseph-the-Righteous, junk.
K—Knock-on-wood, know-it-all.
L—Lazy-bones, leech, liar, lick-plate, locust, log, louse.
M—Melon, midget, misery, mongrel, monkey, mud, mule.
N—Nanny-goat, ninny, nobody, noodle, nuisance.
O—Onion, open-your-mouth, outcast, owl, ox.
P—Pancake, pen-and-ink, pepper, pest, pig, poison, precious, puppy.
Q—Quack, quince.
R—Rag, rat, raw-potato, riff-raff, rogue, rowdy, ruffian.
S—Sabbath-Goy, saint, sausage, scholar, scribbler, scum, slob, slops, smirker, snake, sneak, snout, soak, spy, squirrel, stiffnecked-people, sucker, sweet-tooth, swine.
T—Tattle-tale, thick-head, thief, thunder-and-lightning, toad, tomcat, toothache, tramp, trousers-owner, turkey, turtle.
U—Ugly, ulcer, useless.
V—Villain, vinegar, viper.
W—Wax-in-the-ears, whelp, worm, wretch.
Y—Yellow, yelper.
Z—Zany, zealot, zero.

Age 18.

JANE AUSTEN
born Dec. 16, 1775
Steventon, Hampshire, England

The History of England [*the end is dated Nov. 26, 1791*] *was intended as a skit on the historical abridgements which were fashionable in the eighteenth century* [*and was written*] *for the enjoyment of the Austen family.*

Pinion

Age 15

Selections from THE HISTORY OF ENGLAND, by a Partial, Prejudiced and Ignorant Historian

HENRY THE FOURTH ascended the throne of England much to his own satisfaction in the year 1399, having prevailed on his cousin and predecessor RICHARD THE SECOND to resign it to him, and to retire for the rest of his life to Pomfret Castle, where he happened to be murdered. Be this as it may, King HENRY did not live for ever either; but falling ill, his son the Prince of Wales came and took away the crown; whereupon the King made a long speech, for which I must refer the Reader to Shakespeare's Play.

Things being thus settled between them the King died, and was succeeded by his son HENRY, who grew quite *reformed* and *amiable*, forsaking all his dissipated companions. His Majesty then turned his thoughts to France, where he went and fought the famous Battle of Agincourt. He afterwards married the King's daughter Catherine, a very *agreeable* woman by Shakespeare's account. In spite of all this however, he died, and was succeeded by his son, HENRY VI.

I cannot say much for this Monarch's *sense*. Nor would I if I could, for he was a Lancastrian. It was in this reign that Joan of Arc lived and made such a *row* among the English. They should not have *burnt* her—but they did.

EDWARD THE FOURTH. This Monarch was famous only for his Beauty and his Courage, and he showed his undaunted behaviour in marrying one woman while he was engaged to another. One of his mistresses was Jane Shore, who has had a play written about her, but it is a tragedy and therefore not worth reading.

His Majesty was succeeded by his son, EDWARD V. This unfortunate Prince lived so little a while that nobody had time even to draw his picture. He was murdered by his Uncle's Contrivance, whose name was RICHARD THE THIRD.

The character of this Prince has in general been very *severely* handled by *Historians*. But as he was a *York*, *I* am rather inclined to suppose him a very *respectable* Man. It has been confidently asserted that he killed his two nephews, but it has also been asserted that he did *not* kill his two nephews, which I am inclined to believe true. Whether innocent or guilty, he did not reign long in peace, for HENRY TUDOR, Earl of Richmond, as great a villain as ever lived, made a great fuss about getting the Crown, and having killed the King at the battle of Bosworth, he succeeded to it.

His eldest daughter, however, was married to the King of Scotland and had the happiness of being the grandmother to one of the first Characters in the World. But of *her*, I shall have occasion to speak more at large in future. His Majesty was succeeded by his son Henry whose only merit was his not being *quite* so bad as his daughter Elizabeth.

The Crimes and Cruelties of HENRY VIII are too numerous to be mentioned, and nothing can be said in his vindication, but that his abolishing Religious Houses and leaving them to the ruinous depredations of time has been of infinite use to the landscape of England in general, which was probably a principal motive for his doing it, since otherwise why should a Man who was of no Religion himself be at so much trouble to abolish one which had for ages been established in the Kingdom?

EDWARD VI. As this prince was only nine years old at the time of his Father's death, the Duke of Somerset was chosen Protector of the Realm during his minority. The Duke was on the whole a very amiable Character, and is somewhat of a favourite with me. He was beheaded; of which he might with reason have been proud, had he known that such was the death of Mary Queen of Scotland.

MARY TUDOR. I cannot pity the Kingdom for the misfortunes they experienced during her Reign, since they fully deserved them, for having allowed her to succeed her Brother—which was a double piece of folly, since they might have foreseen that as she died without children, she would be succeeded by that pest to society, that disgrace to humanity, ELIZABETH.

It was the peculiar misfortune of this Woman to have had Ministers. I know that it has been asserted and believed that Lord Burleigh, Sir Francis Walsingham and the rest were deserving, experienced, and able Ministers. But oh! how blinded such writers and such Readers must be to true merit, to merit despised, neglected, and defamed, if they can persist in such opinions when they reflect that these men, these boasted men, were such scandals to their country and to their sex as to allow and assist their Queen in confining for the space of nineteen years, a Woman who had every reason to expect assistance and protection; and at length allowed Elizabeth to bring this *amiable* Woman to an untimely, unmerited, and scandalous Death. She was executed in the Great Hall at Fotheringay Castle (sacred Place!) on Wednesday, the 8th of February, 1587—to the everlasting Reproach of Elizabeth, her Ministers, and of England in general.

JAMES THE FIRST. Though this King had some faults, on the whole I cannot help *liking* him. He was a Roman Catholic, and as I am myself partial to the Roman Catholic religion, it is with infinite regret that I am obliged to blame the Behaviour of any Member of it: yet Truth, being I think very *excusable* in a *Historian*, I am necessitated to say that in this reign, the Roman Catholics of England did not behave like *Gentlemen* to the Protestants.

CHARLES I. The events of this Monarch's reign are too numerous for my pen, and indeed the recital of any events is uninteresting to me; my principle reasons for undertaking the History of England were to abuse Elizabeth (though I am rather fearful of having fallen off in that part of my scheme), and to prove the innocence of the Queen of Scotland, which I flatter myself with having effectually done.

Portrait of Jane by her sister Cassandra.

BEATLES
John Lennon
born Oct. 9, 1940
Liverpool, England
and
Paul McCartney
born June 18, 1942
Liverpool, England

John Lennon was seventeen and Paul McCartney fifteen years of age when they first collaborated as songwriters. Of the over one hundred songs they wrote that first year, only one, "Love Me Do," was recorded (six years later), and quickly became an English hit. [None of these had reached us by press time—Eds.] When George Harrison left school to join the group he was not yet sixteen. Discovery of his true age led to his deportation from Germany, where the group had been playing.

Fisher

John was keen to be successful at art college, and even while he was still at Quarrybank Grammar School he had shown promise of that quite remarkable talent that later revealed itself. . . : He had compiled over 250 short stories, poems, articles and cartoons while still at school—many of which were lost for years until a teacher at his old school was found to have kept a confiscated Lennon notebook titled The Daily Howl. . . . *[It was] the Liverpool pop paper* Mersey Beat *in which much of John Lennon's earliest work—spoofs on current songs, short stories, cartoons, etc.—first appeared under the pen-name Beatcomber.*

Tremlett

About age 21

LIDDYPOOL

Reviving the old tradition of Judro Bathing is slowly but slowly dancing in Liddypool once more. Had you remembering these owld custard of Boldy Street blowing? The Peer Hat is very popularce for sun eating and Boots for Nude Brighter is handys when sailing. We are not happy with her Queen Victorious Monologue, but Walky Through Gallery is goodly when the rain and Sit Georgie House is black (and white from the little pilgrims flying from Hellsy College). Talk Hall is very histerical with old things wot are fakes and King Anne never slept there I tell you. Shout Airborne is handly for planes if you like (no longer government patrolled) and the L.C.C.C. (Liddypool Cha Cha Cha) are doing a great thing. The Mersey Boat is selling another three copies to some go home foreigners who went home.

There is a lot to do in Liddypool, but not all convenience.

NEVILLE CLUB

Dressed in my teenold brown sweaty I easily micked with crown at Neville Club a seemy hole. Soon all but soon people accoustic me saying such thing as

'Where the charge man?' All of a southern I notice boils and girks sitting in hubbered lumps smoking Hernia taking Odeon and going very high. Somewhere 4ft high but he had Indian Hump which he grew in his sleep. Puffing and globbering they drugged theyselves rampling or dancing with wild abdomen, stubbing in wild postumes amongst themselves.

They seemed olivier to the world about them. One girk was revealing them all over the place to rounds of bread and applause. Shocked and mazed I pulled on my rubber stamp heady for the door.

'Do you kindly mind stop shoveing,' a brough voice said.

'Who think you are?' I retired smiling wanly.

'I'm in charge,' said the brough but heavy voice.

'How high the moon?' cried another, and the band began to play.

A coloured man danced by eating a banana, or somebody.

I drudged over hopping to be noticed. He iced me warily saying 'French or Foe.'

'Foe' I cried taking him into jeapardy.

THE MOLDY MOLDY MAN

I'm a moldy moldy man
I'm moldy thru and thru
I'm a moldy moldy man
You would not think it true.
I'm moldy till my eyeballs
I'm moldy til my toe
I will not dance I shyballs
I'm such a humble Joe.

Earliest surviving photograph of Paul and John's pre-Beatles group: the Quarrymen, Liverpool, 1956.

Paul, as the one who always tried to make things happen, was always prepared to play down their likes and dislikes and chat up anyone who looked like helping them. He was trying hard to get them some publicity in the local newspapers so someone like Larry Parnes might hear of them. He has a letter now which he wrote at the time to some journalist called Mr. Low they had met in a pub.

Davies

McCartney Age 18

Dear Mr. Low,

I am sorry about the time I have taken to write to you, but I hope I have not left it too late. Here are some details about the group.

It consists of four boys: Paul McCartney (guitar), John Lennon (guitar), Stuart Sutcliffe (bass) and George Harrison (another guitar) and is called. . . .

This line-up may at first seem dull but it must be appreciated that as the boys have above average instrumental ability they achieve surprisingly varied effects. Their basic beat is off-beat, but this has recently tended to be accompanied by a faint on-beat; thus the overall sound is rather reminiscent of the four in the bar of traditional jazz. This could possibly be put down to the influence of Mr. McCartney who led one of the top local jazz bands (Jim Mac's Jazz Band) in the 1920s.

Modern music, however, is the group's delight, and, as if to prove the point, John and Paul have written over fifty tunes, ballads and faster numbers, during the last three years. Some of these tunes are purely instrumental (such as "Looking Glass Catswalk" and "Winston's Walk") and others were composed with the modern audience in mind (tunes like "Thinking of Linking," "The One after 909," "Years Roll Along" and "Keep Looking That Way").

The group also derive a great deal of pleasure from rearranging old favourites ("Ain't She Sweet," "You Were Meant For Me," "Home," "Moonglow," "You Are My Sunshine," and others).

Now for a few details about the boys themselves. John, who leads the group, attends the College of Art, and, as well as being an accomplished guitarist and banjo player, he is an experienced cartoonist. His many interests include painting, the theatre, poetry, and of course singing, He is 19 years old and is a founder member of the group.

Paul is 18 years old and is reading English Literature at Liverpool University. He, like the other boys, plays more than one instrument—his specialties being the piano and drums, plus, of course . . . [the rest of the letter is missing]

LUDWIG VAN BEETHOVEN
born Dec. 16 or 17, 1770
Bonn, Germany

As a young man.

The first sonatas, published in Bonn (1783), bear the title: "Three sonatas for piano, dedicated to The Most Reverend The Archbishop and Elector-Prince Maximilian Friedrich, my most gracious master, and composed by Ludwig van Beethoven, 11 years of age." The last item was one of his father's advertising tricks, as Ludwig was then actually thirteen years old! The world likes being cheated, and the taste for infant prodigies (in all branches of music) seems never to change!

The book is provided with a fulsome preface addressed to the Archbishop, in which the following lines occur: "From my fourth year music began to be my chief occupation. . . . I have now already reached my eleventh (?) year, and since then the muse has often whispered to me in moments of initiation: 'Attempt it, write down the harmonies of thy soul!' Eleven years, I thought, how will the author's mien suit me? And what will men in the world of art say to this? I was almost on the point of being afraid. Yet—at the bidding of my muse—I obeyed, and wrote."

This monstrous piece of affectation—which must, of course, be regarded in the light of the manners of the time—was fortunately not written by Beethoven himself; it is believed to be the work of the "literary" Neefe [his teacher]. The Ludwig who had composed the sonatas was a little, dark-skinned, pock-marked fellow, with large, brilliant eyes, but with a shy and reserved manner; he sometimes looked untidy and not very clean; he could be abrupt and obstinate, and embittered in mind at the circumstances prevailing at home, which made him both awkward and lonely. He would hardly have written a preface like that quoted above, nor perhaps would he have understood how to fawn like this upon the exalted prince. The publication of the sonatas perhaps earned for him a slight honour and a badly needed income; perhaps they also—owing to the pompous preface—procured him an advancement. At any rate the boy became a "Court musician" the year after, and we can imagine him dressed in a smart uniform, nay, even wearing a bag-wig.

Behrend

Age 11

9 Variationen (C moll)

über einen Marsch von Ernst Christoph Dressler.

(*Der Gräfin von Wolf-Metternich gewidmet.*)

Breitkopf u. Härtel'sche Gesammt-Ausgabe, Serie 17. No. 5. v. 13

Erschienen spätestens im Anfang d. J. 1783 unter dem Titel: *Variations pour le Clavecin sur une Marche de Mr Dresler composées et dediées à son Excellence Madame la Comtesse de Wolfmetternich née Baronne d'Assebourg par un jeune amateur Louis van Beethoven agé de dix ans.* 1780. *A Mannheim chez le Sr Götz, Marchand et Editeur de Musique.* (**Verlagsnummer: 89.**)

Ausgaben. Leipzig, Breitkopf u. Härtel, 9 Ngr. n. Mannheim, Heckel, 36 Kr. Offenbach, André (No. 17), 36 Kr.

Drei Sonaten (Esdur, Fmoll, Ddur). Age 11

(Dem Kurfürsten von Köln, Maximilian Friedrich gewidmet.)

Breitkopf u. Härtel'sche Gesammt-Ausgabe, Serie 16. No. 33—35. v. 12

Erschienen i. J. 1783 unter dem Titel: *Drei Sonaten fürs Klavier dem Hochwürdigsten Erzbischofe und Kurfürsten zu Köln Maximilian Friedrich meinem gnädigsten Herrn gewidmet und verfertiget von Ludwig van Beethoven, alt eilf Jahr. Speier in Rath Bosslers Verlage.* (Verlagsnummer: 21. Hochformat.) Auf der 3. Seite die Widmung:

Erhabenster! Seit meinem vierten Jahre begann die Musik die erste meiner jugendlichen Beschäftigungen zu werden. So frühe mit der holden Muse bekannt, die meine Seele zu reinen Harmonien stimmte, gewann ich sie, und wie mirs oft wohl däuchte, sie mich wieder lieb. Ich habe nun schon mein eilftes Jahr erreicht; und seitdem flüsterte mir oft meine Muse in den Stunden der Weihe zu: »versuch's und schreib einmal deiner Seele Harmonien nieder!« Eilf Jahre — dachte ich — und wie würde mir da die Autormiene lassen? und was würden dazu die Männer in der Kunst wohl sagen? Fast ward ich schüchtern. Doch meine Muse wollt's — ich gehorchte und schrieb. — Und darf ich's nun Erlauchtester! wohl wagen, die Erstlinge meiner jugendlichen Arbeiten zu Deines Thrones Stufe zu legen? und darf ich hoffen, dass Du ihnen Deines ermunternden Beifalles milden Vaterblick wohl schenken werdest? — O, ja! fanden doch von jeher Wissenschaften und Künste in Dir ihren weisen Schüzzer, grosmüthigen Beförderer, und aufspriesendes Talent unter Deiner holden Vaterpflege Gedeihn. — Voll dieser ermunternden Zuversicht wag' ich es mit diesen jugendlichen Versuchen mich Dir zu nahen. Nimm sie als ein reines Opfer kindlicher Ehrfurcht auf und sieh mit Huld Erhabenster! auf sie herab und ihren jungen Verfasser Ludwig van Beethoven. —

Auf einem Exemplar, im Besitz von Prof. Jahn in Bonn, ist von Beethoven's Hand bemerkt: *Diese Sonaten und die Variationen von Dressler sind meine ersten Werke.*

Ausgaben. Wien, Haslinger (mit Op. 1 bez.), à 45 Kr. Leipzig, Breitkopf u. Härtel, No. 1, 2. à 9 Ngr. n. No. 3. 12 Ngr. n.

Age 12

Schilderung eines Mädchens.

Tempo giusto. Breitkopf u. Härtel'sche Gesammt-Ausgabe, Serie 23. No. 14. v. 17

Gedruckt in Bossler's »Blumenlese für Klavierliebhaber« v. J. 1783 (Speyer) mit de Ueberschrift: *Schilderung eines Mädchens, von Herrn Ludwig van Beethoven, alt eilf Jahr.*

Ausgabe. Leipzig, Breitkopf u. Härtel, 3 Ngr. n.

An einen Säugling.

(Gedicht von Wirths.)

Breitkopf u. Härtel'sche Gesammt-Ausgabe, Serie 23. No. 15. v. 17

Erschienen mit der Ueberschrift: *An einen Säugling. Von Herrn Beethoven* — im 2. Theil der »Neuen Blumenlese für Clavierliebhaber — 1784. Speier beim Rath Bossler.« Vgl. »Neue Berliner Musikzeitung« v. J. 1850, S. 196.

Ausgabe. Leipzig, Breitkopf u. Härtel, 3 Ngr. n.

Age 16

EARLIEST SURVIVING LETTER
To Dr. Joseph Wilhelm von Schaden [a lawyer], Augsburg

Age 16.

Bonn, September 15, 1787

Most nobly born and especially beloved Friend!

I can easily imagine what you must think of me. That you have well founded reasons not to think favorably of me I cannot deny. However, before apologizing I will first mention the reasons which lead me to hope that my apologies will be accepted. I must confess that as soon as I left Augsburg my good spirits and my health too began to decline. For the nearer I came to my native town, the more frequently did I receive from my father letters urging me to travel more quickly than usual, because my mother was not in very good health. So I made as much haste as I could, the more so as I myself began to feel ill. My yearning to see my ailing mother once more swept all obstacles aside so far as I was concerned, and enabled me to overcome the greatest difficulties. I found my mother still alive, but in the most wretched condition. She was suffering from consumption and in the end she died about seven weeks ago after enduring great pain and agony. She was such a good, kind mother to me and indeed my best friend. Oh! who was happier than I, when I could still utter the sweet name of mother and it was heard and answered; and to whom can I say it now? To the dumb likenesses of her which my imagination fashions for me? Since my return to Bonn I have as yet enjoyed very few happy hours. For the whole time I have been plagued with asthma; and I am inclined to fear that this malady may even turn to consumption. Furthermore, I have been suffering from melancholia, which in my case is almost as great a torture as my illness. Well, just put yourself in my place; and, if you do, I shall hope for your forgiveness for my long silence. It was extraordinarily kind and friendly of you to lend me three carolins when I was at Augsburg. But I must beg you to bear with me a little longer. For my journey has cost me a good deal and I cannot hope for any compensation here, not even in the smallest way. Fortune does not favor me here at Bonn.

You must forgive me for taking up so much of your time with my chatter, but it has all been very necessary for the purpose of my apology.

I beg you not to refuse from now on your esteemed friendship to me whose most earnest desire is to deserve it, if only to a small extent.

With the greatest respect I remain
your most obedient servant and friend

L. v. Beethoven
Court Organist to the Elector of Cologne

BRENDAN BEHAN
born Feb. 9, 1923
Dublin, Ireland

As a child he read every thing he could lay his hands on. He had a passionate appetite for books. One day his father found him up in bed reading the back of a train ticket which he had picked up off the floor. He could sing ballads for hours. . . . By the time he was nine, he was writing letters to his friends in verse. One day as a result of a joke he played on her, he got Teresa [Byrne] into trouble with the nuns, and wrote her a poem of apology.

O'Connor

Age 9

Teresa I am sorry
If I got you bashed in school.
It was a stupid thing to do
And I feel an awful fool.

I was really raging
When I heard you went to the pics
With, of all the eejits,
Snotty-nosed Paddy Fitz.

I think you were awfully decent
Not to give my name.
Not even to your Da or Ma,
But shouldered all the blame.

Oh, what can I do now, love,
To restore our happiness?
Will I go across to Gill's pub
And to your Ma confess?

Actually, Teresa,
I've just got two and six
So will you stop sulking in the parlour
And go with me to the flicks?

I'll take you to the Drummer
To the ninepenny cushion seats,
And that will leave me with a bob
To get you oranges and sweets.

To give this its proper ending
I'll wind up with yours for ever, Brendan.

Brendan (top) with his brothers and sister: Seamus, Dominic, Brian, Carmel (right front) and friend.

WILLIAM BLAKE
born Nov. 28, 1757
London, England

William's childhood was happy. His father was moderately prosperous and the family was free from want. Moreover, the father seems to have had considerable understanding of the son and did not send him to school, where indeed he would have been completely out of place, for, from an early age, William claimed to have seen visions, and such a lad would have become the butt of his schoolfellows' unthinking wit. When he was only four years old he was set screaming by God, as his wife later reminded him: "You know, dear, the first time you saw God was when you were four years old, and he put his head to the window, and set you a-screaming." Later, when he was about eight or ten years old, he saw a tree filled with angels on Peckham Rye, though when he related this to his father he escaped a thrashing only by his mother's intercession; but he was beaten on another occasion when he ran into the house, saying that he had seen the prophet Ezekiel under a tree. He saw, too, angels walking among haymakers; and to a traveller who was speaking of the splendours of a foreign city, the boy said: "Do you call that *splendid? I should call a city splendid in which the houses were of gold, the pavement of silver, the gates ornamented with precious stones."*

Lister

Before age 14

How sweet I roam'd from field to field
And tasted all the summer's pride,
Till I the Prince of Love beheld
Who in the sunny beams did glide!

He show'd me lilies for my hair,
And blushing roses for my brow;
He led me through his gardens fair
Where all his golden pleasures grow.

With sweet May dews my wings were wet,
And Phoebus fir'd my vocal rage;
He caught me in his silken net,
And shut me in his golden cage.

He loves to sit and hear me sing,
Then, laughing, sports and plays with me;
Then stretches out my golden wing,
And mocks my loss of liberty.

According to B. H. Malkin (A Father's Memoirs of his Child, *1806), who must have got the information from Blake himself, the poem "was written before the age of fourteen." In that case the biographical reality underlying the symbolism may be the proposal his father is known to have made to apprentice Blake to a fashionable painter. He was fourteen when, this scheme having been dropped, he was finally apprenticed to the engraver Basire.*

Bateson

[In] 1772 Blake was indentured as an apprentice to the engraver James Basire for the term of seven years, in the consideration of £ 52 10s for the whole period. The only known copy of the first state of the engraving later known as "Joseph of Arimathea [the disciple who buried Jesus] among the Rocks of Albion," now in the collection of Sir Geoffrey Keynes, bears the inscription in Blake's hand, "Engraved when I was a beginner at Basires / from a drawing by Salvati after Michael Angelo."

Todd

Joseph eventually resolved himself into that strenuous figure in the Blake mythology—the blacksmith Los, who was to hammer into shape systems of religion, philosophy, art and poetry for the benefit of the race.

Wright

About age 15

Joseph of Arimathea among the rocks of Albion.

Two years passed over smoothly enough, till two other apprentices were added to the establishment, who completely destroyed its harmony. Blake, not choosing to take part with his master against his fellow apprentices, was sent out to make drawings. This circumstance he always mentions with gratitude to Basire, who said that he was too simple and they too cunning.

He was employed in making drawings from old buildings and monuments, and occasionally, especially in winter, in engraving from those drawings. This occupation led him to an acquaintance with those neglected works of art, called Gothic monuments. There he found a treasure, which he knew how to value. He saw the simple and plain road to the style of art at which he aimed, unentangled in the intricate windings of modern practice. The monuments of Kings and Queens in Westminster Abbey, which surround the chapel of Edward the Confessor, particularly that of King Henry the Third, the beautiful monument and figure of Queen Elinor, Queen Philippa, King Edward the Third, King Richard the Second and his Queen, were among his first studies. All these he drew in every point he could catch, frequently standing on the monument, and viewing the figures from the top. The heads he considered as portraits; and all the ornaments appeared as miracles of art, to his Gothicised imagination.

About age 16

Malkin

King Edward III.

Queen Eleanor.

But he was not to remain undisturbed. In those days boys from Westminster School were allowed to walk about the Abbey and even to play there. Blake attracted the attention of the boisterous schoolboys, who went out of their way to jeer at him and tease him. At last, when one of them climbed up on a monument level with Blake's platform the better to goad him, the artist grasped him and threw him to the floor. Not content with that, he went straightaway to the Dean and complained about the boys' behaviour. It has been stated that as a result the Abbey was put out of bounds to Westminster boys, but apparently this is untrue.

Lister

WILLIAM CULLEN BRYANT
born Nov. 3, 1794
Cummington, Mass.

Another of the boy's efforts found greater favor. The nation was aroused by the blockades established by England and France in the Napoleonic Wars, these interferences with trade being the subject of violent controversy among the people and the press and Congress. American ships were seized and American seamen impressed into the naval service of England. There were cries for war to protect American commercial interests and to defend the nation's honor. President Jefferson established a policy of neutrality, and to bring the two belligerents to terms decided to use economic pressure through an Embargo Act, passed by Congress in December, 1807, that interdicted practically all seaborne commerce with foreign nations. New England and New York commercial interests were most severely harmed, and in New England, the stronghold of Federalism, the objections to the embargo reached a stage almost of insurrection. The battle raged in town meetings, in newspapers, and in pamphlets. . . . The embargo was also hotly discussed in the Bryant household. Brown

There is some evidence—particularly, perhaps, in the expanded second version (not here printed) which appeared the next year—of some "polishing" by William's father, the Massachusetts physician and legislator Dr. Peter Bryant, and by another local Federalist "poet and scholar" Benjamin Whitwell.

Bryant's own account of the composition of the poem is:

"I had written some satirical lines apostrophizing the President, which my father saw, and, thinking well of them, encouraged me to write others in the same vein. This I did willingly, until the addition grew into a poem of several pages."

How much polishing we shall probably never know, but certainly a boy in an intensely political and intellectual household who had started writing verses at nine and was to produce his most famous poem, "Thanatopsis," at sixteen was capable of unusual things.

Excerpts from THE EMBARGO, A SATIRE
or Sketches of the Times
by a youth of thirteen

Age 13

LOOK where we will, and in whatever land,
Europe's rich soil, or Afric's barren sand,
Where the wild savage hunts his wilder prey,
Or art or science pour their brightest day,
The monster *Vice* appears before our eyes
In naked impudence or gay disguise.

BUT quit the meaner game, indignant Muse,
And to this country turn thy nobler views;
Ill fated clime! condemned to feel the extremes
Of a weak ruler's philosophic dreams;
Driven headlong on to ruin's fateful brink,
When will thy country feel? When will she think?

WAKE Muse of Satire, in the cause of trade,
Thou scourge of miscreants who the laws evade!
Dart thy keen glances, knit thy threat'ning brows,
And hurl thine arrows at fair commerce's foes!

WHEN shall this land, some courteous angel say,
Throw off a weak, and erring ruler's [Jefferson's] sway?
Rise, injured people, vindicate your cause!
And prove your love of Liberty and laws;
Oh wrest, sole refuge of a sinking land,
The sceptre from the slave's imbecile hand!

Oh ne'er consent, obsequious to advance
The willing vassal of imperious France!
Correct that suffrage you misused before,
And lift your voice above a Congress' roar!
And thou [Jefferson], the scorn of every patriot name,
The country's ruin, and her council's shame!
Poor servile thing! derision of the brave!
Who erst from Tarleton fled to Carter's cave;*
Thou, who, when menac'd by perfidious Gaul,
Didst prostrate to her whisker'd minion fall;
And when our cash her empty bags supplied,
Didst meanly strive the foul disgrace to hide;
Go, wretch, resign the presidential chair,
Disclose thy secret measures foul or fair,
Go, search, with curious eye, for horned frogs,
'Mongst the wild wastes of Louisianian bogs;
Or where Ohio rolls his turbid stream,
Dig for huge bones, thy glory and thy theme;
Go scan, Philosophist, thy [Sally's]** charms,
And sink supinely in her sable arms;
But quit to abler hands, the helm of state,
Nor image ruin on thy country's fate!

*In 1781 Jefferson, then governor of Virginia, withdrew to Carter's Mountain to avoid the raiders sent out by Sir Banastre Tarleton.
**Jefferson's slave and alleged mistress.

BUT vain the wish, for hark! the murmuring meed,
Of hoarse applause, from yonder shed proceed;
Enter, and view the thronging concourse there,
Intent, with gaping mouth, and stupid stare,
While in the midst their supple leader stands,
Harangues aloud, and flourishes his hands;
To adulation tunes his servile throat,
And sues, successful, for each blockhead's vote. . . .

RISE then Columbians! heed not France's wiles,
Her bullying mandates, her seductive smiles;
Send home Napoleon's slave, and bid him say;
No arts can lure us, and no threats dismay;
Determin'd yet to war with whom we will,
Choose our own allies or be neutral still.

YE merchants arm! the pirate Gaul repel,
Your prowess shall the naval triumph swell;
Send the marauders shatter'd whence they came,
And Gallia's cheek suffuse with crimson shame. . . .

THEN on safe seas the merchants' barque shall fly,
Our waving flag shall kiss the polar sky;
On canon wings our thunders shall be borne,
Far to the west, or tow'rd the rising morn;
Then may we dare a haughty tyrant's rage,
And gain the blessings of an unborn age. . . .

WHILE thus, all Europe rings with his alarms,
Say, shall we rush, unthinking, to his arms?
No; let us dauntless all his fury brave,
Our fluttering flag, in freedom's gale shall wave,
Our guardian Sachem's errless shafts shall fly,
And terror lighten from our eagle's eye!

HERE then I cease, rewarded, if my song,
Shall prompt one honest mind though guided wrong,
To pause from party, view his country's state,
And lend his aid to stern approaching fate!

In a few years Bryant was to become an apostate to Federalism, adopting the principles of Jeffersonian Democracy and subsequently, when he was editor of the Evening Post, *converting it into an organ of Jacksonianism [and free trade, workingman's rights, free speech and abolition. He also rejected Puritan dogma early for Deism, and became a Unitarian]. Parke Godwin reported that in Bryant's maturer years he was ashamed of his early political lampoons as poems and as expressions of opinion. Asking him if he had a copy of* The Embargo, *Godwin received this testy reply: "No, why should I keep such stuff as that?" Later, told by Godwin that he had borrowed a copy from a friend, Bryant said: "Well, you have taken a great deal of trouble for a very foolish thing."*

Brown

ROBERT BURNS
born Jan. 25, 1759
Alloway, Ayrshire, Scotland

Mauchline, 2d Aug. 1787

You know our country custom of coupling a man and a woman together as Partners in the labors of Harvest.—In my fifteenth autumn [1773], my Partner [Nelly Kirkpatrick] was a bewitching creature who just counted an autumn less.—My scarcity of English denies me the power of doing her justice in that language; but you know the Scotch idiom, She was a bonie, sweet, sonsie lass.—In short, she altogether unwittingly to herself, initiated me in a certain delicious Passion, which in spite of acid Disappointment, gin-horse Prudence and bookworm Philosophy, I hold to be the first of human joys, our dearest pleasure here below.—How she caught the contagion I can't say; you medical folks talk much of infection by breathing the same air, the touch, &c. but I never expressly told her that I loved her.—Indeed I did not well know myself, why I liked so much to loiter behind with her, when returning in the evening from our labors; why the tones of her voice made my heartstrings thrill like an Eolian harp; and particularly, why my pulse beat such a furious ratann when I looked and fingered over her hand, to pick out the nettle-stings and thistles.—Among her other love-inspiring qualifications, she sung sweetly; and 'twas her favorite reel to which I attempted giving an embodied vehicle in rhyme.—I was not so presumptive as to imagine that I could make verses like printed ones, composed by men who had Greek and Latin; but my girl sung a song which was said to be composed by a small country laird's son, on one of his father's maids, with whom he was in love; and I saw no reason why I might not rhyme as well as he, for excepting smearing sheep and casting peats, his father living in the moors, he had no more Scholarcraft than I had.—

Thus with me began Love and Poesy; which at times have been my only, and till within this last twelvemonth have been my highest enjoyment.

from letter to Dr. Moore

Age 14

SONG

(Tune, I am a man unmarried)

O once I lov'd a bonny lass
Ay and I love her still
And whilst that virtue warms my breast
I'll love my handsome Nell.
Fal lal de lal &c.

As bonny lasses I hae seen,
And mony full as braw [fine];
But for a modest gracefu' mien,
The like I never saw.

A bonny lass I will confess,
Is pleasant to the e'e;
But without some better qualities
She's no a lass for me.

But Nelly's looks are blythe and sweet,
And what is best of a',
Her reputation is compleat
And fair without a flaw.

She dresses ay sae clean and neat,
Both decent and genteel;
And then there's something in her gate
Gars [makes] ony dress look weel.

A gaudy dress and gentle air
May slightly touch the heart;
But it's innocence and modesty
That polisses the dart.

'Tis this in Nelly pleases me;
'Tis this enchants my soul;
For absolutely in my breast
She reigns without controul.

LEWIS CARROLL
born Jan. 27, 1832
Daresbury (near Warrington)
England

At Croft Rectory in Yorkshire where his father was installed as Canon in 1843, Lewis Carroll and his brothers and sisters began a series of family magazines, the first of which was Useful and Instructive Poetry. *The piece below was the first poem in issue No. 1 and was written about 1845.*

About age 13

Age 8.

MY FAIRY

I have a fairy by my side
  Which says I must not sleep,
When once in pain I loudly cried
  It said "You must not weep".

If, full of mirth, I smile and grin,
  It says "You must not laugh";
When once I wished to drink some gin
  It said "You must not quaff".

When once a meal I wished to taste
  It said "You must not bite";
When to the wars I went in haste
  It said "You must not fight".

"What may I do?" at length I cried,
  Tired of the painful task.
The fairy quietly replied,
  And said "You must not ask".

  Moral: "You mustn't".

Cover of The Rectory Umbrella, *a Dodgson family magazine, age 18.*

JOHNNY CARSON
born October 23, 1925
Corning, Iowa

Age 18

This is from the 1943 edition of Milestone, *yearbook of Norfolk High School, Norfolk, Nebraska.*

I, *John Carson,* being of sound mind and body (this statement is likely to be challenged by my draft board and the high school faculty), deem it advisable to give you the lowlights of 1942 and 1943.

I can visualize 20 years from now when you sit down by the radio (listening to Roosevelt), with the old 1943 *Milestone* in your trembling hands, and as you glance over those remembrances, you will say to your son—"I wish I could get hold of that *?%")¢/ *Milestone* staff." And then your little son will look at the *Milestone* and say meekly—"Hey, does this stink!"

Be that as it may, I have hereunto set my hand to the task of giving you a month by month, drip by drip, account of Norfolk High School activity during the year. If you like this account, tell my friends. (My friends include my mother, and others who have asked that their names be withheld.)

NOVEMBER was the month when everyone got the bird, and I certainly got it!

This month made all the students very war conscious, with blackouts, etc. In fact, this was one of the few months the students were even awake! All the students enjoyed the blackouts very much. They liked them so well, four unidentified senior boys attempted to put the power plant out of commission.

Gas rationing went into effect, and all the students took it in good spirit—it said in the paper. The limit was four gallons of gas a week, the police told Dan Hoion, when they saw him with a rubber hose in Mr. Burkhardt's gas tank! The football team ended a swell season at Columbus with Al Mather leading the scoring. Mather was arrested for exceeding the thirty-five-mile-an-hour speed limit (on an end run).

JANUARY. A new year brings new classes, new tests, new faces, but the same old teacher! (The only way I'll get out of school now is to be drafted.) This is the month everyone progresses a half-year and becomes a little smarter—I tried explaining to the faculty!

Ward Moore suffered the only real setback, progressing rapidly backwards a half-year in boys' cooking class. They found Ward rolling around on the floor one day because the recipe said to roll in cracker crumbs! I wouldn't say Ward's cookies were very hard, but Larry Skalowsky ran over one of them and blew out two tires!

At this time I would like to say something about the semester tests, but they were afraid the administration might read the *Milestone,* so they wouldn't print it! (Fine chance the administration will read this.)

The month ended with students drooling icicles on the way to school!

FEBRUARY. Month of Washington's birthday. If Washington (who never told a lie) could hear some of the excuses the kids hand Mr. Gerdes every morning, he would turn over in his grave and get up and run for a third term—and probably say, "What, Roosevelt still in?"

Everyone was getting his date to the Junior-Senior banquet. For the benefit of the Sophomores, I will explain in detail how to get a date. The first thing to do is to call up the best-looking girl in school and ask her. After that, call up someone who will go with you! I was turned down so many times, I felt like a bed spread!

Not to mention the Valentine verse I received from my draft board which went like this: "Upon this February morn the draft board wishes to inform, we love you much, and all that stew, but never mind, we'll wait for you!"

APRIL is the time of year when everyone begins to feel stronger, and to recuperate after the winter season. You could tell the teachers were getting stronger. They seemed to throw you out of class harder.

Les France started a commando course designed to toughen you up for the armed forces. He came to school on crutches the next day. (Honest!)

At this time of year, students engage in such activities as track meets, skipping school, class play, skipping school, *Milestone* work, skipping school, and others which include (this will kill you) skipping school!

Junior-Senior field day was held this month, and the boys enjoyed playing such childish games as drop the body, ring around the graveyard, etc. (Any bodies left

John Carson
Class of 1943
Norfolk Senior High School
Norfolk, Nebraska

Minute Men, 1, 2, 3, 4; Thespians 4; Allied Youth 4; Hi-Y 1, 2, 3, 4; features Milestone 4; *features Political 4; Orpheum 1, 2, 4.*

over thirty days became property of the park management!)

MAY. The school year is about to come to a close (and so is this stuff). As you sit reading this gift to the literary world, you will remember Sup't. Burkhardt's praise on the book in his message. Of course, this has nothing to do with the fact that no one had yet seen the book, including the superintendent!

Those of you who failed to make known your observance of Mr. McIntyre's birthday this month may still save face by bringing goodies and sweetmeats to the publications room.

The Senior Class play drew a large crowd recently, and the cast is in line for congratulations for presenting a swell play.

Graduation exercises are about the last activity on the school program, and they are being eagerly looked forward to.

Having been recognized as the epitome of success during my four years (so far) in Norfolk High School, I have been asked to jot down some of my secrets of getting along with the teachers. I oblige with the following:

1. Always hand in daily papers.
2. Laugh at the teacher's jokes.
3. Do an abundance of extra-credit work.
4. Laugh at the teacher's jokes.
5. Never chew gum during classes.
6. Laugh at the teacher's jokes.

(Numbers 1, 3, and 5 may be omitted and no appreciable difference will be noticed!)

Below is a list of the graduating Seniors of '43 who, during the course of the four years they have been confined here, never cheated in a test, never received a ninth period, and never perpetrated dastardly deeds in their minds concerning the bodily welfare of the faculty:

Christopher Porterfield: *Do you have a favorite memento of your mother?*

Dick Cavett: *For several years after I was born she kept a series of clothbound journals called "Scribble-In Books." I knew these books existed, but for a long time couldn't bring myself to read them. Finally I asked my father for them. Most of the entries are little observations of my behavior. Reading them over, I get a double* frisson *from seeing myself through her eyes and, in effect, hearing her voice again.*

Here are a few typical jottings.

Cavett and Porterfield

DICK CAVETT
born Nov. 19, 1936
Gibbon, Neb.

Age 4 months to 5 years

At four months: Laughed out loud. Has developed recently a great aptitude for showing off . . . rears out chest and snorts then awaits laughs. . . . Shows disappointment if the proper appreciation isn't shown.

At eighteen months: Talks in paragraphs rather than sentences. . . . Plays with a Jim Cavett; product of imagination. I hope nothing prophetic. Recites nursery rhymes:

I am a little boy, not very big.
My father's such a bore, I could have been a pig.

Profanity is very evident at times. Where the devil do you suppose he gets it?

At two and a half: In my bath—giggled until he could scarcely speak pointing out part of my anatomy and stammering, "That's what Dadda calls a titty."

At three: Dick has a "wailing chair" wedged between the bookcase and the radio. He retreats there when pressure becomes great against his wishes. Since Christmas candy has been a major issue in this household I can't help ruing the day I ever started sanctioning it for Dick. His apparently unusual intelligence seems to be no assurance against overindulgence. It never seems to work that way. It takes a rustic I guess to be sane in living habits. Do you suppose it is lack of opportunity only that keeps us from harmful vices? Perhaps criminals are not after all so different, but only lack that fear of consequence which makes renunciators of us.

At three: Dick asked, "Where are you before you are born?" Insisted with tears that he had to be someplace before we were married.

At three: Dick: "Do you know who knows who made God?"

"No I don't, Dick."

Dick: "Nobody does but God."

At three: We had quite a "bug" drama. In the process of cutting papers, Dick completely annihilated a box-elder bug. Remorse hit him so forcibly that he was unable to control himself in telling of his crime. An uneasy pillow was his when he tried to sleep.

At four: Moved to Grand Island and, evincing an innate belief in predestination, on being told he probably wouldn't have known his new friend Mary Huston if we had taken the Abbott apt. asserted, "I would have known Mary wherever I had lived."

Couldn't get his conscience in line for a nap because he had pushed Mary. "My head won't let me sleep because I pushed Mary. But I had to do it."

At five: In Dick's falling out of the back of the car I have become more and more aware of my inadequacies. I could borrow his own phrase picked up in his rapid-moving mind heaven knows where, "My golly a hundred, what to do now?" It takes a jolt like that every so often to make me aware of the fact that I'm living my life *now* . . . and what fun and pleasure we are going to have together has to be packed in to the days that are.

Age 4, with his friend, Mary.

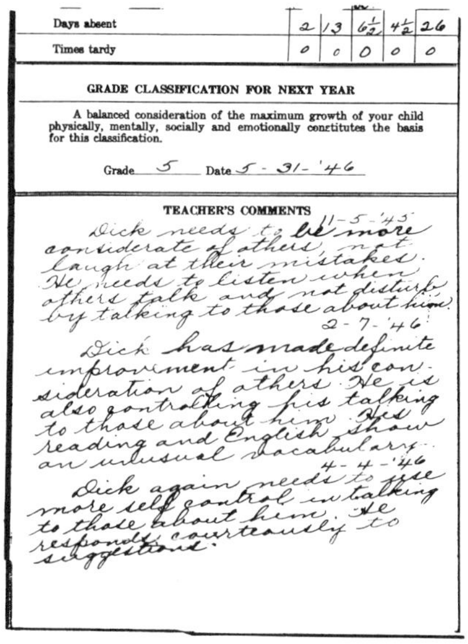

Days absent	2	13	6½	4½	26
Times tardy	0	0	0	0	0

GRADE CLASSIFICATION FOR NEXT YEAR

A balanced consideration of the maximum growth of your child physically, mentally, socially and emotionally constitutes the basis for this classification.

Grade 5 Date 5-31-'46

TEACHER'S COMMENTS

11-5-'45
Dick needs to be more considerate of others, not laugh at their mistakes. He needs to listen when others talk and not disturb by talking to those about him.

2-7-'46
Dick has made definite improvement in his consideration of others. He is also controlling his talking to those about him. His reading and English show an unusual vocabulary.

4-4-'46
Dick again needs to use more self control in talking to those about him. He responds courteously to suggestions.

ANTON CHEKHOV
born Jan. 17, 1860
Taganrog, Russia

Chekhov's father declared himself bankrupt in April 1876 and moved his whole family to Moscow. Anton was left behind to sell off some of the miserable household possessions not confiscated. From here he wrote to his youngest brother Michael.

Taganrog, July, 1876

Age 16

Dear Brother Misha,—I received your letter at the height of the most awful boredom, when I stood yawning at the gate, and therefore you can judge that that huge letter arrived just at the right moment. Your handwriting is good, and in the whole letter I have not found a single mistake in grammar. There is one thing I do not like: why do you call yourself my "insignificant and unnoticeable little brother." Do you admit your insignificance? Not all Mishas, my dear fellow, must be alike. Admit your insignificance, but do you know where? Before God, also before intelligence, beauty, nature, but not before men. Among men one should be conscious of one's dignity. Surely you are not a rogue; you are an honest fellow. Well, respect the honest fellow in you and know that no honest fellow is insignificant. Do not confound "humbling oneself" with "admitting one's insignificance."

George [their cousin] has grown up. He is a nice boy. I often play *babki* (knuckle bones) with him. I have received your letters. You do well to read books. Accustom yourself to reading. In time you will appreciate the habit. Madame Beecher Stowe has squeezed tears from your eyes? I read her once, and re-read her again six months ago with a scientific purpose, and after reading I felt the unpleasant sensation which mortals experience after eating too many raisins or currants.

The promised Dubanos [a dog] has run away and its place of residence is unknown to me. I'll contrive to bring you some other present.

Read the following books: "Don Quixote" (complete in seven or eight parts). It is a fine book. It is the work of Cervantes, whom people put almost on the same level as Shakespeare. I recommend our brothers to read Turgenev's "Don Quixote and Hamlet" if they have not read them. You, my dear, won't yet understand it. If you want to read a travel book that won't bore you, read Goncharov's "Frigate Pallada," etc.

Age 20 (left), with his brother Nikolai.

I send Masha special greetings through you. Do not grieve if I come late. Time runs quickly, however much one boasts of boredom. I shall bring a lodger with me who will pay twenty roubles a month and live under our supervision. . . . Though even twenty roubles is little, taking into consideration the high prices in Moscow and mother's habit of feeding lodgers as God commands. Our teachers charge 350 roubles per annum, and feed the poor youngsters like dogs, on gravy soup from roast meat.

His first literary attempts relate to the time when he was in the upper forms of the grammar school. He contributed to Little Star, *a paper written and edited by the pupils, and composed several numbers of the humorous school paper,* The Stammerer, *which was issued in manuscript. When a pupil of the seventh form he wrote a farce* Not for Nothing Did the Chicken Sing *and a play* Fatherless.

Koteliansky and Tomlinson

Shortly after his arrival in Moscow, writing for those humorous magazines over which he used to pore with delight in the Taganrog library had occurred to Chekhov as the most promising way of adding to his slender resources. Alexander, who two years ago had attempted to place Anton's schoolboy efforts in Alarm Clock, *had now achieved some success as a writer for these magazines; he continued to encourage his brother to try. . . .*

Then, on January 13, 1880, Chekhov read in the "Letter Box" section of the St. Petersburg weekly Dragonfly *laconic but exciting news addressed to him: "Not at all bad. Will print what was sent. Our blessings on your further efforts." Shortly thereafter, a letter arrived from the editor to inform him that he would receive an honorarium of five kopecks a line (about a quarter of a cent a word). Impatiently, Chekhov ran through every succeeding weekly copy of* Dragonfly, *but not until March 9, in issue Number 10, did he find his tale:* A Letter from the Don Landowner Stepan Vladimorovich N., to His Learned Neighbor Dr. Friederick. *It was signed simply ". . . v." His family rejoiced over this first printed work. The twenty-year-old Chekhov's literary career had begun. . . .*

Chekhov lost no time in following up the advantage he had won with the editor of Dragonfly. *Since tales and sketches had to be brief, the payment on each was necessarily small, but if he could publish many of them he had visions of a substantial income to add to the family purse. Now every moment he could steal from his medical studies he spent on writing. He plied* Dragonfly *with manuscripts, and in the course of the remaining months of 1880 nine more of them were printed.*

Simmons

One of these pieces was entitled "My Jubilee."

MY JUBILEE

Age 20

Young friends!

Years ago I suddenly felt in me the presence of that same fire for which Prometheus was chained to the rock. And now it is already three years since I, with great enthusiasm, began sending out my writings, which passed through this purifying Promethean fire, to the four corners of this vast land. I wrote in prose, in verse; I wrote in all different styles, in all different lengths; I wrote thinking of money and without thinking of money. I submitted to all those magazines. But, alas, the envious saw fit not to take my literary products. And even if they printed them it was always as a "Letter to the Editor." Half a hundred stamps I sowed on this "Field" [the title of a magazine]. A hundred I threw into the "Neva" [another magazine and also the St. Petersburg river], tens of them I burned in the "Little Flame" [another magazine]. Five hundred I wasted on "The Dragonfly." To make a long story short: in my entire literary career to this date, I have received exactly 2000 replies! Yesterday I received the last of these which was, in substance, exactly like all the previous ones. Not even a hint at an acceptance. My young friends! The expense of each of my submissions was at least 10 kopeks. So on my literary endeavors I spent 200 rubles. But for 200 rubles I could have bought a horse! My yearly income is only 800 rubles. Imagine!!! And I had to go hungry only because I wrote about nature, love, women's eyes; and also because I attacked the Anglophiles; and because I shared this fire which burns in me, my talent, with these crap artists who sent me back these answers—2000 answers—and not one "Yes"! Hey now! So I suppose we can chalk this up to experience. So today I celebrate my Jubilee on receiving my 2000th answer; and I lift a toast to the end of my literary endeavors, and from now on I rest on my laurels. Either show me somebody else who has received, in three years, as many rejections, or put me on a pedestal for eternity and make me immortal!

Prosaic Poet

This may well have been a wry hint to I.F. Vasilevsky, the sarcastic editor of Dragonfly, *for failures had been accumulating in discouraging numbers. To make matters worse,* Dragonfly's *"Letter Box" rubbed salt in the wounds of authors who had failed. This department of the magazine was a cruel device that spared no would-be contributor's feelings. "You'll receive castor oil instead of an honorarium," it had warned one hopeful author. Now it was hardly less offensive to Chekhov. It rejected one of his manuscripts with: "A few witticisms don't wipe out hopelessly vapid verbiage."* "The Portrait," *it acidly declared, "will not be printed; it doesn't suit us. You've obviously written it for another magazine." And one tale was turned back as "Very long and colorless, like the white paper ribbon a Chinaman pulls out of his mouth." When, at the end of 1880, the "Letter Box" commented on Chekhov's latest contribution: "You don't bloom—you are fading. Very sad. In fact, it's impossible to write without some critical relation to the matter," he lost all patience and decided to break off relations with* Dragonfly.

Simmons

FREDERIC CHOPIN
born March 1, 1810
Zelazowa Wola (near Warsaw)
Poland

About age 16, sketch by Eliza Radziwill.

Music was held in respect in the Chopin family. As a very young child Frederic was apt to burst into tears when he heard a piano. Later, whenever his mother was playing, he liked to crawl underneath the instrument and crouch there for hours, wonder-struck. One night he was discovered seated at the keyboard, and soon his mother was obliged to begin teaching him to play; from the very beginning the boy showed such astonishing aptitude that his parents decided to send him to a professional music teacher. The man chosen was Adalbert (Vojciech) Zywny, a teacher of repute and a picturesque character.

Born in Czechoslovakia, Zywny had followed Prince Casimir Sapieha to Poland and there had become the Court Pianist in the reign of Stanislas Poniatovski. The partition of Poland ruined his career and his hopes. He settled in Warsaw and made a name for himself as a piano teacher. In his long green frock-coat, his wig and top boots, on the move from lesson to lesson from morning till night, fond of his glass of neat vodka and the snuff which he scattered over the keyboard, he was one of the city's "characters," beloved and esteemed by all. He soon became a friend of the family in the Chopin household. . . .

Chopin's schooldays coincided with his first musical successes. His first public appearance was on 24 February 1818, when he played a concerto by Adalbert Gyrovetz; his reception was a triumph. . . .

Meanwhile the composer, too, was beginning to emerge. Frederic improvised music as naturally as he breathed. Zywny wrote down his inspirations.

Boucourechliev

Age 7

CHOPIN'S FIRST PUBLISHED POLONAISE, IN G MINOR, COMPOSED AT THE AGE OF SEVEN

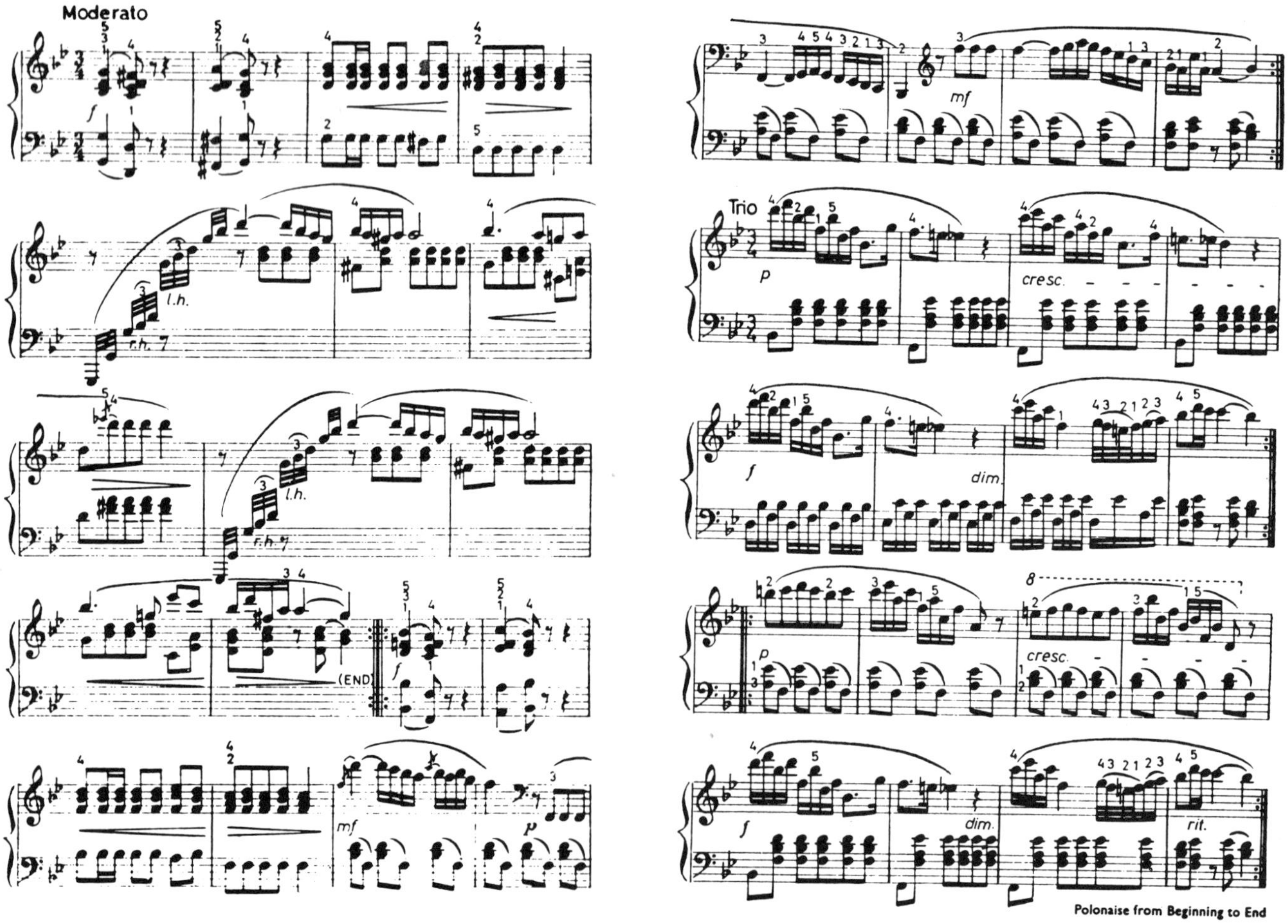

Polonaise from Beginning to End

Two crayon caricatures of a peasant drawn by Frederic "as a youth."

Age 15

CHOPIN'S FIRST PUBLISHED MAZURKA, IN B FLAT, COMPOSED AT THE AGE OF FIFTEEN

WINSTON CHURCHILL
born Nov. 30, 1874
Blenheim Palace
(near Woodstock)
Oxfordshire, England

The Headmaster, Dr. Welldon, however, took a broad-minded view of my Latin prose [in the Entrance Examination to Harrow]; he showed discernment in judging my general ability. This was the more remarkable, because I was found unable to answer a single question in the Latin paper. I wrote my name at the top of the page. I wrote down the number of the question 'I'. After much reflection I put a bracket round it thus '(I)'. But thereafter I could not think of anything connected with it that was either relevant or true. Incidentally there arrived from nowhere in particular a blot and several smudges. I gazed for two whole hours at this sad spectacle: and then merciful ushers collected my piece of foolscap with all the others and carried it up to the Headmaster's table. It was from these slender indications of scholarship that Dr. Welldon drew the conclusion that I was worthy to pass into Harrow. It is very much to his credit. It showed that he was a man capable of looking beneath the surface of things: a man not dependent upon paper manifestations. I have always had the greatest regard for him.

I continued in this unpretentious situation for nearly a year. However, by being so long in the lowest form I gained an immense advantage over the cleverer boys. They all went on to learn Latin and Greek and splendid things like that. But I was taught English. We were considered such dunces that we could only learn English. Mr. Somervell—a most delightful man to whom my debt is great—was charged with the duty of teaching the stupidest boys the most disregarded thing—namely, to write mere English. . . . As I remained in the Third Fourth (B) three times as long as anyone else, I had three times as much of it. I learned it thoroughly. Thus I got into my bones the essential structure of the ordinary British sentence—which is a noble thing. And when in after years my schoolfellows who had won prizes and distinction for writing such beautiful Latin poetry and pithy Greek epigrams had to come down again to common English, to earn their living or make their way, I did not feel myself at any disadvantage.

My Early Life

An early example of Winston's good English (from the Harrovian *of 1890) follows.*

Age 15

COMMEMORATIVE ODE TO INFLUENZA

Oh how shall I its deeds recount
Or measure the untold amount
Of ills that it has done?
From China's bright celestial land
E'en to Arabia's thirsty sand
It journeyed with the sun.

O'er miles of bleak Siberia's plains
Where Russian exiles toil in chains
It moved with noiseless tread;
And as it slowly glided by
There followed it across the sky
The spirits of the dead.

The Ural peaks by it were scaled
And every bar and barrier failed
To turn it from its way;
Slowly and surely on it came,
Heralded by its awful fame,
Increasing day by day.

On Moscow's fair and famous town
Where fell the first Napoleon's crown
It made a direful swoop;
The rich, the poor, the high, the low
Alike the various symptoms know,
Alike before it droop.

Nor adverse winds, nor floods of rain
Might stay the thrice-accursed bane;
And with unsparing hand,
Impartial, cruel and severe
It travelled on allied with fear
And smote the fatherland.

Fair Alsace and forlorn Lorraine,
The cause of bitterness and pain
In many a Gallic breast,
Receive the vile, insatiate scourge,
And from their towns with it emerge
And never stay nor rest.

And now Europa groans aloud,
And 'neath the heavy thunder-cloud
    Hushed is both song and dance;
The germs of illness wend their way
To westward each succeeding day
    And enter merry France.

Fair land of Gaul, thy patriots brave
Who fear not death and scorn the grave
    Cannot this foe oppose,
Whose loathsome hand and cruel sting,
Whose poisonous breath and blighted wing
    Full well thy cities know.

In Calais port the illness stays,
As did the French in former days,
    To threaten Freedom's isle;
But now no Nelson could o'erthrow
This cruel, unconquerable foe,
    Nor save us from its guile.

Yet Father Neptune strove right well
To moderate this plague of Hell,
    And thwart it in its course;
And though it passed the streak of brine
And penetrated this thin line,
    It came with broken force.

For though it ravaged far and wide
Both village, town and countryside,
    Its power to kill was o'er;
And with the favouring winds of Spring
(Blest is the time of which I sing)
    It left our native shore.

God shield our Empire from the might
Of war or famine, plague or blight
    And all the power of Hell,
And keep it ever in the hands
Of those who fought 'gainst other lands,
    Who fought and conquered well.

Age 15, at Harrow.

ROBERT LORD CLIVE
born Sept. 29, 1725
Market Drayton
Shropshire, England

Some lineaments of the character of the man (says Lord Macaulay) were early discerned in the child. There remain letters written by his relations when he was in his seventh year; and from these letters it appears that, even at that early age, his strong will and his fiery passions, sustained by a constitutional intrepidity which sometimes seemed hardly compatible with soundness of mind, had begun to cause great uneasiness to his family. "Fighting," says one of his uncles, "to which he is out of measure addicted, gives his temper such a fierceness and imperiousness, that he flies out on every trifling occasion." The old people in the neighborhood still remember to have heard from their parents how Bob Clive climbed to the top of the lofty steeple of Market Drayton, and with what terror the inhabitants saw him seated on a stone spout near the summit. They also relate how he formed all the idle lads of the town into a kind of predatory army, and compelled the shopkeepers to submit to a tribute of apples and halfpence, in consideration of which he guaranteed the security of their windows. He was sent from school to school, making very little progress in his learning, and gaining for himself everywhere the character of an exceedingly naughty boy. One of his masters, it is said, was sagacious enough to prophesy that the idle lad would make a great figure in the world. But the general opinion seems to have been that poor Robert was a dunce, if not a reprobate. His family expected nothing good from such slender parts and such a headstrong temper. It is not strange, therefore, that they gladly accepted for him, when he was in his eighteenth year, a writership in the service of the East India Company, and shipped him off to make a fortune, or die of fever at Madras.

Timb

It was in his fourth year that George began to evolve the jingles which would one day mature into his songs. His first complete composition was brief, and he asked Jerry [his father] if he would like to hear it. Jerry was enthralled until he heard George's piping voice lilt out:

Damn it to hell!
DAMN it to hell!
Damn it to hell!
DAMN it to hell!

Jerry terminated the audition, suggesting that the lyrics were unsuitable, but he told Nellie [his mother] that what little there was of the tune seemed first rate. . . .

He had been writing songs since his tenth year. Typical of these was his first effort, "The First Floor Front."

McCabe

GEORGE M. COHAN
born July 3, 1878
Providence, R.I.

Age 10

THE FIRST FLOOR FRONT

There's a French girl named McCarthy,
Her first is Mary Ann.
Her mother is her father's wife,
Her father he's a man.
Though Mary's very homely,
She has a pretty face.
And the flat that Mary occupies
Is a most exquisite place.
She has a grand piano,
It makes a fearful noise.
It's pounded every evening
By a gang of girls and boys.
Assembled there at Mary's
For fun they needn't hunt.
They find a whole lot of it
In the first floor front.

CHORUS: There's Kate and Nancy
Billy, Clancy, Dan and Mike Magee.
There's Pat O'Day and Hughie Fay,
All loaded down with glee
There's Jimmy Grogan, Johnny Logan,
Both so big and blimp,
At number three the boulevard,
The First Floor Front.

V. & S. HALL, EAST BROOKFIELD, WEDNESDAY EVENING, JULY 31, 1895.

THE FOUR COHANS
High Class Comedy & Character Artists

In a new and sparkling Comedy, in two acts,

"A YOUNG LADIES' SEMINARY."

CAST OF CHARACTERS:

Prof. Mooney, a light hearted music teacher, JERRY COHAN
Sammie Knary, the seminary's solitary male pupil, GEORGE M. COHAN
Anna Kondher, a charmer fair, an interesting pupil, JOSIE COHAN
Mora Enmore, } Mexicans, MARGARETTA COSTIGAN
Salza Worder, } ALBERT M. CHILDS
Minnie Apolis Jones, assistant preceptress, a theosophist, HELEN F. COHAN

Incidental to the Play, the following Specialties and Songs.

New Girl Coming, - - - SAMMIE
"Broadway Girl," (by G. M. Cohan) - - - ANNA
Sarah Kewe and Sammie, double Song and Dance, - - - SAMMIE and ANNA
New Dance, "The Keating," - - - ANNA
Mr. Walker, (original) - - - SAMMIE
The Dancing Lesson, - - - PROF. MOONEY

OVERTURE, PROF. J. WILLIS MILLIGAN.

Concluding with THE FOUR COHANS' Original Specialty Farce,
"GOGGLES' DOLL HOUSE."
Introducing novel and enjoyable situations, concluding with the wonderful
DANCING DOLLS.

A Special Train will leave North Brookfield at 7.42 p. m., returning from East Brookfield after the show.

Admission, 25 Cents. Reserved Seats, 35 Cents.
Seats on sale at Pepper's in North Brookfield, and at Vizard's in East Brookfield.

In 1893, when he was fifteen, after his older sister Josie had received and accepted an offer to do a single act at Konter and Bials, the leading vaudeville theater in the U.S. (thus breaking up the family act), and later that season at the prestigious Imperial Music Hall at twice the salary the entire Four Cohans had ever earned, George went back into serious song plugging. And he was successful!

M. Witmark & Sons, the greatest song publisher in the country, accepted his song "Why Did Nellie Leave Her Home?" (which Morehouse says he wrote at thirteen). What shock and chagrin when he collected his copies and found they had left the music as it was but had changed the lyrics completely! What had been a vaudeville routine was now a sentimental ballad!

The song (as published), however, became a real hit!

SAMUEL TAYLOR COLERIDGE
born Oct. 21, 1772
Ottery St. Mary
Devonshire, England

The hardships of the sailor! Here at 14, a strange foreshadowing of parts of The Ancient Mariner. *Coleridge himself wrote almost 40 years later about this poem: "This school exercise, written in the 15th year of my age, does not contain a line that any clever schoolboy might not have written, and like most school poetry is a* Putting of Thought into Verse; *for such Verses as* strivings *of mind and struggles after the Intense and Vivid are a fair Promise of better things."*

Age 14

DURA NAVIS

To tempt the dangerous deep, too venturous youth,
Why does thy breast with fondest wishes glow?
No tender parent there thy cares shall sooth,
No much-lov'd Friend shall share thy every woe.
Why does thy mind with hopes delusive burn?
Vain are thy Schemes by heated Fancy plann'd:
Thy promis'd joy thou'lt see to Sorrow turn
Exil'd from Bliss, and from thy native land.

Hast thou foreseen the Storm's impending rage,
When to the Clouds the Waves ambitious rise,
And seem with Heaven a doubtful war to wage,
Whilst total darkness overspreads the skies;
Save when the lightnings darting wingéd Fate
Quick bursting from the pitchy clouds between
In forkéd Terror, and destructive state
Shall shew with double gloom the horrid scene?

Shalt thou be at this hour from danger free?
Perhaps with fearful force some falling Wave
Shall wash thee in the wild tempestuous Sea,
And in some monster's belly fix thy grave;
Or (woful hap!) against some wave-worn rock
Which long a Terror to each Bark had stood
Shall dash thy mangled limbs with furious shock
And stain its craggy sides with human blood.

Yet not the Tempest, or the Whirlwind's roar
Equal the horrors of a Naval Fight,
When thundering Cannons spread a sea of Gore
And varied deaths now fire and now affright:
The impatient shout, that longs for closer war,
Reaches from either side the distant shores;
Whilst frighten'd at His streams ensanguin'd far
Loud on his troubled bed huge Ocean roars.

What dreadful scenes appear before my eyes!
Ah! see how each with frequent slaughter red,
Regardless of his dying fellows' cries
O'er their fresh wounds with impious order tread!
From the dread place does soft Compassion fly!
The Furies fell each alter'd breast command;
Whilst Vengeance drunk with human blood stands by
And smiling fires each heart and arms each hand.

Should'st thou escape the fury of that day
A fate more cruel still, unhappy, view.
Opposing winds may stop thy luckless way,
And spread fell famine through the suffering crew,
Canst thou endure th' extreme of raging Thirst
Which soon may scorch thy throat, ah! thoughtless Youth!
Or ravening hunger canst thou bear which erst
On its own flesh hath fix'd the deadly tooth?

I well remember old Jemmy Bowyer, the plagose Orbilius of Christ's Hospital, but an admirable educer no less than Educator of the Intellect, bade me leave out as many epithets as would turn the whole into eight-syllable lines, and then ask myself if the exercise would not be greatly improved. How often have I thought of the proposal since then, and how many thousand bloated and puffing lines have I read, that, by this process, would have tripped over the tongue excellently. Likewise, I remember that he told me on the same occasion—"Coleridge! the connections of a Declamation are not the transitions of Poetry—bad, however, as they are, they are better than 'Apostrophes' and 'O thou's,' for at the worst they are something like common sense. The others are the grimaces of Lunacy."

S.T.C.

The following history of the Crumb family comics was recounted by Robert Crumb when he was 16 and 17 and published in two 7 x 9" notebooks (in editions of one) as their Arcade *Nos. 3 and 11.* Arcade *was one of a long series of family magazines, started by Charles (his older brother) and Robert (with contributions by their younger sisters and brother: Carol, Sandra, and Maxon).*

ROBERT CRUMB
born Aug. 30, 1943
Philadelphia, Pa.

1950

THE HOMEMADE COMICS OF THE CRUMB FAMILY DURING THE FORTIES WERE SOMEWHAT OF A VAGUE NATURE. THAT IS WHY WE'RE STARTING THIS HISTORY WITH THE YEAR 1950. WE HAD BEEN GRADUALLY WORKING OUR WAY UP FROM WALL SCRIBBLING, ADVANCING TO COLORING BOOKS, THEN MAKING OUR OWN CARTOON PICTURE BOOKS, AND FINALLY REACHING COMIC BOOKS AND USING PENCIL INSTEAD OF CRAYON ABOUT 1949. DURING '49 CAROL, CHARLES, ROBERT AND MAXON DID ALL NATURE OF BOOKS AND COMICS. WHY THEY CHOSE CARTOONS OVER REGULAR ART IS HARD TO SAY. THEY HAD HAD PLENTY OF COMIC BOOKS WHICH THEY DEVOURED EAGERLY, BUT SO HAD MOST KIDS OF THIS SAME PERIOD, WHEN THE CARTOON FIELD WAS AT IT'S BEST, AT LEAST ANIMATED CARTOONS WERE, WHICH THEY SEEMED TO PREFER OVER SERIOUS COMIC-TYPE ART. IN 1950, DURING THE LATTER HALF OF THE YEAR, THINGS BEGAN TO TAKE A MORE DEFINITE SHAPE. CHARLES WAS THE LEADER IN THE FIELD. HE STARTED MAKING UP HIS OWN CHARACTERS. ROBERT CAME ALONG WITH SOME A LITTLE LATER. UP TO THIS TIME ALL THEIR COMICS AND BOOKS WERE CENTERED AROUND THE FAMOUS ANIMATED CARTOON CHARACTERS OF THE DAY, MICKEY MOUSE, ANDY PANDA, MIGHTY MOUSE, BONGO, ETC. "ANIMAL TOWN COMICS" WAS THE FIRST ORIGINAL CRUMB PRODUCTION, MADE BY CHARLES. THE CHARACTERS IN IT WERE ALLY ALLIGATOR, THE MAIN CHARACTER, CHICKY CHICK (LATER CHUCKY CHICK) FUZZY THE BUNNY, MOPSY AND FLOPSY, BLACKY CROW, AND NICKY, ALLY'S NEPHEW. IT IS INDEFINITE JUST HOW MANY ISSUES OF ANIMAL TOWN COMICS" CAME OUT, AS THEY HAVE ALL BEEN LOST. ROBERT CRUMB HAD DIFFY THE MOUSE AND BROMBO THE PANDA LATE IN 1950, AND MADE THEM IN ONLY ONE PRODUCTION, A LITTLE STRING-BOUND, HOMEMADE BOOK CALLED DIFFY IN SHACKTOWN." THE LAST OF THE COMICS USING PROFESSIONAL CHARACTERSWAS A MICKEY MOUSE SERIES BY CHARLES AND A FEW ANDY PANDA COMICS BY ROBERT.

1951

CHARLES DROPPED "ANIMAL TOWN COMICS" IN THE EARLY PART OF 1951. DURING THE MONTHS BEFORE THE STARTING OF FUNNY FRIENDS CHARLES AND ROBERT PRODUCED A FEW "CHUCK AND BOB" COMICS ABOUT THEMSELVES. FINALLY, THE FIRST ISSUE OF "CHUCK CRUMB'S FUNNY FRIENDS" WAS PRODUCED. IT WAS THE START OF A LONG MONTHLY PUBLICATION. THERE WERE FOUR STORIES IN IT. THE FIRST STARRED FUZZY THE BUNNY, A CARRY-OVER FROM "ANIMAL TOWN COMICS" AND HIS SIDEKICK, DONNY DOG. THE SECOND STORY "MARDUKE MONKEY", AND HIS ANTICS WITH HERMAN THE HUNTER, "DANNY PANDA" WAS THE THIRD STORY, "CHUCK AND BOB" A MOUSE A CAT ROUTINE, WAS THE FOURTH.

ROBERT STARTED BROMBO COMICS LATE IN '51 AND THE FIRST ISSUE OF "BROMBO THE PANDA" WAS JANUARY, 1952. IT WAS COMPRISED OF TWO BROMBO STORIES AND A ONE PAGE DIFFY THE MOUSE JOKE. THE FIRST ISSUE WAS NOT MUCH TO TALK ABOUT, NOR MANY OF THE ISSUES WHICH FOLLOWED DURING THE NEXT FEW YEARS.

From Arcade No. 11
January 1961
Age 17

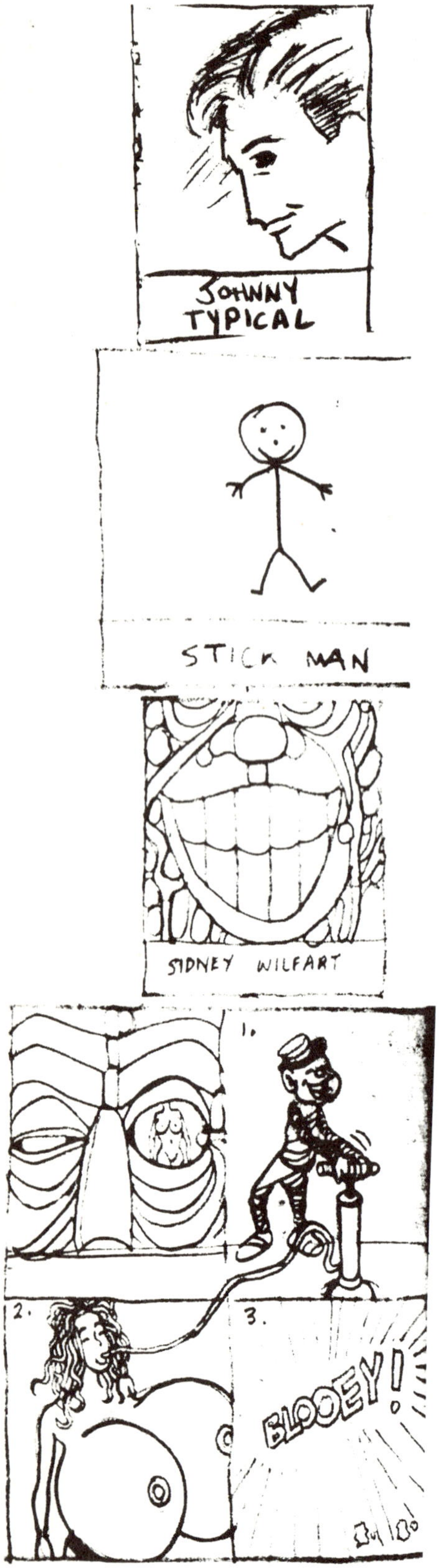

1952

Things started rolling this year. After the first few issues of Brombo the Panda Comics Robert had a bit of a struggle to keep the comic going until the ninth issue when things began to run smoothly. Charles produced eleven issues of Funny Friends with the addition of three new characters, Bonnie Bunny, Mary Monkey, and Wiseguy Weasal . . . Charles teamed up with a friend David Keller and made several issues of "Chemical Kid" comics. Also this year Charles published three Fuzzy the Bunny comics. "Fuzzy in the Army" "Fuzzy Goes to the Moon" and "Fuzzy Goes Out West". These included a second story which was a serial and continued from issue to issue. It was entitled "Fuzzy Bunny Outwits the Phantom Blot".

Other members of the family tried their hand at a monthly schedule comic. Sandra produced "Black-Eyed Susan" comics with such characters as Nosy, Tommy Tulip, Johnny Cougan and others . . . while Maxon stepped forth with "Dizzy Wizzy" comics . . . Characters included Funny Bunny, Jerry Octopus, Chubby the Bear and Tubby Tugboat. Carol got into the act with her "Funny Funnies" . . . characters where the following . . . Campfire Clown . . . Patty and Pogo . . . Twinkle the Pup . . . etc. etc.

This overwhelming spurge of interest in homemade comics eventually led to the forming of the "Animal Town Comics Club" It was kind of an orginazation to discuss problems, ideas, questions concerning homemade comic books. The members and their positions were: Charles Crumb, President, Robert Crumb, Vice President, Carol Crumb, Secretary, Sandra Crumb, Treasurer and Maxon Crumb, was supply boy . . . This club, (although I'm sure we meant well) certainly never accomplished anything. The meetings always ended up in a family brawl, somebody getting hurt, walking out of the meeting, stamping their feet, screaming there head off . . . Among other books and comics produced this year were Nipsy the Bear Comics . . . Animal Town Fun Book . . . Animal Town Christmas Parade . . . The Fisherman and His Wife . . . Brombo and the Beanstalk . . .

1953

Black-Eyed Susan Comics, Dizzy Wizzy Funny Funnies all petered out and so did the goddamn Animal Town Comics Club. However Robert and Charles stuck it out and twelve issues of Brombo the Panda Comics and eleven goddamn issues of Funny Friends where produced this year with the addition of several new titles.

Powerful Panda Comics, Sniff the Panda Comics, and Robert Crumb Comics were new series by Robert Crumb. In addition there were several one shots. These included: Brombo and Sniff in Cardland, Brombo the Panda's Birthday Annual, Spool Land Comics, two issues of Jimmy the Jeep Comics and others. Powerful Panda was adapted into a series of puppet shows which were shown regularly (two or three days a week) to a group of small children at a goddamn summer recreational school in Oceanside, California.

C. Crumb's interprizes this year included four issues of Super Bunny Comics which introduced several new characters. Super Bunny and His Galfriend, a sexy little rabbit named Betty. The villians included Mustache the Weasal and Villianous Vulture with his gang of thieving scum. Other efforts were four issues of Fuzzy the Bunny Comics and five issues of "The Kids of St. Mary's Star of the Sea School" comics . . . These were made up of imaginery adventures of C. Crumbs classmates who attended the Catholic school there in Oceanside.

Robert Fousatt, a friend of C. Crumb's produced several issues of "Super Squirrel Comics" which were of no consquence.

In the latter part of the year a new novelty called Three Dimensional Comics hit the newsstands. All comic book publishers got in on this big money making deal and the Crumb brothers were no exceptions. Charles produced two issues of "Three Dimensional Comics" with featured: "Little Tacos" "The Pig That Flew—Just Once" "Cinderella" and others. Robert produced one issue of "Brombo the Panda 3-D Comics."

However in 1954 the big three dimensional comic craze fizzled out as quickly as it had fizzled in.

(And here the history mysteriously ends—Eds.)

from Arcade No. 11
Age 17

EMILY DICKINSON
born Dec. 10, 1830
Amherst, Mass.

Age 19

Age 15, silhouette by Charles Temple.

THREE VALENTINES

When Elbridge Bowdoin, her father's law partner and ten years her senior, came to call on her at Mount Holyoke [where she was attending school], his conversation, apparently, was somewhere this side of electric. Emily wrote Austin: "Bowdoin, tells me of no news, excepting the following. Cherries are fast getting ripe & the new generation attended the Senior Levee, a short time since, both of which facts, were received by me, with proper resignation. Surely, things must have changed in quiet, peace loving Amherst."

Though older and an all-but-confirmed bachelor, Bowdoin was not so vacuous, it seems, as Emily suggests. He lent the Dickinson girls novels . . . to Mr. Dickinson's displeasure, and further troubled his partner with his liberal politics. . . . Emily thought enough of him and of his sense of humor to send him, in 1850, an exuberant verse valentine urging marriage. It is her earliest known poem and one of the happiest.

Sewall

Awake ye muses nine, sing me a strain divine,
Unwind the solemn twine, and tie my Valentine!

Oh the Earth was *made* for lovers, for damsel, and hopeless swain,
For sighing, and gentle whispering, and *unity* made of *twain.*
All things do go a courting, in earth, or sea, or air,
God hath made nothing single but *thee* in His world so fair!
The *bride,* and then the *bridegroom,* the *two,* and then the *one,*
Adam, and Eve, his consort, the moon, and then the sun;
The life doth prove the precept, who obey shall happy be,
Who will not serve the sovereign, be hanged on fatal tree.
The high do seek the lowly, the great do seek the small,
None cannot find who *seeketh,* on this terrestrial ball;
The bee doth court the flower, the flower his suit receives,
And they make merry wedding, whose guests are hundred leaves;
The wind doth woo the branches, the branches they are won,
And the father fond demandeth the maiden for his son.
The storm doth walk the seashore humming a mournful tune,
The wave with eye so pensive, looketh to see the moon,
Their spirits meet together, they make them solemn vows,
No more he singeth mournful, her sadness she doth lose.
The *worm* doth woo the *mortal,* death claims a living bride,
Night unto day is married, morn unto eventide;
Earth is a merry damsel, and *heaven* a knight so true,
And Earth is quite coquettish, and beseemeth in vain to sue.
Now to the *application,* to the reading of the roll,
To bringing thee to justice, and marshalling thy soul:
Thou art a *human* solo, a being cold, and lone,
Wilt have no kind companion, thou *reap'st* what thou hast *sown.*
Hast never silent hours, and minutes all too long,
And a deal of sad reflection, and *wailing* instead of song?

There's *Sarah,* and *Eliza,* and *Emeline* so fair,
And *Harriet,* and *Susan,* and she with *curling hair!* [Emily herself]
Thine eyes are sadly blinded, but yet thou mayest see
Six true, and comely maidens sitting upon the tree;
Approach that tree with caution, then up it boldly climb,
And seize the one thou lovest, nor care for *space,* or *time!*
Then bear her to the greenwood, and build for her a bower,
And give her what she asketh, jewel, or bird, or flower—
And bring the fife, and trumpet, and beat upon the drum—
And bid the world Goodmorrow, and go to glory home!

Bowdoin was unmoved; he remained a bachelor to the last . . . But he kept the Valentine for forty years.

Sewall

George Gould . . . was a close friend of Austin's [Emily's brother], a classmate, in the same fraternity . . . and his rival on the Amherst oratorical platforms. . . . Such talent may account for the enthusiasm Emily put into the valentine she (presumably) sent him that same year (1850). He was at that time chairman of the editorial board of a new student publication, the Indicator, *published, as he announced in his first statement as editor in June 1849, with the prime object of "our own literary advancement." The following February, the* Indicator *was flooded with valentines from female admirers—and* "one, such *an one" they chose to publish. Since Gould was the only member of the board we know of so closely associated with the Dickinsons, the valentine probably was sent to him.*

It was his colleague Henry Shipley, however, who wrote the comment on it: "I wish I knew who the author is. I think she must have some spell by which she quickens the imagination, and causes the high blood 'run frolic through the veins.' "

Sewall

Age 19

Magnum bonum, "harum scarum," zounds et zounds, et war alarum, man reformam, life perfectum, mundum changum, all things flarum?

Sir, I desire an interview; meet me at sunrise, or sunset, or the new moon—the place is immaterial. In gold, or in purple, or sackcloth—I look not upon the *raiment.* With sword, or with pen, or with plough—the weapons are less than the *wielder.* In coach, or in wagon, or walking, the *equipage* far from the *man.* With soul, or spirit, or body, they are all alike to me. With host or alone, in sunshine or storm, in heaven or earth, *some* how or *no* how—I propose, sir, to see you.

And not to *see* merely, but a chat, sir, or a tete-a-tete, a confab, a mingling of opposite minds is what I propose to have. I feel sir that we shall agree. We will be David and Jonathan, or Damon and Pythias, or what is better than either, the United States of America. We will talk over what we have learned in our geographies, and listened to from the pulpit, the press and the Sabbath School.

This is strong language sir, but none the less true. So hurrah for North Carolina, since we are on this point.

Our friendship sir, shall endure till sun and moon shall wane no more, till stars shall set, and victims rise to grace the final sacrifice. We'll be instant, in season, out of season, minister, take care of, cherish, sooth, watch, wait, doubt, refrain, reform, elevate, instruct. All choice spirits however distant are ours, ours theirs; there is a thrill of sympathy—a circulation of mutuality—cognationem inter nos! I am Judith the heroine of the Apocrypha, and you the orator of Ephesus.

That's what they call a metaphor in our country. Don't be afraid of it, sir, it won't bite. If it was my dog *Carlo* now! The Dog is the noblest work of Art, sir. I may safely say the noblest—his mistress's rights he doth defend—although it bring him to his end—although to death it doth him send!

But the world is sleeping in ignorance and error, sir, and we must be crowing cocks, and singing larks, and a rising sun to awake her; or else we'll pull society up to the roots, and plant it in a different place. We'll build Alms-houses, and transcendental State prisons, and scaffolds—we will blow out the sun, and the moon, and encourage invention. Alpha shall kiss Omega—we will ride up the hill of glory—Hallelujah, all hail!

Yours, truly,
C.

William [Howland], the one who proposed to Vinnie [her sister], was the probable recipient of the other verse valentine of Emily's that survives and the first of her verses to be printed (Springfield Republican, *February 20, 1852, though how it got there is a mystery).*

Sewall

Age 21

"Sic transit gloria mundi,"
"How doth the busy bee,"
"Dum vivimus vivamus,"
I stay mine enemy!

Oh, "veni, vidi, vici!"
Oh caput cap-a-pie!
And oh "memento mori"
When I am *far* from thee!

Hurrah for Peter Parley!
Hurrah for Daniel Boon!
Three cheers, sir, for the gentleman
Who first observed the moon!

Peter, put up the sunshine;
Pattie, arrange the stars;
Tell Luna, *tea* is waiting,
And call your brother Mars!

Put down the apple, Adam,
And come away with me,
So shalt thou have a *pippin*
From off my father's tree!

I climb the "Hill of Science,"
I "view the landscape o'er;"
Such transcendental prospect,
I ne'er beheld before!

Unto the Legislature
My country bids me go;
I'll take my *india rubbers*,
In case the *wind* should blow!

During my education,
It was announced to me
That *gravitation, stumbling*,
Fell from an *apple* tree!

The earth upon an axis
Was once supposed to turn,
By way of a *gymnastic*
In honor of the sun!

It *was* the brave Columbus,
A sailing o'er the tide,
Who notified the nations
Of where I would reside!

Mortality is fatal—
Gentility is fine,
Rascality, heroic,
Insolvency, sublime!

Our Fathers being weary,
Laid down on Bunker Hill;
And tho' full many a morning,
Yet they are sleeping still,—

The trumpet, sir, shall wake them,
In dreams I see them rise,
Each with a solemn musket
A marching to the skies!

A coward will remain, Sir,
Until the fight is done;
But an *immortal hero*
Will take his hat, and run!

Good bye, Sir, I am going;
My country calleth me;
Allow me, Sir, at parting,
To wipe my weeping e'e.

In token of our friendship
Accept this "Bonnie Doon,"
And when the hand that plucked it
Hath passed beyond the moon,

The memory of my ashes
Will consolation be;
Then, farewell, Tuscarora,
And farewell, Sir, to thee!

What Howland had done to deserve such attention is another mystery. He evidently bored Vinnie, and Emily says little about him. But he got along splendidly in Mr. Dickinson's law office, to the point where Emily memorialized the relationship in near-poetic style (to Austin): "Howland is here with father—will stay a while I guess. They go to Northampton together, as it is court there now and seem very happy together in the law. Father likes Howland grandly, and they go along as smoothly as friendly barks at sea—or when harmonious stanzas become one melody. Howland was here last evening—is jolly and just as happy—really I can't think now what is so happy as he."

Sewall

ARTHUR CONAN DOYLE
born May 27, 1859
Edinburgh, Scotland

After that he got what he called "a real money-making proposition." Hard work, long hours, endless prescriptions to make up for the poorest classes of Aston, Birmingham; but he earned some £2 a month. "On the whole I made few mistakes, though I have been known to send out ointment and pill boxes with elaborate directions on the lid and nothing inside." The doctor and his wife liked their assistant, treated him as a son, and he returned to them on two later occasions, seeing a lot of low life, doing all the dispensing, and eventually taking on mid-wifery and the more serious cases in general practice.

While at Birmingham he began to write stories. The urge to do so was strong within him, and when a friend, struck by the vividness of his letters, advised him to try his hand at it, he knocked off an adventure yarn called The Mystery of Sasassa Valley, *sent it to* Chambers's Journal, *and to his amazement received £3 3s. He tried again for the same magazine, but though his next few attempts were not successful, he did not lose heart. "I had done it once and I cheered myself by the thought that I could do it again."*

Pearson

About age 20

CHAMBERS'S JOURNAL

OF

POPULAR

LITERATURE, SCIENCE, AND ART.

Fourth Series

CONDUCTED BY WILLIAM AND ROBERT CHAMBERS.

No. 819. SATURDAY, SEPTEMBER 6, 1879. PRICE 1½d.

THE MYSTERY OF SASASSA VALLEY.

A SOUTH AFRICAN STORY.

Do I know why Tom Donahue is called 'Lucky Tom?' Yes; I do; and that is more than one in ten of those who call him so can say. I have knocked about a deal in my time, and seen some strange sights, but none stranger than the way in which Tom gained that sobriquet and his fortune with it. For I was with him at the time.—Tell it? Oh, certainly; but it is a longish story and a very strange one; so fill up your glass again, and light another cigar while I try to reel it off. Yes; a very strange one; beats some fairy stories I have heard; but it's true sir, every word of it. There are men alive at Cape Colony now who'll remember it and confirm what I say. Many a time has the tale been told round the fire in Boers' cabins from Orange State to Griqualand; yes, and out in the Bush and at the Diamond Fields too.

I'm roughish now sir; but I was entered at the Middle Temple once, and studied for the Bar. Tom—worse luck!—was one of my fellow-students; and a wildish time we had of it, until at last our finances ran short, and we were compelled to give up our so-called studies, and look about for some part of the world where two young fellows with strong arms and sound constitutions might make their mark. In those days the tide of emigration had scarcely begun to set in towards Africa, and so we thought our best chance would be down at Cape Colony. Well—to make a long story short—we set sail, and were deposited in Cape Town with less than five pounds in our pockets; and there we parted. We each tried our hands at many things, and had ups and downs; but when, at the end of three years, chance led each of us up-country and we met again, we were, I regret to say, in almost as bad a plight as when we started.

Well, this was not much of a commencement; and very disheartened we were, so disheartened that Tom spoke of going back to England and getting a clerkship. For you see we didn't know that we had played out all our small cards, and that the trumps were going to turn up. No; we thought our 'hands' were bad all through. It was a very lonely part of the country that we were in, inhabited by a few scattered farmers, whose houses were stockaded and fenced in to defend them against the Kaffirs. Tom Donahue and I had a little hut right out in the Bush; but we were known to possess nothing, and to be handy with our revolvers, so we had little to fear. There we waited, doing odd jobs, and hoping that something would turn up. Well, after we had been there about a month something did turn up upon a certain night, something which was the making of both of us; and it's about that night sir, that I'm going to tell you. I remember it well. The wind was howling past our cabin, and the rain threatened to burst in our rude window. We had a great wood-fire crackling and sputtering on the hearth, by which I was sitting mending a whip, while Tom was lying in his bunk groaning disconsolately at the chance which had led him to such a place.

'Cheer up, Tom—cheer up,' said I. 'No man ever knows what may be awaiting him.'

'Ill-luck, ill-luck, Jack,' he answered. 'I always was an unlucky dog. Here have I been three years in this abominable country; and I see lads fresh from England jingling the money in their pockets, while I am as poor as when I landed. Ah, Jack, if you want to keep your head above water, old friend, you must try your fortune away from me.'

'Nonsense, Tom; you're down in your luck to-night. But hark! Here's some one coming outside. Dick Wharton, by the tread; he'll rouse you, if any man can.'

Even as I spoke the door was flung open, and honest Dick Wharton, with the water pouring from him, stepped in, his hearty red face looming through the haze like a harvest-moon. He shook himself, and after greeting us sat down by the fire to warm himself.

'Whereaway, Dick, on such a night as this?' said I. 'You'll find the rheumatism a worse foe than the Kaffirs, unless you keep more regular hours.'

Dick was looking unusually serious, almost frightened, one would say, if one did not know the man. 'Had to go,' he replied—'had to go. One of Madison's cattle was seen straying down Sasassa Valley, and of course none of our blacks would go down *that* Valley at night; and if we had waited till morning, the brute would have been in Kaffirland.'

'Why wouldn't they go down Sasassa Valley at night?' asked Tom.

'Kaffirs, I suppose,' said I.

'Ghosts,' said Dick.

We both laughed.

'I suppose they didn't give such a matter-of-fact fellow as you a sight of their charms?' said Tom from the bunk.

'Yes,' said Dick seriously—'yes; I saw what the niggers talk about; and I promise you, lads, I don't want ever to see it again.'

Tom sat up in his bed. 'Nonsense, Dick; you're joking, man! Come, tell us all about it. The legend first, and your own experience afterwards.—Pass him over the bottle, Jack.'

'Well, as to the legend,' began Dick—'it seems that the niggers have had it handed down to them that that Sasassa Valley is haunted by a frightful fiend. Hunters and wanderers passing down the defile have seen its glowing eyes under the shadows of the cliff; and the story goes that whoever has chanced to encounter that baleful glare, has had his after-life blighted by the malignant power of this creature. Whether that be true or not,' continued Dick ruefully, 'I may have an opportunity of judging for myself.'

'Go on, Dick—go on,' cried Tom. 'Let's hear about what you saw.'

'Well, I was groping down the Valley, looking for that cow of Madison's, and I had, I suppose, got half-way down, where a black craggy cliff juts into the ravine on the right, when I halted to have a pull at my flask. I had my eye fixed at the time upon the projecting cliff I have mentioned, and noticed nothing unusual about it. I then put up my flask and took a step or two forward, when in a moment there burst apparently from the base of the rock, about eight feet from the ground and a hundred yards from me, a strange lurid glare, flickering and oscillating, gradually dying away and then reappearing again.—No, no; I've seen many a glow-worm and firefly—nothing of that sort. There it was burning away, and I suppose I gazed at it, trembling in every limb, for fully ten minutes. Then I took a step forwards, when instantly it vanished, vanished like a candle blown out. I stepped back again; but it was some time before I could find the exact spot and position from which it was visible. At last, there it was, the weird reddish light, flickering away as before. Then I screwed up my courage, and made for the rock; but the ground was so uneven that it was impossible to steer straight; and though I walked along the whole base of the cliff, I could see nothing. Then I made tracks for home; and I can tell you, boys, that until you remarked it, I never knew it was raining, the whole way along.—But hollo! what's the matter with Tom?'

What indeed? Tom was now sitting with his legs over the side of the bunk, and his whole face betraying excitement so intense as to be almost painful. 'The fiend would have two eyes. How many lights did you see, Dick? Speak out!'

'Only one.'

'Hurrah!' cried Tom—'that's better!' Whereupon he kicked the blankets into the middle of the room, and began pacing up and down with long feverish strides. Suddenly he stopped opposite Dick, and laid his hand upon his shoulder: 'I say, Dick, could we get to Sasassa Valley before sunrise?'

'Scarcely,' said Dick.

'Well, look here; we are old friends, Dick Wharton, you and I. Now, don't you tell any other man what you have told us, for a week. You'll promise that; won't you?'

I could see by the look on Dick's face as he acquiesced that he considered poor Tom to be mad; and indeed I was myself completely mystified by his conduct. I had, however, seen so many proofs of my friend's good sense and quickness of apprehension, that I thought it quite possible that Wharton's story had had a meaning in his eyes which I was too obtuse to take in.

All night Tom Donahue was greatly excited, and when Wharton left he begged him to remember his promise, and also elicited from him a description of the exact spot at which he had seen the apparition, as well as the hour at which it appeared. After his departure, which must have been about four in the morning, I turned into my bunk and watched Tom sitting by the fire splicing two sticks together, until I fell asleep. I suppose I must have slept about two hours; but when I awoke, Tom was still sitting working away in almost the same position. He had fixed the one stick across the top of the other so as to form a rough T, and was now busy in fitting a smaller stick into the angle between them, by manipulating which, the cross one could be either cocked up or depressed to any extent. He had cut notches too in the perpendicular stick, so that by the aid of the small prop, the cross one could be kept in any position for an indefinite time.

'Look here, Jack!' he cried, whenever he saw

that I was awake. 'Come, and give me your opinion. Suppose I put this cross-stick pointing straight at a thing, and arranged this small one so as to keep it so, and left it, I could find that thing again if I wanted it—don't you think I could, Jack—don't you think so?' he continued nervously, clutching me by the arm.

'Well,' I answered, 'it would depend on how far off the thing was, and how accurately it was pointed. If it were any distance, I'd cut sights on your cross-stick; then a string tied to the end of it, and held in a plumb-line forwards, would lead you pretty near what you wanted. But surely, Tom, you don't intend to localise the ghost in that way?'

'You'll see to-night, old friend—you'll see to-night. I'll carry this to the Sasassa Valley. You get the loan of Madison's crowbar, and come with me; but mind you tell no man where you are going, or what you want it for.'

All day Tom was walking up and down the room, or working hard at the apparatus. His eyes were glistening, his cheek hectic, and he had all the symptoms of high fever. 'Heaven grant that Dick's diagnosis be not correct!' I thought, as I returned with the crowbar; and yet, as evening drew near, I found myself imperceptibly sharing the excitement.

About six o'clock Tom sprang to his feet and seized his sticks. 'I can stand it no longer, Jack,' he cried; 'up with your crowbar, and hey for Sasassa Valley! To-night's work, my lad, will either make us or mar us! Take your six-shooter, in case we meet the Kaffirs. I daren't take mine, Jack,' he continued, putting his hands upon my shoulders—'I daren't take mine; for if my ill-luck sticks to me to-night, I don't know what I might not do with it.'

Well, having filled our pockets with provisions, we set out, and as we took our wearisome way towards the Sasassa Valley, I frequently attempted to elicit from my companion some clue as to his intentions. But his only answer was: 'Let us hurry on, Jack. Who knows how many have heard of Wharton's adventure by this time! Let us hurry on, or we may not be first in the field!'

Well sir, we struggled on through the hills for a matter of ten miles; till at last, after descending a crag, we saw opening out in front of us a ravine so sombre and dark that it might have been the gate of Hades itself; cliffs many hundred feet high shut in on every side the gloomy boulder-studded passage which led through the haunted defile into Kaffirland. The moon rising above the crags, threw into strong relief the rough irregular pinnacles of rock by which they were topped, while all below was dark as Erebus.

'The Sasassa Valley?' said I.

'Yes,' said Tom.

I looked at him. He was calm now; the flush and feverishness had passed away; his actions were deliberate and slow. Yet there was a certain rigidity in his face and glitter in his eye which shewed that a crisis had come.

We entered the pass, stumbling along amid the great boulders. Suddenly I heard a short quick exclamation from Tom. 'That's the crag!' he cried, pointing to a great mass looming before us in the darkness. 'Now Jack, for any favour use your eyes! We're about a hundred yards from that cliff, I take it; so you move slowly towards one side, and I'll do the same towards the other. When you see anything, stop, and call out. Don't take more than twelve inches in a step, and keep your eye fixed on the cliff about eight feet from the ground. Are you ready?'

'Yes.' I was even more excited than Tom by this time. What his intention or object was, I could not conjecture, beyond that he wanted to examine by daylight the part of the cliff from which the light came. Yet the influence of the romantic situation and of my companion's suppressed excitement was so great, that I could feel the blood coursing through my veins and count the pulses throbbing at my temples.

'Start!' cried Tom; and we moved off, he to the right, I to the left, each with our eyes fixed intently on the base of the crag. I had moved perhaps twenty feet, when in a moment it burst upon me. Through the growing darkness there shone a small ruddy glowing point, the light from which waned and increased, flickered and oscillated, each change producing a more weird effect than the last. The old Kaffir superstition came into my mind, and I felt a cold shudder pass over me. In my excitement, I stepped a pace backwards, when instantly the light went out, leaving utter darkness in its place; but when I advanced again, there was the ruddy glare glowing from the base of the cliff. 'Tom, Tom!' I cried.

'Ay, ay!' I heard him exclaim, as he hurried over towards me.

'There it is—there, up against the cliff!'

Tom was at my elbow. 'I see nothing,' said he.

'Why, there, there, man, in front of you!' I stepped to the right as I spoke, when the light instantly vanished from my eyes.

But from Tom's ejaculations of delight it was clear that from my former position it was visible to him also. 'Jack,' he cried, as he turned and wrung my hand—'Jack, you and I can never complain of our luck again. Now heap up a few stones where we are standing.—That's right. Now we must fix my sign-post firmly in at the top. There! It would take a strong wind to blow that down; and we only need it to hold out till morning. O Jack, my boy, to think that only yesterday we were talking of becoming clerks, and you saying that no man knew what was awaiting him too! By Jove, Jack, it would make a good story!'

By this time we had firmly fixed the perpendicular stick in between two large stones; and Tom bent down and peered along the horizontal one. For fully a quarter of an hour he was alternately raising and depressing it, until at last, with a sigh of satisfaction, he fixed the prop into the angle, and stood up. 'Look along, Jack,' he said. 'You have as straight an eye to take a sight as any man I know of.'

I looked along. There, beyond the further sight was the ruddy scintillating speck, apparently at the end of the stick itself, so accurately had it been adjusted.

'And now, my boy,' said Tom, 'let's have some supper, and a sleep. There's nothing more to be done to-night; but we'll need all our wits and strength to-morrow. Get some sticks, and kindle a fire here, and then we'll be able to keep an eye on our signal-post, and see that nothing happens to it during the night.'

Well sir, we kindled a fire, and had supper with the Sasassa demon's eye rolling and glowing in front of us the whole night through. Not always in the same place though; for after supper, when I glanced along the sights to have another look at it, it was nowhere to be seen. The information did not, however, seem to disturb Tom in any way. He merely remarked: 'It's the moon, not the thing, that has shifted;' and coiling himself up, went to sleep.

By early dawn we were both up, and gazing along our pointer at the cliff; but we could make out nothing save the one dead monotonous slaty surface, rougher perhaps at the part we were examining than elsewhere, but otherwise presenting nothing remarkable.

'Now for your idea, Jack!' said Tom Donahue, unwinding a long thin cord from round his waist. 'You fasten it, and guide me while I take the other end.' So saying he walked off to the base of the cliff, holding one end of the cord, while I drew the other taut, and wound it round the middle of the horizontal stick, passing it through the sight at the end. By this means I could direct Tom to the right or left, until we had our string stretching from the point of attachment, through the sight, and on to the rock, which it struck about eight feet from the ground. Tom drew a chalk circle of about three feet diameter round the spot, and then called to me to come and join him. 'We've managed this business together, Jack,' he said, 'and we'll find what we are to find, together.' The circle he had drawn embraced a part of the rock smoother than the rest, save that about the centre there were a few rough protuberances or knobs. One of these Tom pointed to with a cry of delight. It was a roughish brownish mass about the size of a man's closed fist, and looking like a bit of dirty glass let into the wall of the cliff. 'That's it!' he cried—'that's it!'

'That's what?'

'Why, man, *a diamond*, and such a one as there isn't a monarch in Europe but would envy Tom Donahue the possession of. Up with your crowbar, and we'll soon exorcise the demon of Sasassa Valley!'

I was so astounded that for a moment I stood speechless with surprise, gazing at the treasure which had so unexpectedly fallen into our hands.

'Here, hand me the crowbar,' said Tom. 'Now, by using this little round knob which projects from the cliff here, as a fulcrum, we may be able to lever it off.—Yes; there it goes. I never thought it could have come so easily. Now, Jack, the sooner we get back to our hut and then down to Cape Town, the better.'

We wrapped up our treasure, and made our way across the hills, towards home. On the way, Tom told me how, while a law-student in the Middle Temple, he had come upon a dusty pamphlet in the library, by one Jans van Hounym, which told of an experience very similar to ours, which had befallen that worthy Dutchman in the latter part of the seventeenth century, and which resulted in the discovery of a luminous diamond. This tale it was which had come into Tom's head as he listened to honest Dick Wharton's ghost-story; while the means which he had adopted to verify his supposition sprang from his own fertile Irish brain.

'We'll take it down to Cape Town,' continued Tom, 'and if we can't dispose of it with advantage there, it will be worth our while to ship for London with it. Let us go along to Madison's first, though; he knows something of these things, and can perhaps give us some idea of what we may consider a fair price for our treasure.'

We turned off from the track accordingly, before reaching our hut, and kept along the narrow path leading to Madison's farm. He was at lunch when we entered; and in a minute we were seated at each side of him, enjoying South African hospitality.

'Well,' he said, after the servants were gone, 'what's in the wind now? I see you have something to say to me. What is it?'

Tom produced his packet, and solemnly untied the handkerchiefs which enveloped it. 'There!' he said, putting his crystal on the table; 'what would you say was a fair price for that?'

Madison took it up and examined it critically. 'Well,' he said, laying it down again, 'in its crude state about twelve shillings per ton.'

'Twelve shillings!' cried Tom, starting to his feet. 'Don't you see what it is?'

'Rock-salt!'

'Rock fiddle; a diamond.'

'Taste it!' said Madison.

Tom put it to his lips, dashed it down with a dreadful exclamation, and rushed out of the room.

I felt sad and disappointed enough myself; but presently remembering what Tom had said about the pistol, I, too, left the house, and made for the hut, leaving Madison open-mouthed with astonishment. When I got in, I found Tom lying in his bunk with his face to the wall, too dispirited apparently to answer my consolations. Anathematising Dick and Madison, the Sasassa demon, and everything else, I strolled out of the hut, and refreshed myself with a pipe after our wearisome adventure. I was about fifty yards away from the hut, when I heard issuing from it the sound which of all others I least expected to hear. Had it been a groan or an oath, I should have taken it as a matter of course; but the sound which caused me to stop and take the pipe out of my mouth was a hearty roar of laughter! Next moment, Tom himself emerged from the door, his whole face radiant with delight. 'Game for another ten-mile walk, old fellow?'

'What! for another lump of rock-salt, at twelve shillings a ton?'

'"No more of that, Hal, an you love me,"' grinned Tom. 'Now look here, Jack. What blessed fools we are to be so floored by a trifle! Just sit on this stump for five minutes, and I'll make it as clear as daylight. You've seen many a lump of rock-salt stuck in a crag, and so have I, though we did make such a mull of this one. Now, Jack, did any of the pieces you have ever seen shine in the darkness brighter than any fire-fly?'

'Well, I can't say they ever did.'

'I'd venture to prophesy that if we waited until night, which we won't do, we would see that light still glimmering among the rocks. Therefore, Jack, when we took away this worthless salt, we took the wrong crystal. It is no very strange thing in these hills that a piece of rock-salt should be lying within a foot of a diamond. It caught our eyes, and we were excited, and so we made fools of ourselves, and *left the real stone behind.* Depend upon it, Jack, the Sasassa gem is lying within that magic circle of chalk upon the face of yonder cliff. Come, old fellow, light your pipe and stow your revolver, and we'll be off before that fellow Madison has time to put two and two together.'

I don't know that I was very sanguine this time. I had begun in fact to look upon the diamond as a most unmitigated nuisance. However, rather than throw a damper on Tom's expectations, I announced myself eager to start. What a walk it was! Tom was always a good mountaineer, but his excitement seemed to lend him wings that day, while I scrambled along after him as best I could. When we got within half a mile he broke into the 'double,' and never pulled up until he reached the round white circle upon the cliff. Poor old Tom! when I came up, his mood had changed, and he was standing with his hands in his pockets, gazing vacantly before him with a rueful countenance.

'Look!' he said—'look!' and he pointed at the cliff. Not a sign of anything in the least resembling a diamond there. The circle included nothing but flat slate-coloured stone, with one large hole, where we had extracted the rock-salt, and one or two smaller depressions. No sign of the gem.

'I've been over every inch of it,' said poor Tom. 'It's not there. Some one has been here and noticed the chalk, and taken it. Come home, Jack; I feel sick and tired. Oh! had any man ever luck like mine!'

I turned to go, but took one last look at the cliff first. Tom was already ten paces off.

'Hollo!' I cried, 'don't you see any change in that circle since yesterday?'

'What d'ye mean?' said Tom.

'Don't you miss a thing that was there before?'

'The rock-salt?' said Tom.

'No; but the little round knob that we used for a fulcrum. I suppose we must have wrenched it off in using the lever. Let's have a look at what it's made of.'

Accordingly, at the foot of the cliff we searched about among the loose stones.

'Here you are, Jack! We've done it at last! We're made men!'

I turned round, and there was Tom radiant with delight, and with a little corner of black rock in his hand. At first sight it seemed to be merely a chip from the cliff; but near the base there was projecting from it an object which Tom was now exultingly pointing out. It looked at first something like a glass eye; but there was a depth and brilliancy about it such as glass never exhibited. There was no mistake this time; we had certainly got possession of a jewel of great value; and with light hearts we turned from the valley, bearing away with us the 'fiend' which had so long reigned there.

There sir; I've spun my story out too long, and tired you perhaps. You see when I get talking of those rough old days, I kind of see the little cabin again, and the brook beside it, and the bush around, and seem to hear Tom's honest voice once more. There's little for me to say now. We prospered on the gem. Tom Donahue, as you know, has set up here, and is well known about town. I have done well, farming and ostrich-raising in Africa. We set old Dick Wharton up in business, and he is one of our nearest neighbours. If you should ever be coming up our way sir, you'll not forget to ask for Jack Turnbull—Jack Turnbull of Sasassa Farm.

FLIRTS AND FLIRTATION.

BY A LADY.

FLIRTATION, strictly defined, is the effort to attract particular attention from the opposite sex by any means, lawful or unlawful; by flatteries, either subtle or gross—according to the tact or taste of the artist—by dress, attitudes, and airs. This, and seeking the society of men, on the part of girls, and adopting a completely different manner towards the two sexes. Accepting this, then, as the true definition of the term, we must be understood, throughout the following remarks, to speak only of what is *unmitigatedly evil* in the practice. What often passes under the name of *harmless* flirtation with those who use it, is not flirting at all, but is merely the pleasant, free, frank intercourse between young men and women with unoccupied hearts, without which society could not get on, as long as the sexes do not live apart in prisons or convents. This we would be very far indeed from condemning. In true flirtation there is always the element of coquetry, which entirely separates it from any other kind of intercourse between the sexes.

Flirtation may be called a game between two people, carried on, as the Germans say, 'unter vier Augen' (under *four eyes*).

In some cases, but not often, the game develops affection on both sides, or only on one; and when the latter, it must very quickly come to an end, after perhaps much suffering, especially if the attachment be on the woman's side. Flirting seems to be indulged in by most young people as their way of life, sometimes for the mere pleasure of it, or for the gratification of vanity and love of conquest, but more often with the ulterior design on the part of women of securing a husband. Men as a rule are not so given to aimless flirtations as women. They are either passably indifferent to most of the girls they meet, or else fall violently in love with one or another, from time to time, so that they have at least the merit of being, or believing themselves to be sincere, while the fancy lasts. With men, moreover, flirtation lacks the obnoxious element of indelicacy, which is usually inseparable from the same practice in a woman. She should always be the wooed, never the wooer. If a pleasurable, flirting is also an exhausting excitement, and requires great pains on a woman's part, unless she be what is termed a finished coquette, an adept in the art, who exercises it from mere love of power; though she may not have the smallest special regard for the individual man at the time being, and would perhaps repulse any serious demonstration on his part.

This kind of flirting is not very often met with in real life. It seems chiefly confined to the heroines of sensational novels and verse. The more commonplace style is that of the girl who flirts merely because it seems 'the thing' to do, or because others do it, or that she may be admired, or have a beau, or get settled in life. How much of really enjoyable intercourse with men do girls deprive themselves of, by this almost invariable intro-

WILLIAM E. B. DU BOIS
born Feb. 23, 1868
Great Barrington, Mass.

When he was fifteen, Du Bois began writing a column for a black newspaper, the New York Globe *(later known as the* New York Freeman, *and still later, the* New York Age*). Edited by one of the leading black intellectuals of the day, T. Thomas Fortune, the newspaper carried a number of news columns from cities and towns in the East. Du Bois reported on the social and cultural life of the blacks in Great Barrington.*

Lester

Age 15

Age 19, a junior at Fisk.

April 14, 1883

. . . The citizens of the town are forming a Law and Order society to enforce the laws against liquor selling, which have been sadly neglected for the last year or two. It would be a good plan if some of the colored men should join it. By the way, I did not notice many colored men at the town meeting last month: it seems that they do not take as much interest in politics as is necessary for the protection of their rights. . . .

September 29, 1883

The political contest is near at hand, and the colored men of the town should prepare themselves accordingly. They should acquaint themselves with the political status and attitude of the candidates toward them, particularly their representatives. The choice of Governor should also demand a good share of their attention. Those who voted for Gen. Butler last year, "just to see what he would do," have found it a pretty costly experiment. They will see that while preaching economy, and refusing the necessary appropriations to charitable institutions, he has spent an immense sum of money on needless investigations, such as Tewksbury and the like. The colored men may well ask themselves how they have been benefited by his administration, although he professes to be their friend. A political office should not be the goal of one's ambition, but still, if anyone wishes an office and is worthy of it, it should not be denied him on account of color. We had an example of this here a short time ago, when a colored man, along with a number of white men, applied for the position of night watchman. After an examination the applicants melted down to one white man, a strong Democrat, and the colored man, a Republican. A committee composed wholly of Republicans was chosen to decide between the two candidates, and they selected the white man. The colored men of Great Barrington hold the balance of power, and have decided the election of many officers for a number of years. If they will only act in concert they may become a power not to be despised. It would be a good plan if they should meet and decide which way would be most advantageous for them to cast their votes.

The debate which I spoke of in my last letter ["Ought the Indian to have been driven out of America?"] took place last Wednesday evening at the house of Mr. William Crosly. It was contested warmly on both sides and strong arguments were brought up. It was finally decided in favor of the affirmative. After the debate the ladies of Zion Church held their monthly supper. Mr. Wm. Chinn has returned from Washington. The First Congregation Church, which was dedicated here last Friday, is the handsomest church in the county, and compares with any in the State. The organ, which was given by Mr. Timothy Hopkins, of San Francisco, is one of the most complete in the world. Miss Frances Newport has returned from Pittsfield, where she has been during the Summer. Miss Hattie Sames returned to Providence last Tuesday. Mr. H. Hines and wife of Norfolk, Conn., were visiting friends in town last week. Mr. William Adams of Hartford, Conn. stopped here a short time and departed for Petersburg, Va. last Thursday. . . .

October 20, 1883

There is on foot a movement looking toward the holding of a county convention of the colored Republicans of this county, which is meeting with general favor and regarded as a move in the right direction. There also seems to be a general regret that among all of our people here there are no business men among us, and the desire to remedy this evil is becoming more and more manifest. Miss Isabella Jones, of Stockbridge, was visiting friends in town last week. Miss Lizzie Young will shortly leave here for Brooklyn, N.Y. The monthly supper at the A.M.E. Zion Sewing Society will be held at the residence of Mr. J. Cooley on the 17th. Mr. J.T. Burghardt, of Amherst, arrived today. Mrs. Jackson, of New York, was the guest of Miss Frances Newport last week and on Friday evening agreeably entertained a select company of friends. Mrs. Crossly also held a small reception on the evening of the 2nd inst. at their residence.

January 26, 1884

The ladies hereabouts commenced the leap year season by inviting the gentlemen to a sleigh ride and surprise party at Mr. A.W. Austin's, in Stockbridge, on the 17th inst. There were about twenty-five present, and the time was very pleasantly passed in playing games, and with music, and finally the climax was capped by one of those inimitable suppers which the ladies of this place know so well how to prepare. There is to be a ball given at Northrop's Hall at Lee on the 23d inst, and a festival the following night. It is hoped there will be a good attendance at both. The children's singing class is having good success under the direction of Mrs. McKinsley, and we hope to hear from them soon. There are about ten members. The last monthly supper of the Zion Society was very successful, both financially and otherwise. Mr. I.M. Burghardt, of Meriden, Conn, was in town a short time ago.

February 23, 1884

Age 16

. . . The annual town meeting draws near and colored voters had best begin to look toward their interests. . . .

August 2, 1884

At the closing of exercises of the Southern district school of this place Master Elijah Austin, a colored boy, won the prize of a gold dollar, for being the best reader. He is to be congratulated on his success. . . .

August 23, 1884

. . . On the eleventh inst. quite a large party started from here about 8:30 P.M. to Lake Buel. After a delightful drive of six miles the Lake was reached about 10 P.M. From that time until midnight the carriages kept arriving from this place, Stockbridge, Lee, and other places. Dances, boating and promenading was indulged in until supper was served and the festivities ceased about 3 A.M. This is the third annual ride to the Lake and we do not hesitate to pronounce it the best. The Gilbert family, a company of eight colored singers, gave an entertainment for two successive evenings at Sumner Hall, Aug. 13 and 14. The time of their coming was unlucky, it being at the same time with the St. James Church fair, yet there was a fair audience both nights. The concert was first-class in every respect and the singing of four-year-old "Baby Gilbert" was especially noted. It is hoped they will make us another call at some more favorable time. Miss Julia Newport of Amherst is visiting with her mother, Mrs. M. Newport. The warmer weather is filling the town with summer boarders and the hotels have their full quota. Mr. Alexander Du Bois [his grandfather], the well known steward, passed his eighty-first birthday in his cottage at New Bedford, receiving calls from a few friends.

September 27, 1884

Messrs. Cooley & Mason, our enterprising caterers to the public appetite, will reopen their restaurant at the Agricultural Fair which takes place here Sept. 24th, 25th and 26th. Theirs is the only colored establishment on the ground, and we wish them the same success this year that has attended them in their former ventures. . . .

October 18, 1884

A party of nine from this place spent the evening very pleasantly with Mr. H. Jackson, of South Lee, on the 9th last. The trustees of the A.M.E. Zion Church have succeeded in making an advantageous exchange of land for the site of the church with Dr. Samuel Camp. The piece has a fine situation on Elm street, in the heart of the town. Quarterly conference will be held here on the first Sunday in November, Rev.

Mr. J. F. Lloyd, of Waterbury, Conn., presiding. Mrs. M. Newport returned recently from a visit to Amherst. Singing schools are now held at Mrs. McKinsley's on Thursday evenings. All are invited to join and have a good time. In the political parade held there recently the colored voters marched with the white, and were neither tucked in the rear nor parcelled off by themselves. There was a colored ball held in Sanford's Hall, under the management of Gilbert Don and C.F. Jackson, on the second night of the Agricultural Fair. It was a complete success both financially and otherwise. Mr. James T. Burghardt, of Amherst, paid us a visit a short time ago.

November 22, 1884

Rev. J.F. Lloyd, of Middletown, Conn., conducted the quarterly meeting of the A.M.E. Zion Church at the residence of Mrs. J. McKinsley last Sabbath. The society has been incorporated recently, and it is expected that work upon the church edifice will commence at no far distant day. Mr. Lloyd on the day of his departure took tea at Mr. Wm. Crosley's with a few friends. Mrs. Mary Jackson and Mr. W. Crosley were admitted to the church on probation. Mr. Frank Whiting, a cousin to Mrs. Mark Hopkins has kindly offered to teach a class of colored people in Bible study at the residence of Mr. Crosley on Sunday afternoons at 2:00 p.m.

December 6, 1884

The wedding bells of Berkshire were again awakened from their long silence on Thanksgiving night, to celebrate the marriage of Miss Henrietta, niece to Mr. and Mrs. Chas. Way of Stockbridge, to Mr. Wellington Crockett of Lenox. Throughout the evening carriages kept arriving at the spacious residence of Mr. Way until the house was literally filled with the elite of Berkshire, both white and colored. The ceremony was performed at 8 P.M. by the Rev. Mr. Lloyd of Lee. The bride was attired in a traveling suit of poplin and margon velvet. The bridesmaids wore white merino, trimmed with satin. The groom and groomsmen appeared in the regulation suits. After the ceremony a bountiful supper was served, along with champagne, wine and cigars for the gentlemen. At 10:15 the bridal pair took a hack for Lenox, where they will take up their residence. The presents were especially handsome, and many were sent from friends in North Adams, Pittsfield, Boston and Philadelphia. Below is a partial list: Check for $100, bride's father-in-law; furnished cottage in Lenox, together with the stage route between Lenox and Pittsfield, from the same to the groom; silver cake basket, cut glass cake basket, a fine engraving, silver pickle dish, two glass sets, a number of fruit plates, silver butter dish and knife, set of knives, water pitcher, eight large lamps, two very fine toilet sets, bronze candle stick, two dozen damask linen towels and many others. . . .

Among the most encouraging signs of the advancement of the colored race here was the formation of a club for literary and social improvement to be known as the Sons of Freedom. We call upon all members of the race who sincerely wish for its advancement to join the ranks.

January 10, 1885

On Christmas night there was a tree at the residence of Mrs. M. Newport, there being present many young folks of the town. At 8 P.M. a procession of them was formed in the parlor, where the tree was laden with presents. Miss Hattie Sumea played the march, while the Misses Freeman and Gracie Jackson led the liliputian band, consisting of seven couples, followed by the adults. When the tree was surrounded Messrs. Burghardt and Mason proceeded to divest it of its burdens, to the gratification of all. The remainder of the evening was spent in jollification till a late hour. Not content with one night's enjoyment Mr. W.M. Crosley filled his cosy dwelling on the evening of the 26th with about thirty-five guests. The evening's entertainment was declared one of the most enjoyable of the season. The last meeting of the Sons of Freedom at the House of Mr. Mason was especially interesting. The study of United States history was profitably continued, after which the gentlemen were summoned by the hostess to a lunch, which was also ably discussed. All the gentlemen were called upon by the president to reply to a general toast, after which the meeting adjourned, to meet with Mr. W.E. Gardner on the 5th inst. On New Year's night this same club, under the lead of President Mason, made calls upon lady friends. Fourteen different residences were favored and the result was a surprise both to receivers and received.

January 31, 1885

. . . Your correspondent had the honor of being elected president recently of the high school lyceum, of which he is the only colored member. . . .

Callender's Colored Minstrels along with the Hyer Sisters and Tom McIntosh entertained a crowded house here last Wednesday night with a program which was first class in every respect.

ALLEN WELSH DULLES
born April 7, 1893
Watertown, N.Y.

Age 8

THE BOER WAR, A HISTORY

Chapter I. The Boers and British in South Africa

In the year 1652 the Boers landed on Cape of Good Hope, Finding no people but a few Indians which they had to fight before they could have the land to themselves, but as soon as they had conquered the Indians they set to work to build towns and houses. But the smallpox got among the Dutch so there was room for the new commers; but after a little the Dutch found that there was some gold at a place called Johannesburg.

In 1806 Britain sent trupes which were defeated by the dutch and they took Cape town. But in the year 1814 Britain paid a large sum of six millions to restore Cape town and some other South African land. I think if Britain had known sooner that there was going to be war she would not have paid so much. At this time in south Africa the Dutch, French and German numbered thirty thousand; they were slave holders and the slaves were about as many. Britain did not hear about the gold right away but as soon as he did hear he sent trupes.

If Britain had been a little quicker he might of had the gold. At this time Britain had very few men and they did not stand any chance of beating the Dutch. After a while the Dutch found out that the English were going to make war on them so the dutch got there men ready to fight and made ready for war. That is one thing that helped them very much for if they were not ready to fight the British could come in and capture them. There would not be any quarreling if it was not for the gold. It was not right for the british to come in and get the land because the Boers came first and they had the first right to the land. If Britain had got there first then they could have the land. But it looks now as if the Boers were being driven out of the land. It is not because there is not enough room on the earth for there is room for every body to be comfortable, but the reasen is that every nation wants more land than each other even if they have'nt enough people to cover the space. There is not very much gold but England wants to be richer so she will not loose much money by the war. Britain has not been fighting as hard as she could since 1652, but she would fight a battle or too but there has'nt been any real fighting till 1899 then she began to fight because she saw that the Dutch were getting land and gold. The British were sly enough to go and get in the land when the Dutch were being killed by the small pox.

When the Boers came to the land they expected to make themselves into a country, and after they had cultivated they began to dig for gold, and in the year 1884 they met with success and that attracted England's atention but British began to steal in and to spread out. For the British could not have the Dutch getting gold, so she had to go and meddle with them which brought on war between Britain and the Dutch.

Chapter II. The First Year of Fighting

On Oct. 11 1899 the Boers forces crossed the frontiers and began war. On Dec. 18 1899 Lord Roberts was ordered to South Africa to take charge of the British trupes and Kitchner as chief staff. . . .

Chapter III. The Farm Burning

The British found that if they could not fight the Boers out of their land that they would burn them out, so they began to burn the land, but they could not burn the houses and have the poor women and children starve to death, so they had to huddle them altogether and tried to feed them as well as they could so that they could get the land. This camp where they kept the women and children is called a concentration camp. It sounds very bad to think of having everything burned up and it *was* very bad, for you would have to leave your house and go and be all in one camp and they probely got very bad food. Some people think that the British rule is not very bad, but you have to do just what they say, and you cannot feel free to do what you want, like you could if they had their own rule. Many babies died in the concentration camp and the women were all the time crying because they could not see their husbands. . . .

Dulles, Allen Welsh; lawyer, diplomat; *b.* Watertown, N.Y., 7 April 1893; *s.* of Rev. Allen Macy Dulles and Edith Foster; *m.* 1920, Clover Todd; one *s.* two *d. Educ.:* Princeton University. B.A., 1914, M.A., 1916, George Washington Univ. LL.B., 1926; Brown Univ. LL.D., 1947; Temple University LL.D., 1952; Columbia University LL.D., 1955; Princeton University LL.D., 1957; George Washington University LL.D., 1959; Boston College LL.D., 1961; University of South Carolina, LL.D., 1962; Williams College, LL.D., 1965. Educational work Allahabad, India, 1914-1915; entered U.S. Diplomatic Service, 1916, and served at Vienna, Berne, American Peace Delegation, Paris, Berlin, 1919; American Commission, Constantinople, 1920; Chief of Division of Near Eastern Affairs, Dept. of State, 1922-26; Deleg. to Intl. Conf. on Arms Traffic, Geneva, Switzerland 1925; member of Deleg. Geneva Disarmament Confs., 1926-27 and 1932 and 1933; resigned from Diplomatic Service, 1926, to take up practice of law with Sullivan and Cromwell, N.Y. City; Dir. Council on For. Relations. War work in Europe with the U.S. Office of Strategic Services, 1942-45. U.S. Central Intelligence Agency: Deputy Director, 1951-1953, Director, 1953-61; resumed law practise with Sullivan & Cromwell, 1962; Member, President Commn. on the assassination of Pres. Kennedy, 1963-64. Presbyterian. Medal of Merit, Medal of Freedom, 1916; Officer of Legion of Honor, 1947; Order of SS. Maurizio e Lazzaro, Italy, 1946; Belgian Cross of Officer of Order of Leopold, 1948. National Security Medal, 1961. *Publications:* Can We Be Neutral? (with Hamilton Fish Armstrong), 1939; Germany's Underground, 1947; The Craft of Intelligence, 1963; The Secret Surrender, 1966; Great True Spy Stories, 1968. *Address:* (home) 2723 Q St., N.W., Washington 7, D.C., U.S.A. *Clubs:* Century (New York); Metropolitan, Alibi (Washington).

Died 30 Jan. 1969.

Chapter IV. The Second Year of Fighting

England ought to be content if she owned the mines where gold is, but no, she wants to have the land to. She is all the time picking into little countries. A little time ago she was trying to make war on Venezuela and now South Africa, and trying to squeeze the life out of the Boers, but she is finding it hard work to do it; all her crack soldiers are being cut up by the Boers.

One day the British tied 10 billy goats to try the afects of some lideight shels and so he fired about 20 at them and then went up to see how many were left and he found that there were 11—one had been born. . . .

Chapter V. DeWet's Escape

On Feb 9 1902 Kitchner thought that he had the Wily Boer in a trap; the march began on Feb. 15, the hole force in various directions, till he had DeWet in a trap. But DeWet and some other men and a number of cattle were together, and at one o'clock DeWet mixed up with the cattle, rushed for the standt-Lindley block house line. Many attempts to brake the line were made durin the night, very few Boers escaped. 10 dead Boers were picked up in the morning near Heibron but the total losses were 283 men and 700 tired horses. . . . A year ago Lord Kitchner reported that there were only 13,000 Boers and this year he reported that the Boer total losses are 18,000 men in the last year, that shows that Kitchner's reports cannot be trusted at all. . . .

Chapter VI. The Enportment of Horses to South Africa

During the latter part of the war the Americans have been enporting horses to South Africa for the British to use. The people who are having it done dont know how much it helps the British. They think if they send 1,000 horses to South Africa that it wont be much to 300,000 trupes but they think that they can get money and not help the British very much, but they keep on doing it till it does amount to sumthing. I think that England is big enough to get her own horses and if not she ought not to have started the war, for she cant depend on other nations to supply England with horses. This enportment of horses to South Africa is not done by the government but by private people for the reason the Government can not stop it.

Chapter VII. The Last

Before I end this history I want to say a little about the Boer prisoners in the Bermudas. The Bermudas are nearly in the middle of the Atlantic ocean. There are 5,000 prisoners there, and among them are about 100 prisoners whose ages are from sixty six to nearly eighty and about 200 young men under 16 and the youngest of them all is a little boy a little over nine. But very few of these young men and old men were ever really fighting against the British, but the British just came in and captured them and sent them to the prison camp in South Africa and then to the Bermudas. The British never let the Boer officers on parole but the Boers think that they ought to have the same privileges that the United States did to the Spanish officers. They have very little food. They were accustomed to all the food they wanted in South Africa and the little supply that they were now receiving had great effect on their health. The British are trying now never to let them go back to their own land. It was a very cruel thing for England to do to go and take the Boers from their land when they were not fighting the English and probably never let them go back to South Africa again. This war has cost England a great many men and a large sum of money.

One of the greatest Boers in all South Africa is Mr. Styne, he is a great general as well as a great man. He has encouraged the Boers in their long fighting and if the Boers get their independence he ought to have part of the credit. Some people think that the Boers treated the Zulus so badly, but the British did most of it, but the Boers had to fight them or they would be tortured. If the gold mine in Johannesburg failed the British would soon get tired of fighting for the land and go back to England. The Boers want peace but England has to have the gold and so she goes around fighting all the little countries, but she never dares to fight eather China or Russia. Al the people that have their independence should like to see the Boers win for England is trying to take it from the Boers.

All this talk about the Boers having slaves is not true for the Boers have not had any slaves since 1832, for a Boer captain told me so. America cannot say anything about the slavery for the Americans let men have slaves in the Philipens now.

The Boers are very industrious and are hard workers and are very fond of the Bible, but the Boer prisoners are not even allowed to have the Psalms for they think it will incurage them. They love their country especially and they ought to have it in spite of the wicked English who are trying to rob them of it. I hope that the Boers will win for the Boers are in the wright and the British are in the wrong in the War.

ALBRECHT DÜRER
born May 21, 1471
Nuremberg, Germany

Age 13

Doubtless in a moment of pride in later years at such a remarkable achievement for a boy of 13, the artist inscribed the drawing with the words, "This I drew of myself in a mirror the year 1484, when I was still a child. Albrecht Dürer." Apart from being his first self-portrait, it represents one of the earliest self-portraits in the history of art. Moreover, whereas other artists waited until maturity to indulge in this self-examination, Dürer showed an unusually precocious curiosity in the world around him as well as in himself.

The boy looks to the right, pointing like a St. John at the foot of the Cross, a witness to the event. The other hand is tucked behind, the artist thus avoiding the difficulty of portraying the actual hand used for drawing. A similar silver point drawing of the artist's father, probably by the father, though often claimed as the work of the son, shows the same glassy stare, owing to the eyes having been added afterwards, and uses a similar arrangement of the hands, except that the right hand holds a silver statuette, acknowledging his profession as goldsmith. Probably the young Dürer took his father's drawing as a model of how to solve the problems of self-portraiture. One can still clearly see the free underdrawing as he felt his way towards a definition of the head and arms. [The hair on the right side of the portrait was probably by a later, less-skilled hand.] Though Dürer may have failed to equal his father's technical proficiency, he surpassed him in the freshness and naturalness of expression. The father was portrayed within the convention of Flemish art, but in the son's portrait a new personality shows signs of breaking through.

White

Self-portrait at age 13.

MARY BAKER EDDY
born July 16, 1821
Bow (near Concord), N.H.

This ingenuous little Puritan ditty, with something both sprightly and otherworldly about it, is revealing. Its twelve-year-old author might use the conventional language of piety . . . but a very real and original young person comes through the lines.

The year she wrote it revivals were held in the Old North Church in Concord and in Abraham Burnham's church in Pembroke, and the heady revivalistic atmosphere may well have precipitated a religious crisis for her. But the poem shows her suspended in a sense between two worlds: the religious world represented in different ways by her parents and the literary world represented by Albert Baker [her older brother], then an undergraduate at Dartmouth.

Peel

Age 12

RESOLUTIONS FOR THE MORNING

I'll rise in the morn and drink in the dew,
  From flowers that bloom in the vale—
So mildly dispensing their charms ever new,
  Over hillocks, and flowery dales.

I'll gaze on the orb in yon eastern sky,
  For loftier thoughts 'twill invite!
His beams can enlighten the spiritual eye,
  And inspire my pen as I write.

I'll form resolutions with strength from on high,
  Such physical laws to obey,
As reason with appetite, pleasures deny,
  That *health*, may my efforts repay.

I'll go the alter of God and pray,
  That the reconciled smiles of His son
May illumine my path through the wearisome day,
  And *cheer* me with *hope*, when 'tis done.

I'll greatful remember the blessings I've shared,
  And make this my daily request:
Increase thou my faith, my vission enlarge,
  Clothe me with the garment of peace.

I'll earnestly seek for deliverance from
  Indulgence in sinful mirth:
From *thoughtlessness*, vanity, all that is wrong,
  With *ambition*, that binds me to earth.

And O, I'll remember my *dear absent* friends,
  Though distance may part us the while,
I'll breathe forth a prayer for their *spiritual* gain,
  That goodness, may sorrow beguile.

To these resolutions should I but prove true
  Through faith, free from spiritual pride,
I'll love to acknowledge my days *must be few*
  For they'll waft me away to my God.

At the age of nine or ten, he told me, he wrote "a few little verses about the sadness of having to start school again every Monday morning." He gave them to his Mother and hoped they had not been preserved. At about fourteen he wrote "some very gloomy quatrains in the form of the Rubaiyat*" which had "captured my imagination." These he showed to no one and presumed he destroyed.*

Valerie Eliot

T. S. ELIOT
born Sept. 26, 1888
St. Louis, Mo.

"Song" was done as a school exercise when Eliot was attending Smith Academy (which his grandfather had founded) in St. Louis in 1905. It is his earliest known surviving poem.

Age 16

SONG

If space and time, as sages say,
Are things that cannot be,
The fly that lives a single day
Has lived as long as we.
But let us live while yet we may,
While love and life are free,
For time is time, and runs away,
Though sages disagree.

The flowers I sent thee when the dew
Was trembling on the vine
Were withered ere the wild bee flew
To suck the eglantine.
But let us haste to pluck anew
Nor mourn to see them pine,
And though the flowers of life be few
Yet let them be divine.

[*Written underneath in Tom's hand: "Doggerel License No. 3,271,574"*]

Age 17.

DUKE ELLINGTON
born April 29, 1899
Washington, D.C.

Age 4.

James P. was the great rag pianist of the day. His piano roll of his own "Carolina Shout" *was must listening. Duke slipped the Swiss-cheese-like paper on his piano's roller, slowed its speed down and followed every hill and dale its playing made upon the instrument's keyboard, pressing his fingers down after J.P.'s, pedaling after Johnson, until he had learned to shout* "Carolina." *When James P. Johnson came to Washington to supplant the piano roll with his person, Duke was ready. Johnson sat his barrelly figure down at the piano, flashed his infectious grin, tossed back his bullfrog face, and, with eyes shining, hopped, stomped and strutted through the strident figures of his celebrated composition. It was at a big gathering, and the large crowd yelled and clapped its approval. Duke followed, addressed the piano in more sedate fashion, as was fitting in the younger man, the comparative unknown. But he was the local boy and sentiment was with him, his gang was behind him. He rolled over a few bars. He strode into it, and with hands leaping from the piano in the impressive manner he had learned from watching Dishman, Bowser and friends, "he ran him right out of the joint," as one of the witnesses recalls the event.*

From running the great J.P. right out of the joint, it was an easy step to the confidence necessary to compose his own rag. Working after school at the Poodle Dog Café, a high ranking soda fountain "establishment," right around the corner from the Washington Senators' ballground, it was logical to call it the "Soda Fountain Rag." *Now all that was necessary was the opportunity to play it.*

One day the heavy-drinking pianist at one of the cafés, a "whiz" of a pianist but even more brilliant a drinker, drank so much he knocked himself right out. Duke sprang to his place, and without a moment's hesitation to clear away the prostrate form of the overcome piano-shouter, he jumped into the opening bars of "Soda Fountain Rag." *He played it as a one-step, two-step, waltz, and as a fox-trot, slow, middle-tempo and up. "They never knew it was the same piece," and "I was established. Not only did I write my own music, but I had a repertory!" Duke became more interested in this repertory, in his piano altogether, than he was in his painting, and in 1917 he left high school just a few months before graduation.*

Ulanov

Age 16

SODA FOUNTAIN RAG

By
EDWARD DUKE ELLINGTON

JULES FEIFFER
born Jan. 26, 1929
Bronx, N.Y.

Jules' mother was a fashion designer and she brought home a large dress catalog for him so that he could draw on the backs of its pages.

The full (tabloid-sized) page (verso) was designed as a "week-end supplement strip."

Feiffer confesses to being influenced greatly by radio. "I Love a Mystery" (WEAF) was his favorite show.

He is particularly proud of his signature on this strip and says he has never lettered better (worse, yes—better, no).

As a young boy.

Age 11 or 12

DAREDEVIL
ADVENTURERS
STOP THIEF!
ALLEZ OOP!
OOP!
I GOT IT!
RRRRIP
GIMME!
IMGETTIN' OUT OF HERE!
STOP!
WHATS UP?
THAT FELLER TRIED TO STEAL THE MAP.. HE GOT HALF OF IT!
HE DIDN'T GET THE IMPORT_ ANT PART!
THATS GOOD!
FROM NOW ON WE'VE GOT TO BE CAREFUL!
GET THE MEN UP WE'RE STARTING NOW!
MEANWHILE, DUNKAN REPORTS TO CRAFT..
GOT THE MAP?
I ONLY GOT HALF OF IT!
THIS IS THE WRONG HALF.. GET THE GOOD HALF OR ELSE..
6-9
TO BE CONT'D

At the age of about six, Bobby Fischer, who has become the greatest chessplayer in history, learned the game from his sister. By the time he reached his early teenage years, he was one of the finest chessplayers in the United States. The brilliant game below is his first published effort, played when he was 13. The next year he startled the world by going on to win the U.S. Championship.

Frank Brady

BOBBY FISCHER
born March 9, 1943
Chicago, Ill.

Age 13

United States Junior Championship
Lincoln, Nebraska
1956

WHITE	*BLACK*
Carl L. Grossguth-	Fischer
1. P-K4	P-QB4
2. N-KB3	P-Q3
3. P-Q4	PxP
4. NxP	N-KB3
5. N-QB3	P-QR3
6. B-K2	P-K4
7. N-N3	B-K2
8. B-K3	0-0
9. Q-Q2	P-QN4
10. P-B3	B-K3
11. P-N4	P-Q4!
12. P-N5	P-Q5
13. PxN	BxP!
14. 0-0-0	PxB
15. QxQ	RxQ
16. N-B5	N-B3!
17. NxB	PxN
18. KR-B1?	P-N5

(18. KR-N1 P-N5 19. N-R4 N-Q5 20. R-N2 or 18. P-QR3 offer sterner resistance—Collins in *Chess Life*)

19. N-R4	N-Q5
20. RxN	RxR!?
21. B-Q3	R/1-Q1
22. K-Q1	B-N4
23. K-K2	B-B5
24. P-KR3	R-QB1
25. R-Q1	R-B3
26. P-N3	K-B2
27. P-R4	K-B3
28. P-R5	P-R4
29. N-N2	RxB!

(30. KxR R−B6+ 31. K-K2 RxBP+; 30. RxR RxP+; 30. NxR RxP+ 31. K-K1 B−N6+ 32. K−B1 P−K7+; 30. PxR R−B7+ —Collins)

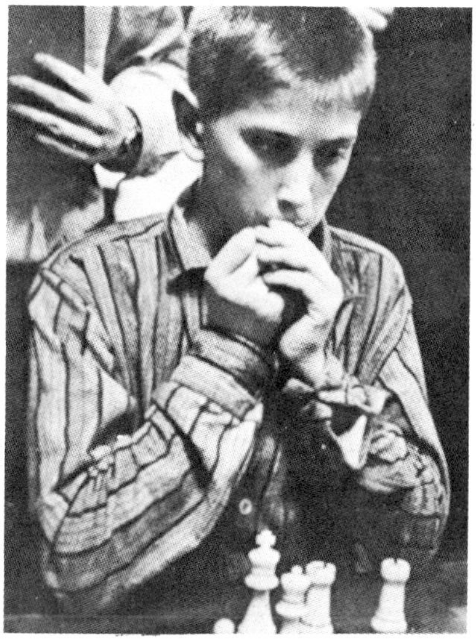

Fischer was a nervous tournament player when he was a teenager; biting his nails during a complicated position, jumping up and down and pacing back and forth between moves. As he matured, he developed a sangfroid *that marked him as one of the most controlled players the game has ever known.*

MARJORY FLEMING
born Jan. 15, 1803
Kirkcaldy, Scotland

She was made out of thunder-storms and sunshine, and not even her little perfunctory pieties and shopmade holinesses could squelch her spirits or put out her fires for long. Under pressure of a pestering sense of duty she heaves a shovelful of trade godliness into her journals every little while, but it does not offend, for none of it is her own; it is all borrowed, it is a convention, a custom of her environment, it is the most innocent of hypocrisies; and this tainted butter of hers soon gets to be as delicious to the reader as are the stunning and worldly sincerities she splatters around it every time her pen takes a fresh breath.

Twain

No more fascinating infantile author has ever appeared, and we may certainly accept the moderate anticipation of her first biographer, that if she had lived she might have written books. Unfortunately she had an attack of measles, and when apparently recovering was taken ill and died after three days of "water on the brain," Dec. 1811 [*a month before her ninth birthday*].

Stephens

Age 6-8

A pencil sketch by Miss Isa Keith.

I love in Isas [her cousin and tutor] bed to lie
O such a joy & luxury
The botton of the bed I sleep
And with great care I myself keep
Oft I embrace her feet of lillys
But she has goton all the pillies

I confess that I have been more like a little young Devil then a creature for when Isabella went up to stairs to teach me religion and my multiplication and to be good and all my other lessons I stamped with my feet and threw my new hat which she made on the ground and was sulky an was dreadfuly passionate but she never whipped me but gently said Marjory go into another room and think what a great crime you are committing letting your temper git the better of you but I went so sulkely that the Devil got the better of me but she never whip me

I am now going to tell you about the horible and wret[ched] plaege that my multiplication give me you cant concieve it—the most Devilish thing is 8 times 8 & 7 times 7 it is what nature itselfe cant endure

I have a delightl pleasure in view which is the thoughts of going to Braehead where I will walk to Craky-hall wich puts me In mind that I walked to that delightfull place with that a delightfull place young man beloved by all his [blot] friends and espacialy by me his loveress but I must not talk any longer about hin any longer for Isa said it is not proper for to speak of gentalman but I will never forget him

I am very very glad that satan has not geven me boils and many other Misfortunes

To Day I bronunced a word which should never come out of a ladys lips it was that I caled John [her brother] a Impudent Bitch and afterwards told me that I should never say it even in joke but she kindly forgave me because I said that I would not do it again I will tell you what I think made me in so bad a homour is I got 1 or 2 cups of that bad bad sina tea to Day

Isa is teaching me to make Simecolings nots of interrgations peorids & commoes &c;

As this is Sunday I must begin to write serious thoughts as Isabella bids me. I am thinking how I should Improve the many talents I have. I am very sory I have threwn them away it is shoking to think of it when many have not half the instruction I have because Isabella teaches me to or three hours every day in reading and writing and arethmatick and many other things and rligion into the bar gan. On sunday she teaches me to be virtuous.

The weather is very mild & serene & not like winter A sailor called here to say farewell, it must be dreadfull to leave his native country where he might get a wife or perhaps me, for I love very him very much & wth all my heart, but 0 I forgot Isabella forbid me to speak about love.

Now am I quite happy: for I am going tomorrow to a delightfull place, Breahead by name, belonging to Mrs Crraford, where their is ducks cocks hens bublyjocks 2 dogs 2 cats & swine. & which is delightful; I think it is shoking to think that the dog & cat should bear them & they are drowned after all. I would rather have a man dog then a women dog because they do not bear like women dogs, it is a hard case it is shoking.

I will never again trust in my own power. for I see that I cannot be good without Gods assistence.

My dear Isa

I now sit down on my botom to answer all your kind and beloved letters which you was so good as to write to me.

This is the first time I ever wrote a letter in my Life.—There are a great many Girls in the Square and they cry just like a pig when we are under the painfull necessity of putting it to Death.—Miss Potune a Lady of my acquaintance praises me dreadfully.—I repeated something out of Deen Sweft and she said I was fit for the Stage and you may think I was primmed up with majestick Pride but upon my word I felt myselfe turn a little birsay birsay is a word which is a word that William composed which is as you may suppose a little enraged.

Marjory and Sir Walter Scott.

STEPHEN FOSTER
born July 4, 1826
Lawrenceville
(near Pittsburgh)
Pennsylvania

As a boy.

At the age of seven years he accidentally took up a flageolet in the music store of Smith and Mellor, Pittsburgh, and in a few minutes he had so mastered its stops and sounds that he played "Hail Columbia" in perfect time and accent. He had never before handled either a flageolet or a flute.

It was not long after this that he learned, unaided, to play beautifully on the flute. He had the faculty of bringing those deep resonant tones from the flute which distinguished the natural flautist from the mechanical performer.

Morrison Foster

When he was nine years old a Thespian company was formed, composed of boys of neighbor families, Robinsons, Cuddys, Kellys and Fosters. The theatre was fitted up in a carriage house. All were stockholders except Stephen. He was regarded as a star performer, and was guaranteed a certain sum weekly. It was a very small sum, but it was sufficient to mark his superiority over the rest of the company. "Zip Coon," "Long-Tailed Blue," "Coal-Black Rose," and "Jim Crow" were the only Ethiopian songs then known. His performance of these was so inimitable and true to nature that, child as he was, he was greeted with uproarious applause, and called back again and again every night the company gave an entertainment, which was three times a week. They generally cleared enough to enable the whole party to buy tickets to the old Pittsburgh Theatre on Saturday nights, where they could be seen in the pit listening to the acting of Junius Brutus Booth, Augustus A. Addams, Edwin Forrest, Oxley, Conner, Logan, Proctor, William and John Sefton, Mrs. Drake and Mrs. Duff.

Morrison Foster

Age 10

Youngstown, Jan. 14, 1837

My Dear Father
I wish you to send me a commic songster for you promised to. if I had my pensyl I could rule my paper. or if I had the money to by Black ink But if I had my whistle I would be so taken with it I do not think I would write atall. there has been a sleighing party this morning with twenty or thirty cupple. Dr. Bane got home last night and told us Henry was coming out here. I wish Dunning would come with him tell them both to try to come for I should like to see them both most two much to talk about.
I remane your loving son
Stephen C. Foster

Towanda, Thursday [1841]

Age 14

My Dear Brother [William, age 34].
As you wish to have me go to Athens for fear I will not learn enough in this place, I will tell you what my ideas were on the subject.

Mr. Vosberry is a very good mathematition, and as he has quit keeping school, he is going to ocupy a private room in the house of Mr. Elwell.

Mr. Kettle will be here tomorrow and will stop at Bartlett & Fords. he will have a room there but will not be in it in the daytime as his paint room will be at another house. Mr. Ford says he will board me and give me as good a room as I wish for $2.00 per week.

If you will let me board here (while you stay) and room with Kettle I will promise not to be seen out of doors between the hours of nine & twelve A.M. and one & four P.M. Which hours I will attribute to study, such as you please to put me into. I will also promise not to pay any attention to my music untill after eight Oclock in the evening after which time Mr. Kettle will probably be in the room as he cannot paint after dark. I dont se how I could have a better chance for study. & the above price is as cheap as I could live in Athens that lonesome place—I can go over to recite in the forenoon at about 10 oclock and in the afternoon at 4—do please consent.

Your affectionate & grateful brother
Stephen

(PS) Please pay Mr. D. Mitchell $3.00 which I borowed from him to pay for pumps, subscription &c for the exhibition. I allso owe Mr. Vandercook a very small amount.

Dont pay Mr. Herrick for fire in my room as I have not had any since you payed him last.

July 24, 1841, Canonsburg

Age 15

My Dear Brother,

I arrived here on last Tuesday, and found among the quantity of Students of this institution, several of my old acquaintances. . . .

The tuition instead of being $5.00 amounts to $12.50 and boarding $2.00 per week.

Pa paid my tuition bill in advance, as is customary at this place. Their is several other bills which I have not paid as I have not the means. Such as 2 or $3.00 for joining one of the literary societies, as all of the studens belong to them I was requested to joiin one and put it of for a couple of weeks, for as Pa has not much more than the means of geting along I thought I would write you this letter that you might considder over the matter. I will also have to pay boarding bill at the end of every month which will amount to $8.50 that is at the end of four weeks and a half which generally makes a month, and if you see fit to send me a little of the bino. once in a while I will insure you their is no inducements here to make me spend any money unnecesarily. I will allso have to pay about $1.25 per week for washing as I have to keep myself very clean here.

I would inform you in the meantime I need another summer coat or two and especially for Sunday. . . .

Aug. 28, 1841

. . . I hope you will pardon me for writing to you so extensively on the money subject. But at the same time I will let you know that a boy comes out mighty thin in Canonsburg without some of it in his pocket. . . .

It was while at Athens [Academy] that he first gave publicity to an effort at composition. He wrote a piece for the college commencement, and arranged it for four flutes. He took himself the leading part, and three others of the students the remaining ones. He called it "The Tioga Waltz." Its performance was very satisfactory to the audience, and was rewarded with much applause and an encore.

Morrison Foster

THE TIOGA WALTZ.

Composed and arranged for four flutes, by STEPHEN C. FOSTER, at the age of thirteen years.
Performed at the College Commencement, Athens, Pa., 1839,
by himself and three other students.

BENJAMIN FRANKLIN
born Jan. 17, 1706
Boston, Mass.

Three years after Benjamin Franklin went to work as an apprentice printer, James Franklin [his elder brother] brought out the first issue of The New-England Courant. . . .

"He had some ingenious Men among his Friends who amus'd themselves by writing little Pieces for this Paper, which gain'd it Credit, and made it more in Demand; and these Gentlemen often visited us. Hearing their Conversations, and their Accounts of the Approbation their Papers were receiv'd with, I was excited to try my Hand among them. But being still a Boy, and suspecting that my Brother would object to printing any Thing of mine in his Paper if he knew it to be mine, I contriv'd to disguise my Hand, and writing an anonymous Paper I put it in at Night under the Door of the Printing House. It was found in the Morning and communicated to his Writing Friends when they call'd in as usual. They read it, commented on it in my Hearing, and I had the exquisite Pleasure, of finding it met with their Approbation, and that in their different Guesses at the Author none were named but Men of some Character among us for Learning and Ingenuity."

Young Benjamin signed his contribution to the paper "Silence Dogood," and then proceeded to create a character to go with the name. Silence described herself as the widow of a country minister, who was "an Enemy to Vice, and a Friend to Vertue. . . . A hearty Lover of the Clergy and all good Men, and a mortal Enemy to arbitrary Government and unlimited Power." She also admitted she had "a natural Inclination to observe and repove the Faults of others, at which I have an excellent Faculty." Fourteen letters over the signature of Silence came from the sixteen-year-old Franklin's pen between April and October of 1722. Perhaps the best of them was the fourth [printed on May 14], in which the apprentice printer took revenge for being denied a college education.

Fleming

Young Ben Franklin (with hat) in his brother's printing shop in Philadelphia. Everyone is congratulating him for his first weekly newspaper column, except his jealous brother James (right).

Age 16

An sum etiam vel Graecè loqui vel Latinè docendus?—
Cicero

Discoursing the other Day at Dinner with my Reverend Boarder, formerly mention'd, (whom for Distinction sake we will call by the name of Clericus,) concerning the Education of Children, I ask'd his Advice about my young Son William, whether or no I had best bestow upon him Academical Learning, or (as our Phrase is) *bring him up at our College:* He perswaded me to do it by all Means, using many weighty Arguments with me, and answering all the Objections that I could form against it; telling me withal, that he did not doubt but that the Lad would take his Learning very well, and not idle away his Time as too many there now-a-days do. These Words of Clericus gave me a Curiosity to inquire a little more strictly into the present Circumstances of that famous Seminary of Learning; but the Information which he gave me, was neither pleasant, nor such as I expected.

As soon as Dinner was over, I took a solitary Walk into my Orchard, still ruminating on Clericus's Discourse with much Consideration, until I came to my usual Place of Retirement under the *Great Apple-Tree;* where having seated my self, and carelessly laid my Head on a verdant Bank, I fell by Degrees into a soft and undisturbed Slumber. My waking Thoughts remained with me in my Sleep, and before I awak'd again, I dreamt the following DREAM.

I fancy'd I was travelling over pleasant and delightful Fields and Meadows, and thro' many small Country Towns and Villages; and as I pass'd along, all Places resounded with the Fame of the Temple of LEARNING: Every Peasant, who had wherewithal, was preparing to send one of his Children at least to this famous Place; and in this Case most of them consulted their own Purses instead of their Childrens Capacities: So that I observed, a great many, yea, the most part of those who were travelling thither, were little better than Dunces and Blockheads. Alas! alas!

At length I entred upon a spacious Plain, in the Midst of which was erected a large and stately Edifice: It was to this that a great Company of Youths from all Parts of the Country were going; so stepping in among the Crowd, I passed on with them, and presently arrived at the Gate.

The Passage was kept by two sturdy Porters named *Riches* and *Poverty*, and the latter obstinately refused to give Entrance to any who had not first gain'd the Favour of the former; so that I observed many who came even to the very Gate, were obliged to travel back again as ignorant as they came, for want of this necessary Qualification. However, as a Spectator I gain'd Admittance, and with the rest entred directly into the Temple.

In the Middle of the great Hall stood a stately and magnificent Throne, which was ascended to by two high and difficult Steps. On the Top of it sat LEARNING in awful State; she was apparelled wholly in Black, and surrounded almost on every Side with innumerable Volumes in all Languages. She seem'd very busily employ'd in writing something on half a Sheet of Paper, and upon Enquiry, I understood she was preparing a Paper, call'd *The New-England Courant*. On her Right Hand sat *English*, with a pleasant smiling Countenance, and handsomely attir'd; and on her left were seated several *Antique Figures* with their Faces vail'd. I was considerably puzzl'd to guess who they were, until one informed me, (who stood beside me,) that those Figures on her left Hand were *Latin*, *Greek*, *Hebrew*, &c. and that they were very much reserv'd, and seldom or never unvail'd their Faces here, and then to few or none, tho' most of those who have in this Place acquir'd so much Learning as to distinguish them from *English*, pretended to an intimate Acquaintance with them. I then enquir'd of him, what could be the Reason why they continued vail'd, in this Place especially: He pointed to the Foot of the Throne, where I saw *Idleness*, attended with *Ignorance*, and these (he informed me) were they, who first vail'd them, and still kept them so.

Now I observed, that the whole Tribe who entred into the Temple with me, began to climb the Throne; but the Work proving troublesome and difficult to most of them, they withdrew their Hands from the Plow, and contented themselves to sit at the Foot, with Madam *Idleness* and her Maid *Ignorance*, until those who were assisted by Diligence and a docible Temper, had well nigh got up the first Step: But the Time drawing nigh in which they could no way avoid ascending, they were fain to crave the Assistance of those who had got up before them, and who, for the Reward perhaps of a *Pint of Milk*, or a *Piece of Plumb-Cake*, lent the Lubbers a helping Hand, and sat them in the Eye of the World, upon a Level with themselves.

The other Step being in the same Manner ascended, and the usual Ceremonies at an End, every Beetle-Scull seem'd well satisfy'd with his own Portion of Learning, tho' perhaps he was *e'en just* as ignorant as ever. And now the Time of their Departure being come, they march'd out of Doors to make Room for another Company, who waited for Entrance: And I, having seen all that was to be seen, quitted the Hall likewise, and went to make my Observations on those who were just gone out before me.

Some I perceiv'd took to Merchandizing, others to Travelling, some to one Thing, some to another, and some to Nothing; and many of them from henceforth, for want of Patrimony, liv'd as poor as Church Mice, being unable to dig, and asham'd to beg, and to live by their Wits it was impossible. But the most Part of the Crowd went along a large beaten Path, which led to a Temple at the further End of the Plain, call'd, *The Temple of Theology*. The Business of those who were employ'd in this Temple being laborious and painful, I wonder'd exceedingly to see so many go towards it; but while I was pondering this Matter in my Mind, I spy'd *Pecunia* behind a Curtain, beckoning to them with her Hand, which Sight immediately satisfy'd me for whose Sake it was, that a great Part of them (I will not say all) travel'd that Road. In this Temple I saw nothing worth mentioning, except the ambitious and fraudulent Contrivances of Plagius, who (notwithstanding he had been severely reprehended for such Practices before) was diligently transcribing some eloquent Paragraphs out of Tillotson's *Works*, &c., to embellish his own.

Now I bethought my self in my Sleep, that it was Time to be at Home, and as I fancy'd I was travelling back thither, I reflected in my Mind on the extream Folly of those Parents, who, blind to their Childrens Dulness, and insensible of the Solidity of their Skulls, because they think their Purses can afford it, will needs send them to the Temple of Learning, where, for want of a suitable Genius, they learn little more than how to carry themselves handsomely, and enter a Room genteely, (which might as well be acquir'd at a Dancing-School,) and from whence they return, after Abundance of Trouble and Charge, as great Blockheads as ever, only more proud and self-conceited.

While I was in the midst of these unpleasant Reflections, Clericus (who with a Book in his Hand was walking under the Trees) accidentally awak'd me; to him I related my Dream with all its Particulars, and he, without much Study, presently interpreted it, assuring me, *That it was a lively Representation of* HARVARD COLLEGE, *Etcetera*.

I remain, Sir, Your Humble Servant,

Silence Dogood

SIGMUND FREUD
born May 6, 1856
Freiburg, Moravia

When he was nine years old he passed an examination that enabled him to attend high school (Sperl Gymnasium) a year earlier than the normal age. He had a brilliant career there. For the last six of the eight years he stood at the head of his class. He occupied a privileged position and was hardly ever questioned in class. . . .

There is no doubt that young Sigmund was engrossed in his studies and was a hard worker. Reading and studying seem to have filled the greater part of his life. Even the friends who visited him, both in school years and later, were at once closeted in the "cabinet" for the purpose of serious discussion, much to the pique of his sisters who had to watch the youths pass them by. A notable feature was his preference for comprehensive monographs on each subject over the condensed accounts given in the textbooks. . . .

When, at the age of seventeen, he was graduated with the distinction summa cum laude, *his father rewarded him with a promise of a visit to England, which was fulfilled two years later. From a contemporary letter to a friend, Emil Fluss, we happen to know some details of the examination.*

Jones

Age 17

Vienna 16.6.1873
At night

Age 16, with mother.

Dear Friend

If I didn't shrink from making the silliest joke of our facetious century, I would just say: "The *Matura* [the final examination before graduation] is dead, long live the *Matura.*" But I like this joke so little that I wish the second *Matura* [the orals] were over, too. Despite secret qualms of conscience and feelings of remorse I wasted the week following the written exam, and ever since yesterday I have been trying to compensate for the loss by filling up thousands of old gaps. You never would listen when I accused myself of laziness, but I know better and feel there is something in it.

Your curiosity over the *Matura* will have to be content with cold dishes as it comes too late and after the meal is finished, and unfortunately I can no longer furnish an impressive description of all the hopes and doubts, the perplexity and hilarity, the light that suddenly dawned upon one, and the inexplicable windfalls that were discussed "among colleagues"—to do this the written exam is already of far too little interest to me. I shall refrain from telling you the results. That I sometimes had good and sometimes bad luck goes without saying; on such important occasions kind Providence and wicked Fate are invariably involved. Events of this kind differ from the ordinary run of things. Briefly, since I don't wish to keep you on tenterhooks about something so unattractive: for the 5 papers I got *exc., good, good, good, fair.* Very annoying. In Latin we were given a passage from Virgil which I had read by chance on my own account some time ago; this induced me to do the paper in half the allotted time and thus to forfeit an *exc.* So someone else got the *exc.*, I myself coming 2nd with *good.* The German-Latin translation seemed very simple; in this simplicity lay the difficulty; we took only a third of the time, so it failed miserably. Result: *fair.* Two others managed to get *good.* The Greek paper, consisting of a 33-verse passage from *Oedipus Rex,* came off better: [I was] the only *good.* This passage I had also read on my own account, and made no secret of it. The maths. paper, which we approached in fear and trembling, turned out to be a great success: I have written *good* because I am not yet positive what I was given. Finally, my German paper was stamped with an *exc.* It was a most ethical subject on "Considerations involved in the Choice of a Profession," and I repeated more or less what I wrote to you a couple of weeks ago, although you failed to confirm it with an *exc.* Incidentally, my professor told me—and he is the first person who has dared to tell me this—that I possess what Herder so nicely calls an *idiotic* style—i.e. a style at once correct and characteristic. I was suitably impressed by this amazing fact and don't hesitate to disseminate the happy event, the first of its kind, as widely as possible—to you, for instance, who until now have probably remained unaware that you have been exchanging letters with a German stylist. And now I advise you as a friend, not as an interested party, to preserve them—have them bound—take good care of them—one never knows.

This, dear friend, was my written Matura. Please wish me loftier aims and less adulterated success and more powerful rivals and greater zeal. Oh, to think of all the good wishes that could be heaped upon me without anything improving by one iota! Whether the *Matura* was easy or difficult I cannot judge; just assume that it was jolly.

I have been to the exhibition twice already. Interesting, but it didn't bowl me over. Many things that seemed to please other people didn't appeal to me because I am neither this nor that, not really anything completely. Actually, the only things that fascinated me were the works of art and general effects. A great comprehensive panorama of human activity, as the newspapers profess to see, I don't find in it, any more than I can find the features of a landscape in an herbarium. On the whole it is a display for the aesthetic, precious and superficial world, which also for the most part visits it. When my "martyr" (this is what we call the *Matura* among ourselves) is over, I intend to go there every day. It is entertaining and distracting. One can also be gloriously alone there in all that crowd.

Needless to say, I am telling you all this with the purely malicious intention of reminding you how uncertain it is when you will be able to see all this splendour, and yet how painful the parting is bound to be when the moment comes. I can well understand your feelings. To leave one's beloved home, fond relatives—the most beautiful surroundings—ruins in the immediate neighbourhood—I must stop or I shall become as sad as you—after all, you know best what you have got to part from! I bet you wouldn't mind if your future employer didn't tear you away from the joys of home for another month. Oh Emil, why are you a prosaic Jew? Journeymen of Christian-Germanic disposition have composed the most beautiful poems under similar circumstances.

You take my "worries about the future" too lightly. People who fear nothing but mediocrity, you say, are safe. Safe from what? I ask. Surely not safe and secure from being mediocre? What does it matter whether we fear something or not? Isn't the main question whether what we fear exists? Admittedly more powerful intellects are also seized with doubts about themselves; does it therefore follow that anyone who doubts his virtues is of powerful intellect? In intellect he may be a weakling yet at the same time an honest man by education, habit, or even self-torment. I don't mean to suggest that if you find yourself in a doubtful situation, you should mercilessly dissect your feelings, but if you do you will see how little about yourself you're sure of. The magnificence of the world rests after all on this wealth of possibilities, except that it is unfortunately not a firm basis for self-knowledge.

In case you cannot understand me (for my thoughts are following a certain drowsy philosophy), just ignore what I have said. Unfortunately I wasn't able to write during the day, in 23 days that day will come, the longest of days on which, etc. Since in the brief interval I am supposed to quaff knowledge in great gulps, I am left with no opportunity of writing commonly intelligible letters. I take comfort in the thought that I am not writing to a common intelligence, and beg to remain with every possible expectation

Yours
Sigmund Freud

For several days Herr Bretholz, his elder daughter and his nephew, a sage from Czernowitz, have been our daily visitors. Do you know the last? He really is a sage; I have enjoyed him very much.

Sig. Freud

INDIRA GANDHI
born Nov. 19, 1917
Allahabad, India

"Indu" was only four when her grandfather Motilal and father Jawaharlal were jailed for the first time for their allegedly seditious activities against the British Government. When the two Nehru men went to the magistrate's court to stand trial and did not return home, the child's sense of loss was overwhelming. She had sat in Motilal's lap as the court went through the ritual of a trial, and she was inconsolable when both were taken away to prison and she had to return home without them. The frequency of similar occurrences in the years that followed did not entirely blunt Indira's feelings of outrage and shock whenever there was a new imprisonment. That after a while her mother was taken away almost as often as her father strongly accentuated her grief.

When the child in her got the better of her grim sense of earnestness and she took out her dolls and toys, she almost always played at politics. Her fantasies seldom related to such usual childhood themes as a marriage between two dolls or acquisition of such riches as a glittering set of glass bangles or a trayful of favorite sweets. Her mind was always involved with the independence movement, and she would make her dolls enact aspects of the fight with the British that she had seen herself or heard her elders describe. Her small doll house would sometimes represent the store that had chosen to ignore the Mahatma's plea and was still selling foreign goods. She would station a number of dolls clad in white *khadi* all around the recalcitrant shop as Congress Party workers supposedly picketing its various entrances and urging shoppers to boycott it the way Indira had seen her mother and aunts do so often. At other times she would play at a more serious kind of game. A set of tiny clay dolls would be British soldiers—so identified by the round, brown pith helmets that they wore. Another set of dolls were given tiny red turbans to identify them as the Indian policemen who acted according to their British employers' bidding. The soldiers would carry guns and the policemen long wooden clubs. Facing the foreign rulers and their native minions would be a row of dolls dressed in white homespun *khadi* and carrying nothing but the Congress Party flag. She would move this row forward in an act of defiance while she herself shouted some of the slogans heard at political meetings and demonstrations. The authorities, too, would move forward menacingly, brandishing the guns and clubs. When the people were undaunted, the soldiers and policemen would act with expected brutality and beat up the demonstrators. The latter would fall on the ground only to rise again, carrying the flag aloft and shouting for freedom even more vigorously. All such games always had a happy, satisfying ending. In the shop-picketing game, all customers would turn away disgustedly, leaving the "bad" shopkeeper no option but to close down. In the confrontation with the police, the doll demonstrators always won, with the pretended British authorities retreating in confusion and leaving behind helmets, turbans, and *lathis* as convincing proof of rout.

Bhatia

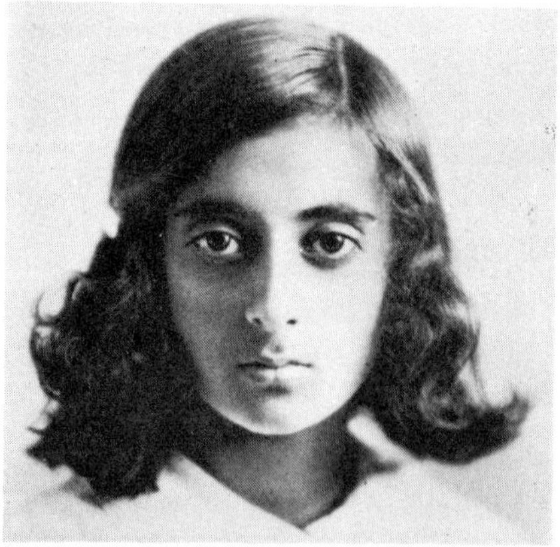

Age 9.

ALLEN GINSBERG
born June 3, 1926
Newark, N.J.

It was around Christmas 1943 that the seventeen-year-old rustic from Paterson, New Jersey, then newly enrolled at Columbia and living on the seventh floor of the Union Theological Seminary, first ventured "Way down south in Greenwich Village/Where one meets the uptown spillage/Poets, artists, writers, fakers,/And interior decorators. . . ." He wore a red shirt and a red bandana and he thinks this poem may have been inspired by the redoubtable Minetta Tavern.

A NIGHT IN THE VILLAGE

Age 17

In Greenwich Village, night had come.
The darkened alleyways were dumb—
The only voices we could hear
Were lonely echoes, sounding clear
From basement bars, where reddish light
Obscenely sweated in the night,
Where Neons called to passers-by
"Enter, drink, and dream a lie,
Escape the street's reality,
Drink gin and immortality."

I smiled to my comrades two:
We found a door and entered through;
We stumbled to a smokey brawl,
Reality fled beyond recall.
We sat down jesting, wit in flower,
Disputed wildly, burned the hour;
We drank a river of delight,
While pleasure's flame was kindled bright;
Memory came, and memory flew,
Dreams were lost, and born anew . . .

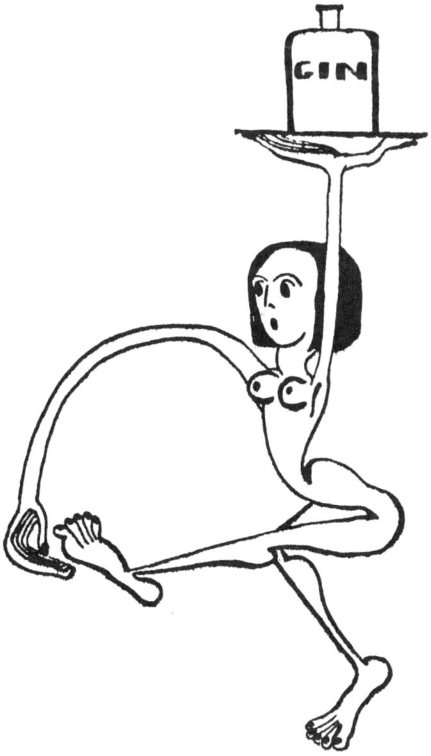

Suddenly it seemed, I woke—
My throat was tight, as if to choke
My tongue from talk; though in my ear
The bawdy bawl was ringing clear,
Its meaning I no longer guessed;
My heart was thundering in my breast,
I looked up horrified to see
Eternity glaring down at me!
I looked about in wild alarm—
Death met my glance. He raised his arm:
Futility, mirrored everyplace,
Dwelled in every person's face—
In every visage was that taint,
Underneath a Woman's paint,
Undisguised by colored lead,
Leered a mocking white Death's head.
Under a lurid light, the room
Was flushed with shame and vivid doom.

Reflected in a whiskey glass,
Fate's yellow eyes were molten brass;
In undertones, beneath a note,
Death spoke out of the singer's throat;
While, staring through a drunkard's eyes,
Fate confounded drinker's lies:
For all the drinks that they had tried,
Death still sat there at their side.
And Death peered with contemptuous calm
From the barman's open palm.
Thus, waiting patiently, alas,
Conferring there, and clinking glass,
And toasting Death, their drinking mate,
Bent Time, Futility, and Fate.

A woman's laughter rent the gloom—
And back came once again the room.

About age 17.

JOHANN WOLFGANG GOETHE
born August 28, 1749
Frankfurt-on-Main, Germany

The young E. K. L. Isenburg von Buri [son of the Privy Councillor of Isenburg-Birstein and 17 years old at the time of these letters] had at the estate Neuhof on the Main, almost three leagues from Offenbach, founded a Secret Society (Geheimbund) *[supposedly in 1747]. It was called the Arcadian Society* (Arcadische Gesellschaft), *after the Roman Society* (Accademia degli Arcadi), *of merely literary purpose. It was dedicated to God and Virtue, and on its seal was an Apollo with lyre and aureole. . . .*

Buri was the first President (Archon) *of the Bund, and no one under fifteen could be Archon. A candidate to be received into the Society's membership must be over twelve and of "the proper worthiness." The Archon by himself was the first grade; the three next were the Praepositors* (Aufseher), *then the Noble Freemen* (edle Freien)*—who must be of noble blood and who had all the rights of the Proctors, —third, the Freemen* (Freien). *None of these grades could exceed twelve in number. Lowest of all was the grade of the ordinary members—the Commons* (die Gemeinen), *with no limit of number. At a later time, girl members appear. . . . The alternating place of assembly was called* Philandria*—probably Love of* Mankind, *not Love of* Men *is meant. The Archon might of his own authority enroll members. . . .*

Düntzer

Age 14

Age 16.

To Ludwig Ysenburg von Buri, Neuhof

Frankfort, 23 May, 1764

Wohlgebohrner, insonders Hochzuehrender Herr,

Ew. Wohlgebohrn will wonder when a stranger ventures to prefer a request to you. Yet you might kindly refrain from astonishment at all those who recognize your merits. For you may well be assured that your character itself has the power of making hearts your own in lands still more distant than where I live.

You see from my opening that for the time I am concerned for nothing but your acquaintance, until you prove whether I am worthy of being your friend and joining your Society.

Do not be displeased with my boldness, and forgive me for it; I cannot act otherwise, for were I to remain longer silent, and admire your great qualities in secret as I have hitherto done, it would cause me the greatest regret in the world. None of my friends who know you are willing to grant me this inestimable pleasure. Perhaps a little envy may be answerable for this. But there just occurs to me the best reason: they are not willing to bring to your acquaintance any person who has my failing, lest by that means you should be made responsible for it. You, honoured sir, will know that we are glad to conceal our shortcomings when we seek to gain access to a person whom we respect. But I have this in common with the wooer in Raabener, that I declare my faults beforehand. I know, indeed, that my chattering will be tedious to you, yet it can't be helped; you must have experience of it some time, either before or after we become acquainted. One of my chief faults is that I am somewhat impetuous. You know, I dare say, what the choleric temperament is; on the other hand no one forgets an injury more easily than I. Moreover I am very much given to laying down the law, yet when I have nothing to say I can let things alone. But I will gladly place myself under discipline if it is carried out as one may expect from your discernment. At the very beginning of my letter you will find my third fault, namely, that I write as familiarly to you as if I had already known you a hundred years; but what of that? this is simply a thing that I cannot unlearn. I hope that your mind, that does not tie itself to trifles like etiquette, will forgive me for it; but be assured that I will never leave due respect out of sight.

One thing more occurs to me; I have also this fault in common with the abovementioned person, that I am very impatient, and do not like to remain long in uncertainty. I beg you to come to a decision as quickly as possible.

These are my principal faults. Your sharp-sighted eyes will detect a hundred small ones in me, which, however, as I hope, will not put me beyond your favour, but everything will speak for me; and my faults as well as my zeal will show you that I am and constantly will remain your most devoted servant,

Joh. Wolfgang Goethe

P.S. Should you be in doubt about my age, I may say for your satisfaction that my years are about the same as those of *Alexis*. I complain of him very much, in that hitherto he has from day to day put off introducing me to your acquaintance. If you are good enough, as I hope and most earnestly request you, to honour me with a reply, be so kind as to put my Christian name upon the address. I live in the great *Hirsch-Grabe*. Farewell.

About age 20 in his attic at Frankfurt. Probably a self-portrait.

To L. Ysenburg von Buri

Sir, Frankfort, 2 June, 1764

I will reserve all my delight and all my joy until I have the honour of seeing you, for my pen is not capable of expressing it. You are altogether too kind to me, in that you give me such speedy hope of being acquainted with you, when I believed that this good fortune was so far distant from me. I am very much indebted to you therefor.

Alexis is one of my best friends. He can tell you enough from personal experience. I have enjoined him to impart all simply needful facts. He must omit none of my faults, but also not be silent about what is good in me. But, with all that, I request that you will give yourself the trouble to put me to the proof; for sensible as Alexis is withal, something might still remain concealed from him, that might be displeasing to you. I am somewhat like a chameleon. Then is my Alexis to be blamed if he has not regarded me from all points of view? Enough of this.

You may set yourself to disclaim as you will, you still betray yourself quickly enough. You disown perfections, and in the very same moment they shine in your actions.

Your prudence is laudable. Far from its offending me, it is, the rather, pleasing to me, and in fact contributes perhaps to my credit. Were your society of such a nature that every one who proposed could enter it without scrutiny, merely by introducing himself, it would at once be the greatest piece of stupidity; could this be an honour for me? Oh, no! But since you first choose, test, and scrutinize, this tends to the greatest pleasure for me, if you will indeed still accept me. You compare yourself with the *Herrn von Abgrund*, but this comparison is false, and in fact very false. If you go over the whole character and hold yourself in contrast, you will do nothing but find points which do not agree with one another. He makes a secret out of an affair which is not one; and is distrustful in the most exaggerated degree, but you are so with reason. That your prudence is not in the least exaggerated I will prove by an example.

We have many blockheads in our town, as you without doubt will know very well. Suppose, now, that it occurred to such a one to make your acquaintance. He requests his tutor to compose a letter; and it must be a most agreeable letter. He does so, and the young gentleman sets his name to it. By that means you acquire a high idea of his learning, and take him up without examination; but when you look at him in the light, you find that instead of a well-instructed man, your acquaintance has been augmented by a calf's-head.

That is undeniable! Now it is quite possible that I am such a one; thus your prudence is well applied.

On this occasion I write nothing more, except only the most confident assurance that I am and will always remain, sir, your most devoted servant,

Joh. Wolfgang Goethe

Alas, his application was rejected "because of his vices." He had been involved in a somewhat mysterious affair in which he was persuaded to write "a passionate love letter in verse in order to mystify a certain love-sick young man." The case actually came to trial but the records have been destroyed. It was during this affair that Wolfgang (at fourteen) met his beloved Gretchen.

NIKOLAI GOGOL
born March 31, 1809
Sorochintsy (near Poltava)
Ukraine

His head buzzed with ideas; every style was right: in rapid succession he produced an epic poem, Russia Under the Tartar Yoke; *a romantic drama à la Schiller, called* The Brigands; *and a satire on the inhabitants of Nezhin [his high school],* A Few Words on Nezhin, Where the Law Is Not Made for Fools. *This was a work in five parts: "(1) dedication of a chapel in the Greek cemetery, (2) election of a Greek magistrate, (3) the fair for gluttons, (4) dinner at the home of the marshal of nobility, (5) a students' gathering." In addition, there were "occasional" poems ridiculing students and teachers. But, increasingly, Nikolai and his "circle" were turning to the sentimental genre. . . .*

Since his friends [wrote] too, some market for the output became necessary. Handwritten magazines were created to exhibit the school's literary production: The Star, The Northern Dawn, The Literary Meteor, The Dunghill of Parnassus. *Of some of these endeavors (total circulation: one copy), Nikolai Gogol was the editor in chief. He inundated them with his poems and prose, and illustrated them with his drawings. His readership was composed of the remainder of his class. The magazine was borrowed back and forth, and passed from hand to hand; passages were read aloud. . . .*

Nothing remains of all the early works mentioned above, whose titles alone have survived in the memoirs of his contemporaries.

Troyat

About age 20

About age 18.

In his list of the trades he could ply [in St. Petersburg] in order to keep body and soul together, Nikolai Gogol made no mention of writing; but he had never written as much as during these months at Vasilyevka.

First he wanted to polish off a verse idyl, *Hans Kuechelgarten* which he had begun at school. He had taken the subject from a work by Vos, *Louise*, translated by Teryaev in 1820. For style, he had consulted Pushkin and Zhukovsky. But no matter how he tried, his hand remained lethargic, his rhymes were like glue, the whole thing reeked of *ennui*. On one side the author described the patriarchal bliss of a German family illumined by the angelic Louise, who was in love with Hans. On the other, he set Hans, a tormented dreamer swimming in a romantic stew. Hans suffered from some undefined malaise:

> In the tempest of his heart,
> Vaguely he wondered
> What he wanted, what he sought,
> To what goal tended his wild soul,
> Filled with love and impatience,
> As though seeking to embrace the whole earth.

Hans, a combination of Goethe's Werther, Pushkin's Lensky, and Chateaubriand's René, had several things in common with his creator too. At every turn, the private preoccupations of Nikolai Gogol invaded his work. What he had said in prose in his letters to his mother, his uncle Kosyarovsky, and his friend Vysotsky, was repeated in verse in the poem. Like Nikolai Gogol, Hans Kuechelgarten felt a sudden need to escape the confines of his narrow life and accomplish some magnificent deed, "to leave a trace of his passage on earth."

> It's settled. Why should I
> Leave my soul to perish here,
> Seek no other goal,
> Not strive for the best,
> Condemn myself to obscurity unknown,
> A creature half alive to all?

The scorn Nikolai Gogol felt for the petty people of Nezhin, Hans Kuechelgarten extended to the rest of the universe:

How venomous their breath,
How false the beating of their hearts,
How perfidious their minds,
And how hollow ring their words!

Also, Hans Kuechelgarten's joy at the thought of returning home is none other than that of Nikolai about to leave school for good:

So the imprisoned pupil
Awaits his desired release.
His studies are soon over.
His mind floods with dreams.
He is borne aloft by thoughts.
Here he is, free, independent,
Delighting in himself and the world.
But as he parts from his companions,
Whose efforts, laughter, and peaceful
Nights he has shared,
He muses, gloom invades him,
And, weighted down by sadness,
He sheds a furtive tear.

Gogol's first published work, the narrative poem Hans Kuechelgarten *(1829), drew two short comments from contemporary periodicals. F. V. Bulgarin, the editor of* Northern Bee, *took exception to the publisher's (in fact Gogol's own) introductory note to the poem and wondered why the publisher had been "proud to acquaint the public with this new talent." Pride, Bulgarin thought, was hardly justified; indeed, the public would have remained happy enough had the acquaintance never been made. N. A. Polevoy, in his turn, published a note in the* Moscow Telegraph, *choosing for his target another sentence from the publisher's introduction. "This poem," the introduction read, "was not written for the public; reasons important to the author alone have led to its publication." The author's private reasons might have been valid, Polevoy commented, but there were much more weighty reasons why the poem should not have been published.*

Both comments represented routine exercises in snubbing a youthful talent and did not differ from hundreds of other short notes in the Bibliography and Criticism sections of contemporary periodicals. They were characteristic of the reviewers' preference for supercilious wit over serious analysis. Not that Hans Kuechelgarten *merited deep consideration; but the critics might at least have offered constructive criticism instead of mere flippancy. As is well known, Gogol reacted to the notices by destroying as many copies of the poem as he could lay his hands on [by burning them in the wood stove of a hotel room he had hired for that day].*

Debreczeny

OLIVER GOLDSMITH
born Nov. 10, 1730
near Ballymahon
County Longford, Ireland

there was Company at his fathers at that time he was turnd of seven they were attended at tea by a little boy who was desired to hand the Kettle—but the handle being to hot the boy took up the skirt of his coate to put between him & it but unfortunately the Ladys perceived some thing which made them Laugh immodarately whether from the akwardness of the turn or anything that might be seen there I cant say but the Docter [Oliver] immeadietly perceived there cause of Laughter & inform^d his father who promised him a reward of Gingerbread to write some thing on it and as it was one of his earliest productions that can be recollected tho perhaps not fit for the Publick I shall insert it here

Mrs. Hodson (Goldsmith's sister)

Age 7

Thesues did see as Poets say
Dark Hell & its abysses
But had not half so Sharp an Eye
As our young Charming Misses

For they c^d through boys breeches peep
And view what ere he had there
It seemd to Blush & they all Laugh_d
Because its face was all Bare

They laughed at that
Which some times Else
Might give them greatest pleasure
How quickly they c^d see the thing
Which was their darling treasure

Some have dated this poem at age 12. Friedman places it among the "unauthenticated" poems.

In effect Alexander [was] orphaned at the age of thirteen. . . . In short order [he] became a clerk in the office of Nicholas Cruger, a New York merchant who operated a trading firm in St. Croix. . . . The only personal letter that has survived from the time . . . is one he sent to Edward Stevens, a young friend who had been sent to school [at Kings College, later called Columbia] in New York.

Kline

ALEXANDER HAMILTON
born probably Jan. 11, 1755
on Nevis, British West Indies

St Croix Novemr. 11th 1769 **Age 14**

Dear Edward

This just serves to acknowledge receipt of yours per Cap Lowndes which was delivered me Yesterday. The truth of Cap Lightbourn & Lowndes [New York-based ship captains] information is now verifyd by the Presence of your Father and Sister for whose safe arrival I Pray, and that they may convey that Satisfaction to your Soul that must naturally flow from the sight of Absent Friends in health, and shall for news this way refer you to them. As to what you say respecting your having soon the happiness of seeing us all, I wish, for an accomplishment of your hopes provided they are Concomitant with your welfare, otherwise not, tho doubt whether I shall be Present or not for to confess my weakness, Ned, my Ambition is prevalent that I contemn the grov'ling and condition of a Clerk or the like, to which my Fortune &c. condemns me and would willingly risk my life tho' not my Character to exalt my Station. Im confident, Ned that my Youth excludes me from any hopes of immediate Preferment nor do I desire it, but I mean to prepare the way for futurity. Im no Philosopher you see and may be jusly said to Build Castles in the Air. My Folly makes me ashamd and beg youll Conceal it, yet Neddy we have seen such Schemes successfull when the Projector is Constant I shall Conclude saying I wish there was a War.

I am Dr Edward Yours Alex Hamilton

PS I this moment receivd yours by [Captain] William Smith and am pleasd to see you Give such Close Application to Study.

It was a natural disaster, however, not a war . . . that gave Hamilton his chance to escape ledgers and account books. On August 31, 1772, a hurricane swept St. Croix, and a few days later Hamilton wrote an account of the storm in a letter to his father. A copy of the letter reached Hugh Knox, a Presbyterian minister and journalist on the island, and Knox arranged to have the letter published [in the Royal Danish American Gazette *of Oct. 3, 1772]. It was this letter that won the boy local fame and an opportunity to leave Nicholas Cruger's Countinghouse. . . . Impressed by Hamilton's obvious intelligence and talents, several wealthy residents of St. Croix subscribed to a fund for the young man's education [in New Jersey to prepare, and then at Kings College, New York City].*

Kline

St. Croix, Sept. 6, 1772 **Age 17**

Honoured Sir,—I take up my pen just to give you an imperfect account of the most dreadful hurricane that memory or any records whatever can trace, which happened here on the 31st ultimo at night.

It began about dusk, at North, and raged very violently till ten o'clock. Then ensued a sudden and unexpected interval, which lasted about an hour. Meanwhile the wind was shifting round to the South West point, from whence it returned with redoubled fury and continued so till near three o'clock in the morning. Good God! what horror and destruction—it's impossible for me to describe—or you to form any idea of it. It seemed as if a total dissolution of nature was taking place. The roaring of the sea and wind—fiery meteors flying about in the air—the prodigious glare of almost perpetual lightning—the crash of the falling houses—and the ear-piercing shrieks of the distressed, were sufficient to strike astonishment into Angels. A great part of the buildings throughout the Island are levelled to the ground—almost all the rest very much shattered—several persons killed and numbers utterly ruined—whole families running about the streets unknowing where to find a place of shelter—the sick exposed to the keenness of water and air—without a bed to lie upon—or a dry covering to their bodies—our harbour is entirely bare. In a word, misery in all its most hideous shapes spread over the whole face of the country.—A strong smell of gunpowder added somewhat to the terrors of the night; and it was observed that the rain was surprisingly salt. Indeed, the water is so brackish and full of sulphur that there is hardly any drinking it.

My reflections and feelings on this frightful and melancholy occasion are set forth in following self-discourse.

Where now, Oh! vile worm, is all thy boasted fortitude and resolution? what is become of thy arrogance and self-sufficiency?—why dost thou tremble and stand aghast? how humble—how helpless—how contemptible you now appear. And for why? the jarring of the elements—the discord of clouds? Oh, impotent presumptuous fool! how darest thou offend that omnipotence, whose nod alone were sufficient to quell the destruction that hovers over thee, or crush thee into atoms? See thy wretched helpless state and learn to know thyself. Learn to know thy best support. Despise thyself and adore thy God. How sweet—how unutterably sweet were now the voice of an approving conscience;—then couldst thou say—hence ye idle alarms—why do I shrink? What have I to fear? A pleasing calm suspense! a short repose from calamity to end in eternal bliss?—let the earth rend, let the planets forsake their course—let the sun be extinguished, and the heavens burst asunder—yet what have I to dread? my staff can never be broken—in omnipotence I trust.

He who gave the winds to blow and the lightnings to rage—even him I have always loved and served—his precepts have I observed—his commandments have I obeyed—and his perfections have I adored.—He will snatch me from ruin—he will exalt me to the fellowship of Angels and Seraphs, and to the fulness of never ending joys.

But alas! how different, how deplorable—how gloomy the prospect—death comes rushing on in triumph veiled in a mantle of ten-fold darkness. His unrelenting scythe, pointed and ready for the stroke.—On his right hand sits destruction, hurling the winds and belching forth flames;—calamity on his left threatening famine, disease, distress of all kinds.—And Oh! thou wretch, look still a little further; see the gulf of eternal mystery open—there mayest thou shortly plunge—the just reward of thy vileness.—Alas! whither canst thou fly? where hide thyself? thou canst not call upon thy God;—thy life has been a continual warfare with him.

Hark! ruin and confusion on every side.—'Tis thy turn next: but one short moment—even now—Oh Lord help—Jesus be merciful!

Thus did I reflect, and thus at every gust of the wind did I conclude,—till it pleased the Almighty to allay it.—Nor did my emotions proceed either from the suggestion of too much natural fear, or a conscience overburdened with crimes of an uncommon cast.—I thank God this was not the case. The scenes of horror exhibited around us, naturally awakened such ideas in every thinking breast, and aggravated the deformity of every failing of our lives. It were a lamentable insensibility indeed, not to have had such feelings,—and I think inconsistent with human nature.

Our distressed helpless condition taught us humility and a contempt of ourselves.—The horrors of the night—the prospect of an immediate cruel death—or, as one may say, of being crushed by the Almighty in his anger—filled us with terror. And everything that had tended to weaken our interest with Him, upbraided us, in the strongest colours, with our baseness and folly.—That which, in a calm unruffled temper, we call a natural cause, seemed then like the correction of the Deity.—Our imagination represented him as an incensed master, executing vengeance on the crimes of his servants.—The father and benefactor were forgot, and in that view, a consciousness of our guilt filled us with despair.

But see, the Lord relents—he hears our prayers—the Lightning ceases—the winds are appeased—the warring elements are reconciled, and all things promise peace.—The darkness is dispelled—and drooping nature revives at the approaching dawn. Look back, Oh, my soul—look back and tremble.—Rejoice at thy deliverance, and humble thyself in the presence of thy deliverer.

Yet hold, Oh, vain mortal!—check thy ill-timed joy. Art thou so selfish as to exult because thy lot is happy in a season of universal woe?—Hast thou no feelings for the miseries of thy fellow-creatures, and art thou incapable of the soft pangs of sympathetic sorrow?—Look around thee and shudder at the view.—See desolation and ruin wherever thou turnest thine eye. See thy fellow-creatures pale and lifeless; their bodies mangled—their souls snatched into eternity—unexpecting—alas! perhaps unprepared!—Hark the bitter groans of distress—see sickness and infirmities exposed to the inclemencies of wind and water—see tender infancy pinched with hunger and hanging to the mother's knee for food!—see the unhappy mother's anxiety—her poverty denies relief—her breast heaves with pangs of maternal pity—her heart is bursting—the tears gush down her cheeks—Oh sights of woe! Oh distress unspeakable!—my heart bleeds—but I have no power to solace!—Oh ye, who revel in affluence, see the afflictions of humanity, and bestow your superfluity to ease them.—Say not, we have suffered also, and with-hold your compassion. What are your sufferings compared to these? Ye have still more than enough left.—Act wisely.—Succour the miserable and lay up a treasure in Heaven.

I am afraid, sir, you will think this description more the effort of imagination, than a true picture of realities. But I can affirm with the greatest truth, that there is not a single circumstance touched upon which I have not absolutely been an eye-witness to.

Our [Governor] General has several very salutary and human regulations, and both in his public and private measures has shown himself *the man*.

At Harvard, Hearst was a regular cut-up. He became a member of the Hasty Pudding (dramatic) Society and business manager of the Lampoon. *He wrote several unsigned short verses for the magazine and made many cartoon suggestions. The magazine prospered under his tutelage.*

WILLIAM RANDOLPH HEARST
born April 29, 1863
San Francisco, Calif.

Age 20-22

In the Presidential election of 1884, Hearst cast his first ballot and went all out for Cleveland and Hendricks, the Democratic candidates. When their victory was belatedly confirmed, Hearst organized a celebration such as staid old Harvard had never experienced. He hired several bands of music, bought wagonloads of beer, set off fireworks in all directions and raised such a blazing ["The house was fired—just a little, not much." W.R.H.], ear-splitting, rip-roaring, all-night racket as to scandalize Cambridge and almost cost his expulsion. It was the first outburst of that Hearstian genius for fireworks, brass bands and spectacular demonstrations which afterward were to startle and entertain the populace so frequently.

Some days later, with a cherubic smile wreathing his countenance, Hearst stood before a choleric dean and was informed that the college authorities had decided he might, for a period of some months, be able to give more undivided attention to his studies as a nonresident of Cambridge. This process was known as "rustication." . . .

As we have indicated, Hearst was always in more or less of a muddle with the Harvard faculty. But it was not until the middle of his [junior] year, at the beginning of the Christmas holidays of 1885, that he was actually expelled. The specific cause was an unpalatable practical joke, concocted in the early morning hours after Hearst and a few heel-kicking buddies had been over Boston-way until dawn. . . .

Just at breakfast time, messenger boys rang the doorbells at the homes of certain members of the faculty [among them such lights as William James and Josiah Royce] and delivered stout packages gay with ribbons and holly. The scholarly gentlemen, a little thrilled with the mystery of the proceedings, opened their gifts. Each package contained a chamber pot, adorned with the recipient's name and photograph. This was Will Hearst's l'envoi to Harvard.

Winkler

In a Hasty Pudding Society production at Harvard.

ERNEST HEMINGWAY
born April 9, 1899
Oak Park, Ill.

This story, published in the February 1916 issue of [*Oak Park High School's literary magazine*] Tabula, *shows his early concern with nature and violence . . . that he had formed the basis of his style, even as a junior in high school, and had chosen his subject matter of violence and manliness before his World War I experiences.* [*It*] *deals with the raw material Hemingway lived with each summer* [*in Michigan, where he had several Ojibwa friends*].

Montgomery

Age 16

Leaving Michigan for a reporter's job on the Toronto Star.

JUDGMENT OF MANITOU

Dick Haywood buttoned the collar of his mackinaw up about his ears, took down his rifle from the deer horns above the fireplace of the cabin and pulled on his heavy fur mittens. "I'll go and run that line toward Loon River, Pierre," he said. "Holy quill pigs, but it's cold." He glanced at the thermometer. "Forty-two below! Well, so long, Pierre." Pierre merely grunted, as, twisting on his snowshoes, Dick started out over the crust with the swinging snowshoe stride of the traveler of the barren grounds.

In the doorway of the cabin Pierre stood looking after Dick as he swung along. He grinned evilly to himself, "De tief will tink it a blame sight cooler when he swingin by one leg in the air like Wah-boy, the rabbit; he would steal my money, would he!" Pierre slammed the heavy door shut, threw some wood on the fire and crawled into his bunk.

As Dick Haywood strode along he talked to himself as to the travellers of the "silent places." "Wonder why Pierre is so grouchy just because he lost that money? Bet he just misplaced it somewhere. All he does now is to grunt like a surly pig and every once in a while I catch him leering at me behind my back. If he thinks I stole his money why don't he say so and have it out with me! Why, he used to be so cheerful and jolly; when we agreed at Missainabal to be partners and trap up here in the Ungave district, I thought he'd be a jolly good companion, but now he hasn't spoken to me for the last week, except to grunt or swear in that Cree lingo."

It was a cold day, but it was the dry, invigorating cold of the northland and Dick enjoyed the crisp air. He was a good traveller on snowshoes and rapidly covered the first five miles of the trap line, but somehow he felt that something was following him and he glanced around several times only to be disappointed each time. "I guess it's only the kootzie-ootzie," he muttered to himself, for in the North whenever men do not understand a thing they blame it on the "little bad god of the Cree." Suddenly, as Dick entered a growth of spruce, he was jerked off his feet, high into the air. When his head had cleared from the bang it had received by striking the icy crust, he saw that he was suspended in the air by a rope which was attached to a spruce tree, which had been bent over to form the spring for a snare, such as is used to capture rabbits. His fingers barely touched the crust, and as he struggled and the cord grew tighter on his leg he saw what he had sensed to be following him. Slowly out of the woods trotted a band of gaunt, white, hungry timber wolves, and squatted on their haunches in a circle round him.

Back in the cabin Pierre as he lay in his bunk was awakened by a gnawing sound overhead, and idly looking up at the rafter he saw a red squirrel busily gnawing away at the leather of his lost wallet. He thought of the trap he had set for Dick, and springing from his bunk he seized his rifle, and coatless and gloveless ran madly out along the trail. After a gasping, breathless, choking run he came upon the spruce grove. Two ravens left off picking at the shapeless something that had once been Dick Haywood, and flapped lazily into a neighboring spruce. All over the bloody snow were the tracks of My-in-gau, the timber wolf.

As he took a step forward Pierre felt the clanking grip of the toothed bear trap, that Dick had come to tend, close on his feet. He fell forward, and as he lay on the snow he said, "It is the judgment of Manitou; I will save My-in-gau, the wolf, the trouble."

And he reached for the rifle.

ADOLF HITLER
born April 20, 1889
Braunau, Upper Austria

Age 14.

The cartoon he drew of one of his High School teachers was, by contrast, anything but peaceful: it showed his dislike of the new school no less than the contempt in which he held his teachers. The arrogant and overbearing man is drawn with the corners of his mouth pulled down, his brows furrowed, his cold little eyes squinting, and his remoteness emphasized by his formal suit with its ridiculously stiff collar. As a finishing touch, the 11-year-old Hitler had sardonically placed an ice-cream cone—a symbol of infantilism—between the teacher's rigid fingers.

Maser

Age 11

[Hitler and Kubizek] quarreled rarely, perhaps because they were both so devoted to art that they saw no reason to dispute about something so much greater than themselves. The mild-mannered Kubizek was content to watch and listen, accompanying his friend everywhere. There came a time when they knew every street in the city and all the surrounding villages. They climbed all the neighboring hills, even the Freinberg, which the people of Linz seldom visited because they thought there were better views from the other hills. They visited the baroque monastery of Saint Florian, where Anton Bruckner was buried, and Adolf went into raptures over the beauty of the design. Sometimes they wandered beside the Danube in search of high rocks, from which they could look down at the dark, swirling waters below. Adolf enjoyed these excursions outside of Linz, but he was emphatically a city-dweller without any desire to live in the countryside. He told Kubizek: "I'll never live in a village like Leonding again!"

One day Adolf decided to build a house where they could both live for the rest of their lives, studying art in peace and harmony. They would find a beautiful woman to serve as housekeeper, and every summer they would make the grand tour of Germany, studying the great cathedrals and whatever other buildings took their fancy. Adolf designed the house with a tower, a spiral stairway, ornamental doorways leading to a vast music room, and comfortable rooms for friends who cared to visit them. In the brilliantly lighted hall a beautiful servant would welcome their guests. Some preliminary sketches for the palatial house have survived.

Payne

Age 17

POPE JOHN XXIII
born Nov. 25, 1881
Sotto il Monte, Bergamo
Bruscio District, Italy

In 1892, their landlord's brother, Canon Morlani of Bergamo Cathedral, got him a boarder's place in the town seminary, where he slowly established a reputation for diligence and good conduct. In June 1895, at the age of thirteen, he received the tonsure, and from this point we begin to know something about him, for he marked the event by opening a spiritual diary, published after his death under the title of Giornale dell'Anima.

This work has led to some misapprehension about the nature of Roncalli's character and spirituality. Its publication, in fact, disturbed many progressive Catholics, who had much admired his pontificate, for it seemed to reflect a quite exceptionally simple, even naive, approach to the religious life. . . .

This view tends to be confirmed by a cursory reading of the diary. Roncalli began it on the instructions of his superiors. It was not a private document but a training exercise, to be periodically produced for inspection and comment. . . . Though Bergamo was undoubtedly a progressive town by the standards of late-nineteenth-century Italian Catholicism, the seminary was exceptionally strict, and Roncalli's spiritual and academic training was conducted on very narrow lines. . . .

The main object of the diary was to identify his moral failings, and to record his progress in eliminating them. Most of his "sins" appear pretty humdrum: gossiping in the kitchen at home, drowsing during meditations, taking too long a siesta, eating too much fruit, failing to wear his heavy clerical clothes while out walking–the natural failings of a jovial, extrovert youth with a tendency to put on too much weight. Sex, as he later recalled, did not worry him very much, an impression confirmed by the diary, though he went through the usual exercises. . . .

This is a boy of sixteen, repeating by rote the precepts of his spiritual adviser. In preparing for a life of clerical celibacy, it is necessary to acquire certain patterns of behavior which soon become instinctive and cease to be irksome. Roncalli seems to have taken to them easily, without acquiring the ingrained suspicion of women characteristic of many celibates; his relationships with women throughout his mature life were open, friendly, unselfconscious and entirely innocent.

Johnson

Age 15 and 16

OF HOLY PURITY

Through the grace of God and the intercession of my Mother, Mary most holy, I am convinced of the inestimable worth of holy purity and of my own very great need of it, called as I am to the angelic ministry of the priesthood. In order to preserve this shining mirror free from all stain, I have in these holy Exercises, with the approval of my Spiritual Father, written down the following resolutions, which I desire to keep most scrupulously. I offer them to the Virgin of Virgins by the hands of those three angelic youths, Aloysius Gonzaga, Stanislaus Kostka and John Berchmans, my special protectors, so that she, through the merits of these three lilies of chastity, so precious in her sight, may deign to bless these resolves and grant me the grace to put them into practice.

(1) First of all, I am profoundly convinced that holy purity comes as a grace from God, and that without this grace I am incapable of it, and so in this matter I will start on the sure foundation of humility, distrusting myself and placing all my confidence in God and most holy Mary. Therefore every day I will pray to the Lord for the virtue of holy purity, and I will pray to him with particular fervour at holy communion, since it is in the Eucharist that he offers me the "grain that shall make the young men flourish, and new wine the maidens." I will have a tender love for the Queen of Virgins. I will always offer the Hour of Prime of the Little Office, the first Hail Mary of the Angelus and the first decade of the rosary for the acquiring and preserving of holy purity. I will also ask Joseph, Mary's most chaste spouse, to help me, addressing to him twice a day the prayer "O Guardian of Virgins," and I will cultivate a devotion to the three saintly youths I have mentioned, whose purity I will try to copy in my own life.

(2) I will take pains to mortify my own feelings severely, keeping them within the bounds of Christian modesty; to this end I will set a special guard on my eyes, which St. Ambrose called "deceitful snares" and St. Anthony of Padua "thieves of the soul," avoiding, as far as possible, large gatherings of people for feasts, etc., and when I am obliged to be present on these occasions I will make quite sure that nothing that even suggests the sin against holy purity may offend my eyes: on such occasions they shall remain downcast.

(3) I will also take care to behave with the greatest decorum when I am passing through towns or other places full of people, never looking at posters or illustrations, or shops which might contain indecent objects, bearing in mind the words of Ecclesiasticus: "Do not look around in the streets of a city; nor wander about in its deserted sections."

And even in the churches, besides behaving with edifying decorum during the sacred functions, I will never gaze at beautiful things of any sort, such as pictures, carvings, statues or other objects of art which, however slightly, offend against propriety, and particularly where paintings are concerned.

(4) With women of whatever station in life, even if they are related to me or are holy women, I will be particularly cautious, avoiding their familiarity, company or conversation, especially if they are young women. Nor will I ever fix my eyes on their faces, mindful of what the Holy Spirit teaches us: "Do not look intently at a virgin, lest you stumble and incur penalties for her." So I will never confide in them in any way, but when I have to speak with them I will see that my speech is "dry, brief, prudent and correct."

(5) I will never hold in my hands or look at books containing frivolities or immodest pictures, and if I find any of these dangerous objects, even in my companions' hands, I will tear them up or burn them, unless by so doing a graver scandal should ensue.

(6) Besides giving an example of perfect modesty in my own speech, I must also, when with my family, try to keep the conversation free from subjects ill-befitting holy purity, never allowing anyone, especially in my presence, to speak of love-making or use any coarse or indecent words or sing love songs. I will always gently rebuke any immodesty on the part of others, and if they should persist I will go right away from them, showing my deep displeasure. In the seminary I will be most careful in this respect and on my guard to prevent any demonstrativeness or particular friendships among my companions, and all those acts and words which, though acceptable in the world, are unbecoming for clerics.

(7) At table, whether speaking or eating, I will never be greedy or immoderate; I will always find an opportunity for a little mortification; as regards the drinking of wine I will be more than moderate, because in wine lies the same danger as in women: "Wine and women lead intelligent men astray."

(8) I will likewise observe the greatest modesty with regard to my own body at all times and in every movement of my eyes, hands and mind, etc., both in public and in private. To this end, then, and to remove any occasion for these movements, however innocent, at night before falling asleep I will place the rosary of the Blessed Virgin around my neck, fold my arms crosswise on my breast, and see that I find myself still lying in this position in the morning.

(9) In everything I will always remember that I must be as pure as an angel, and I will so bear myself that in everything about me, in my eyes, words and actions, may be seen that holy modesty shown in the highest degree by Saints Aloysius, Stanislaus and John Berchmans, a modesty that is pleasing, that commands reverence and is the expression of a chaste heart and soul, beloved of God.

(10) I will not forget that I am never alone, even when I am by myself: God, Mary and my Guardian Angel see me; and I am always a seminarist. When I am in danger of sinning against holy purity, then more urgently than ever will I appeal to God, to my Guardian Angel and to Mary, with my familiar invocation: "Mary Immaculate, help me." Then I will think of the scourging of Jesus Christ and of the Four Last Things, mindful of the Holy Spirit's words: "In all you do remember the end of your life, and then you will never sin."

HELEN KELLER
born June 27, 1880
Tuscumbia, Alabama

Miss Sullivan began to teach Helen Keller on March 3, 1887. [Four months later] while she was on a short visit away from home, she wrote to her mother. Two words are almost illegible, and the angular print slants in every direction.

Macy

Age 7

Huntsville, Alabama, July 12, 1887

Helen will write mother letter papa did give helen medicine mildred will sit in swing mildred did kiss helen teacher did give helen peach george is sick in bed george arm is hurt anna did give helen lemonade dog did stand up.

conductor did punch ticket papa did give helen drink of water in car

carlotta did give helen flowers anna will buy helen pretty new hat helen will hug and kiss mother helen will come home grandmother does love helen

good-by

Helen reading.

Helen and Anne Sullivan.

JACK KEROUAC
born March 12, 1922
Lowell, Mass.

Throughout the winter and spring of his year at Horace Mann [which he was attending on a scholarship] he wrote music notes for the school paper, mostly about popular swing bands like Glenn Miller. He amused his young literary friends by writing what they considered pornographic love stories, and in the spring of 1940 Jack remembered, "I scored all the winning touchdowns in the fall so they put me at the top of the literary magazine in the spring" with a story . . . "Une Veille de Noel." . . . The school yearbook announced that "Brain and Brawn found a happy combination in Jack, a newcomer to school this year."

Charters

About age 18

About age 18, at Horace Mann School.

About age 17, at Lowell High School.

UNE VEILLE DE NOEL

The bartender ran the towel along the bar and cleared it of empty glasses. Mike, seated at the bar in front of the pudgy barkeep, whistled softly as he fiddled with his glass of beer. He lifted it from the bar and gazed intently at the little ring of moisture it left on the mahogany surface.

"The world," he said. "The world is at my feet, and this barroom is the Universe." Mike was gray at the temples.

"All roads are blocked outside of Newark, and the Weather Bureau warns all motorists to refrain from driving unless absolutely. . . ."

"Two beers!" shouted one of the two college students seated at the other end of the bar.

". . . Necessary," blared on the radio. The bartender liked to play his little radio set loud, especially during the news and weather reports. He brought the two glasses of beer over to the college boys and squinted out over their heads at the storm outside. By the red light of the sign "BAR" he could make out the soft and billowy drifts of snow leaning against the sides of the buildings. He whistled with the music that had now begun on the radio and watched the specks of snow which swept by the aura of reddish light.

Mike stared dully at the coins he had scattered out before him on the bar. There was enough money there to supply him with beers for the rest of the evening.

"Some storm!" commented the bartender, as he returned to the middle of the bar where Mike was sitting.

"Yesterday, it was in the air. Tonight, it is here. What more do you expect? What more can you comment on?"

"I dunno," grinned the barkeep. "All I know is that it is some blizzard."

"I suppose it is."

Over by the radio, at the other end of the bar, an old man sat dozing. Both his withered hands rested on the bar, but his head was erect as he nodded sleepily. The radio played on.

The bartender spoke: "If the Rangers can tighten up their defense tonight and the Blackhawks can down Boston over in Chicago, there might be a chance. . . ."

"Two beers!" interrupted one of the college students.

The barkeep filled up two glasses and carried them over. He dropped the empty ones in the hot water pan underneath the bar and said to Mike: "They don't say much, do they?" He had returned to the middle of the bar.

"Glib," muttered Mike.

The old man by the radio shifted in his stool and went back to his horizontal slumber. Mike stared at him with his intelligent, faded blue eyes.

"Doesn't he ever do anything but sleep?"

"I guess not," answered the bartender, grinning. "The poor old codger. I let him in every night, away from the cold. He just sits there all night, and then when I close up, he shuffles out without a word. I guess he sleeps in the subways."

"Where does he sleep daytimes?" asked Mike, draining his glass.

"I dunno," grinned the barkeep. "I dunno."

Mike stared at the old man. "He might have been a great savant. Who knows? He might have been a great preacher. Liked to sleep too much all his life—ruined his brilliant career, I imagine. . . ."

The door flung open, letting in a cold wind and some particles of snow. A woman in a brown coat, without a hat, entered. A little black dog followed, and she stamped her feet clear of snow as she closed the door behind her. The dog trotted up to Mike and ran a warm tongue along the man's big wrists.

"Merry Christmas!" shouted the woman, cheerfully, shaking the snow from her black hair.

"Merry Christmas!" shouted back the grinning bartender. "A Merry Christmas to you, Midge!" The bartender turned, smiling, and filled a glass with brew.

Midge walked up with long strides, shaking the snow from her coat, and sat on the stool next to Mike's. Her face was flushed from the cold, her hair glistening with crystals of snow. She looked at Mike with misty gray eyes and said: "What's the matter Old Man?" She sipped from the glass.

The two college students stared at her momentarily with bleary eyes, then proceeded to drain their glasses. They clomped the empty glasses down on the bar, and one of them smacked his lips.

"Two beers!" he ordered.

"Right," said the bartender. "What you been doing tonight, Midge? Where's the kid?" The bartender carried the two beers over to the other end of the bar.

"Oh, he went to a show with the two bits Mike gave him at supper time," answered the woman. Mike turned and peered at his wife.

"What show did he go to?"

"Don't worry about Joey. I guess he knows what he wants."

"Pretty husky little fella for six," commented the barkeep, smiling. "Is he coming in tonight?"

"Yes," muttered Mike. "I always have him come and get me, to take me home. Sort of 'Nellie-take-father-home' affair, isn't it? Well, so what." Mike turned away from his wife and brooded over the moist circle formed by the bottom of his glass. He thought of the world again.

The barkeep looked at the woman with kind eyes. She looked at Mike lovingly and laid a hand on his arm, but he did not respond. The old man by the radio began to snore. A minute ticked away.

"Two beers!" shouted one of the college students.

Outside, the silent snow fell upon a silent world. Graceful drifts were forming everywhere—forming in lines that sloped gently, as snow will do. The sign "BAR" shone on. Greenwich Village lay placidly in the midst of the Christmas hush.

The door of the barroom opened slowly. A thin figure of a man appeared, and a draft of cold air played about the room. He closed the door behind him and walked to the bar with soft footsteps. His face was white, despite the cold. His hands were extremely white, thought Midge, as she watched him sit on the stool. The stranger smiled kindly at the barkeep. The barkeep mechanically began to wipe the top of the bar, and grinned.

"Merry Christmas! What'll you have?"

The stranger's face lit up into a faint smile, and his long white fingers fumbled with the wet hat-brim. His hair was thick and curly.

"Nothing, thank you. I just came in to wish you a Merry Christmas. I don't drink," he said. His words were low, soft, yet seemed to penetrate to the furthest recesses of the room. They were spoken with slow precision.

The old man by the radio awoke violently and stared about him bewilderedly. Then his gaze fell upon the stranger; and he slowly got off the stool and stood tottering, holding on to the edge of the bar.

The two college students put down their glasses of beer and stared—neither of them spoke.

The dog pattered up to the stranger and began to run his tongue across the man's snow-covered shoes. The man looked down at the beast benevolently with deep brown eyes, and dropped down one of his ivory hands to pat it on the head. Midge watched the long fingers stroke with amazing flexibility, with tender exactitude. There was no noise except for the radio. Some Spanish music or something.

Mike gripped his young wife's hand suddenly and scrutinized the stranger with fearful intentness. His face was tense, bewildered. He ran his thick fingers through his graying hair.

The barkeep's grin was wiped clear off his face. He could only fumble with his towel.

"Well," smiled the stranger, "I guess I'll be going now. Merry Christmas."

The man got up, turned deliberately, and opened the door. He disappeared into the night. No one uttered a word. The dog whined at the door.

"Let's go home," said one of the college students.

They got up, left their money on the bar, and headed for the door. It opened, and a little boy ran into the barroom.

"Daddy!" he greeted. "The show was great. And Christmas is great, too. You see all sorts of pretty things on Christmas. I just saw an angel come out of here just now. Do you know him, Daddy?"

The door was ajar, the air rushed in carrying snow. There was a long pause.

"Yes," said Mike, slowly, holding his wife's hand. "I guess I know him, all right."

RUDYARD KIPLING
born Dec. 30, 1865
Bombay, India

The Rudyard Kipling who set sail from England [for India] in September 1882 was still a schoolboy alike in years and in much of his behaviour. He was noisy, talkative, inquisitive, and largely given to pranks and inordinate laughter. But along with this went two things: the generous admixture of emotional precocity which had made Flo Garrard so important to him when so young, and the habit of constant association with artists and writers. "All the people one was taken to see either wrote or painted pictures," he records—and adds as an afterthought: "or, as in the case of a Mr. and Miss de Morgan, ornamented tiles." During his schooling, holidays not spent with the Burne-Joneses or the Poynters were passed in the care of three sisters who "took charge of schoolgirls and young students;" and these ladies had known Carlyle and were themselves much immersed in literary pursuits and literary society. They must have looked forward to Rudyard's becoming a writer. And so, too, must his parents out in India. One of his first discoveries when he arrived there was that, without letting him know, they had caused to be printed for private circulation a number of his poems, under the title of Schoolboy Lyrics *(1881). He is said to have sulked for three days when this was divulged to him.*

Stewart

About age 15

TWO SIDES OF THE MEDAL

"I will into the world, I will make me a name,
I will fight for truth, I will fight for fame,
I will win pure love, and when I die
The world shall praise me, worthily."

He entered the world—he fought for fame;
They twined him the thorny wreath of shame.
I met him once more full suddenly;
His face was seamed with misery.

"Have you fought for truth? have you worked in vain?
Have you gained pure love without a stain?
Is your name yet great? Will it ever be?
Are you praised of all men, worthily?"

He did not answer—he did not speak,
But waited awhile with a reddened cheek,
Then, trembling, faltering, and looking down—
Good heavens, he asked me for half a crown!

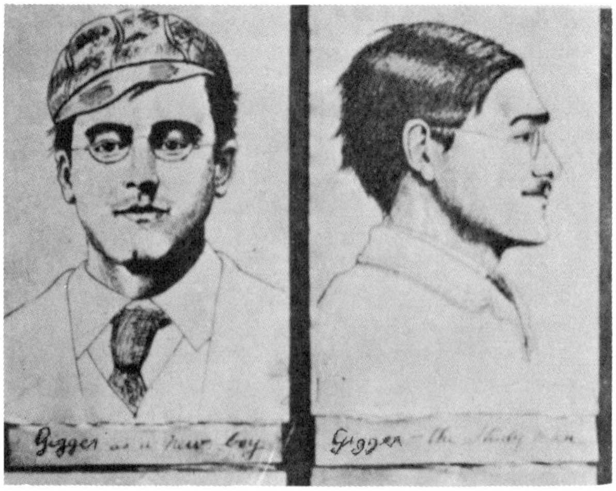

Gigger as a new boy   Gigger – the Study Man.

Sketches by G.C. Beresford, a classmate.

Gigger The Editor

Gigger knows his way about

THE LESSON

We two learned the lesson together,
  The oldest of all, yet so new
To myself, and I'm wondering whether
  It was utterly novel to you?

The pages—you seemed to have known them,
  The pictures that changed 'neath our eyes;
Alas! by what hand were you shown them,
  That I find you so womanly wise?

Is it strange that my hand on your shoulder
  In the dusk of the day should be placed?
Did you say to yourself, "Were he older
  His arm had encircled my waist?"

If it be so, so be it, fair teacher;
  I sit at your feet and am wise,
For each page of the book is a feature,
  And the light of the reading, your eyes.

We have met, and the meeting is over;
  We must part, and the parting is now;
We have played out the game—I, boy-lover,
  In earnest, and you, dearest, how?

PAUL KRASSNER
born April 9, 1932
Brooklyn, N.Y.

Age 7

Room 204

PE. 6–9412

Local Union #816 Used Brick Chauffeurs
WELFARE FUND
364 WEST 34th STREET, NEW YORK 1, N. Y.

Tuli & Sylvia,

The best I can come up with is this Valentine's greeting I gave to my mother when I was seven as I recall:

Do you believe in Cupid--
Or aren't you that stupid?

Okay?
love, Paul

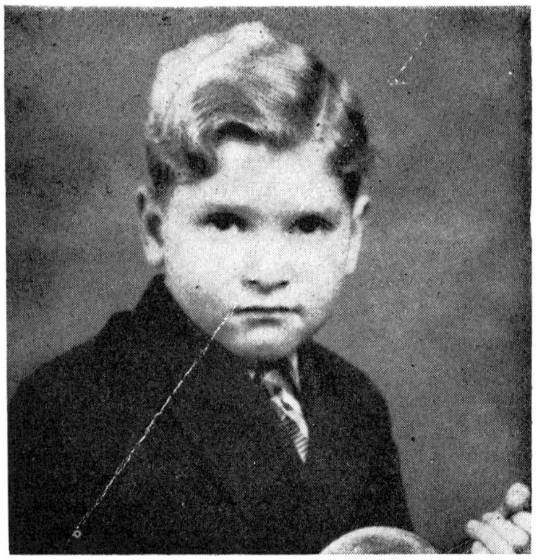

Paul Krassner, age six, is believed to be the youngest concert artist in any field to appear at Carnegie Hall.

My first short story. I think it reflects a specific "proletarian" ideology or outlook very strong in the second generation, of immigrants' children, then attending the New York City free colleges. It was published in Pulse, *the "literary-art magazine" of Brooklyn, CCNY, Queens and Hunter Colleges, for December 1942.*

TULI KUPFERBERG
born Sept. 28, 1923
New York, N.Y.

GOD BLESS THE CHILD

Age 19

Child, you are today;
For you there was no
Yesterday—
And you shall be gone
Tomorrow
—Betty Rothwax

He opened his eyes. This was Tuesday. He had four more days to work until the weekend. Twenty past seven. His mother came in and said, "It's twenty past seven." She started hitting the pillow of the bed his old man had slept in. It sounded like a cannon.

From New Utrecht High School yearbook.

"I'll get up at ha' past," he said.

"And make sure you're not late again," she said. Boom!

At ha' past his mother shoved him and he sat up. He dressed in a stupor, but by the time he was eating he knew what he was doing. Juice and coffee and an A&P donut.

Walking to the subway he knew that today must be a nice day. He caught the 8:05 and found his usual spot, standing, leaning against the far door. He slept on and off till 34th Street. He remembered how Jack used to stand and sleep next to him. Jack had been drafted last week.

At 34th Street he was pushed out. He joined the fast moving herd and he felt like bellowing. They pushed him into the street. This was going to be a nice day. The air was like cool lettuce. The sky was like Bucks County. The street was like 30th Street. He was there. Around the corner and into the building. Old, chipped, ragged, twisted—into the elevator.

Joe, the colored elevator boy, said, "Hello, hello, hello." He said, "Hello, Joe." Everyone had told him not to lend Joe any money that first afternoon he had come in. "Joe is a chiseler." Joe had paid him back the quarter he had lent him before the week was up.

While it waited on the ground floor for more passengers, the mouths in the elevator ground out a queer hodgepodge of language. "Seterday, yeah, two bits, you should uv seen Myrtle's face."

Joe pushed the door shut. It jammed. He got it. The faces froze as the elevator went up. At the different floors, the leaving crowds made sounds like noble chorals, dying in the distance. *His* floor.

He had to push someone to get out. "Sorry," he said. *Why the hell am I hurrying.* He slowed down with a jerk and strolled down the corridor. The sound of his braggadocio heels played self esteem music into his waiting ears.

He pushed open the door to the Acme Ribbon Company. Heads revolved on cervical axes, and his fellow workers noted that he was here. "Hey Frank, Irwin the pimp is here. Hello Irwin. The mid-week pimp. You're behind on your union dues, Sady."

Irwin made his way to the back of the shop. Over his head the paralyzed rolls of material hung; cardboards, paper, wood, boxes, miscellany, dust. They formed an arch and he walked under them almost proudly. He took off his clothes while talking to Frank. "We're going to work on organdy today." "O yeah," said Irwin. He put on the shoes that were holey, the shirt that was torn, and the pants that stunk. Now I'm ready to work, he thought. He went to the timeclock. His card number? What's the difference what number. He punched down hard, viciously. He felt he was punching through himself. Henry blew the whistle and it was on.

The factory, the tomb of dead wasted motion, had been still. Now noise came riding on a tank. Horribly, noise on a tank. Grrr. Ingggg. Teeekong. Zukta. Zuuukta.

Teeeekong. Zuuukta. Louder and deafening louder still. If you listen you go mad. If you don't you are dead.

You had been talking and saying sweet human things and then the tank came and mowed down your humanity . . . Don't talk, WORK!

Irwin was at his machine. He pressed his foot on the pedal. The ribbon began running from his hands onto the spool. Round and round. Organdy, faster, faster, he couldn't see the color. The machine was hitting a terrible rhythm. He knew he couldn't keep it up. Flitcracksh! Bumble, bumb. The main spool upset. Get your damn foot off the pedal! The ribbon piled itself into nice knots. He got down on his knees and started untying it. Good thing the boss didn't see it. His knees hurt. Three minutes and it was fixed. Slow, a little faster. Hmmm. Hmmm. Damn! The ribbon cut him. A cutblood. Red blood stained the organdy ribbon. The boss came. "Why can't you be careful. Cut off that piece wid blood on it. You got a bandaid? . . . Slow, aldetime slow I'm telling you."

He went slow. All the time slow. Organdy ribbon, miles of organdy ribbon spinning. And the light laughed at it shinily. How many miles of ribbon? Where is this ribbon going? Where did it come from? How many people are going to use this ribbon? Where are they? Who and what are they and who am I? Slowly, ever slowly the organdy ribbon flows. He was hypnotized by the organdy rhythm. He was losing consciousness. STOP! I'm a human being.

It's only 9:30. Christ. Here you are God, goods. What's good for you is bad for me.

He watched the organdy spin in dull fascination. He wanted it to spin faster. He wanted it to spin the fastest in the world. *He* was working this machine. *He* would show it. *He* would become the fastest bilex machine operator in the world. The boss would make him foreman and kick Henry out. Billy Rose of bilex, OUCH. It cut him again. You bloody bastard. He sucked it to his lips. You frmicommsukm. He stopped his machine to look around. 10:20. Everybody was working. Slaves. Round and round. Over and over. The same, the same. He was bored. He was dulled. He was bored. His head was spinning now. He didn't know what he was doing. Fast. Ahhh stop. Stretch. He should put tape on his fingers. He rubbed his eyes. Opened them. He rubbed his eyes again. Now he was alive. He bent over the machine. His muscles ached. Over and over again the same muscles. His back ached. He was alive and time was passing. His hands and his feet hurted him. His arches. He was tired. His arches pained him. He only looked at the ribbon, he didn't notice it. He was living precious hours of his short life.

Is this the thing the Lord God made and gave to have dominion over sea and land?

Wheee, beeee, hheee, heeee. Twelve o'clock! The machines listened. Slobberly, regretfully, finally they slowed down. They were silent sad. The silence made a big sound in your ears. Lunch! All retired mutely to the back. O punch yourself out first. Punch the flesh back in yourself. Brown rolls and yellow eggs. Stretch out on the bench. "Oh could I sleep. Dimag got three for four. Louis left for Ohio, armament aircraft. Hey Frank, Henry got his Questionnaire. Yeah. Haha."

"Hey, Frank," said Irwin, "goin' down for a Pep?"

The voices on the elevator and the voices in the street were still writing symphonies.

"Hey, I'm takin' that dame out I picked up in Coney last week."

"Ya think you'll get anything?"

"Ah, who the hell knows. Ya think ya have to get somethin out of a girl to enjoy her company?"

"Are you kiddin?"

Frank and Irwin went to the park. "This is a nice day," said Frank. "When I get my vacation, I think I'll go fishin' one day." They sat there ten minutes, and then it was time to go.

"Wait," said Irwin, "I want to get a iced coffee in the automat." "Ah, hurry up," said Frank walking in with him.

They punched in two minutes late. "Iced coffee you wanted," said Frank. "Look at the boss' face."

"Irwin," said the boss. "It's a little slow with rolling today, so we'll put you on shipping for the time being."

And they gave him little wooden spools, metal clips and a hammer, and they told him bang. And he did bang verily. And the sound of metal on metal did ring in his ears many times. And he had thoughts of deafness if he kept this up. And had not Will, the departed stock boy, broke his finger in the selfsame circumstances. Was not Archie, the router in the photo engraving place, nearly granite-stone deaf from the sound of the machine from years and whirs. And he felt danger for his wrist, for it hurt him long, and he had always to lift the heavy hammer and bang down hard. Hard. And the machines made a mighty clamor and shout. And he did curse every time he struck a blow, and he felt therefore good.

BANG!
THEM THAT'S GOT SHALL GET
THEM THAT'S NOT SHALL LOSE
SO THE BIBLE SAYS
AND IT STILL IS NEWS
MAMA MAY HAVE
PAPA MAY HAVE
BUT GOD BLESS THE CHILD
THATS GOT HIS OWN.
THATS GOT HIS OWN.

"Don't hit it that way," said the boss. "Like this." BANG, said the boss. BANG! BANG! "One shot, O.K.?" . . . O.k.

Bing bang bing bing bang bing bang bing bangbing bing bang bing bing cling bang thirty minutes, 324 bangs. BANG! . . . "Alright, put that down. You're going out."

Going out! Where there was air and trees and quiet. And people living! Where there were people living.

"Take these rolls to Premo Ribbon. You know where. On Madison, 63 Madison."

Hop, roll the rolls into the cart. Jokingly down the

elevator into the street. No, the boss wasn't watching. Stop for a soda.

Jollily down Madison. 63. The street rolls with him. It's a nice day. Buildings have funny appearances. People are unhurried. Everybody's going somewhere, though. The sky is blue. I'm not, are you? 63 Madison. What the hell. No 63. Damn. 68? Must be. "Premo? What you talkin' 'bout man? No such Premo here." In panic to the drugstore. Phone book. Did he say 36? No he didn't say 36. But . . . here it is. PREMO, 36 Mad. Licketysplit, loaded wagon passed the lights to 36. Up the el. Acme Ribbon. Sign here, dear. Goodbye. Too bad the organization of our society is such that I can't fall in love with you. I'd love to you know. Maybe you would too.

Jauntily back up Madison. Fine buildings. Cages though. Fine people in the street though. Hustle bustle break a muscle. Hurleyburley my name ain't Shirley. The great scene. The moving tides of people, the dynanimity. I'm part of it. Stinking me. Lookit. Stinking me. Looka me. I'm a very insignificant part of all this. No, I'm not. Without guys like me? There'll always be jerks like you. O yeah? Yeah. . . . Well I'm a part of it anyway. A part of the great story of the greatest city of the greatest civilization of the world. . . . Did you ever here of the Samoans? Yeah? Well they had a happier civilization than ours . . . Yeah? Mm, so we can't go to Samoa can we? If you join the navy. Shut up stinkhead.

I'm part of it. I'm walking up Madison with my wagon. People have to get out of my way if I want them to, but I don't want them to. Nice shops on Madison, now up 30th. Dirty hotels. But I won't live in that kind of a hotel. The Waldorf, that's for me. Near Times Square. Near everything. The Martha Washington, The Gramercy Park, No. 1 Fifth Avenue, Sutton Place, Tudor City.

I got to go up but I hate like hell to do it. But I got to. My spirits fall with the elevator rise.

"What took you so long."

I had to wait in the place.

"Ah that place is so inefficiency. Irwin, take care of the cutting machine now."

The cutting machine is a big slow slumbering monster. It cuts with heat. It cuts the ribbon and it burns your hands. Oil it with hot green, yellow grease. Lead the ribbon through its intricacies. Start it. You keep each thread going into its box. You tear the ribbon apart because the machine doesn't cut and it sticks together. Ho. Go. There it goes. Starts off fast. At the warmup stage. Going faster now. Turning it on. Rip that stuck. Separate the two lines. Ho stuck. Ho boxes. Ho stuck. A flap over! Ribbon stuck, starts burning. Stop the machine! The boss yells. "It always sticks," lamely.

"You don't catch it fast enough," from the boss.

Silence from you. Deep, embittered, not-my-fault silence.

The boss tinkers with the machine. "All right," says the boss. "The machine will run itself now. Go back to spooling and take a look every once in a while at the machine. Bring the stuff to Jerry."

Forty cents an hour. The minimum he pays. The minimum he pays, the minimum he'll get. Forty cents an hour I'm selling my life for. I'm selling my life for two-thirds of a cent a minute.

We head for the machine and trip on the ribbon. We crawl, drag ourselves through the air and clutch for the sky. We hit a bench and our shin embraces the side. Ouch. God damn. "What's there in it for the poor man?" *What's in it for the poor man. What's in it for the poor man.*

"Only a few hours before his electrocution he asked that his final statement, with its faulty English, in barely legible longhand, be given to the newspapers."

Have you thought about some people are allowed a chance over and over again then there are others allowed little chance, some no chance at all . . .

In my case I worked hard from sun up until sundown trying to make a living for my family and it ended in death for me.

The penitentiary all over the United States are full of people who was poor tried to work and have something, Couldn't so that made them steal and rob.

Irwin went to the machine. He bowed humbly before it. And fed it almost tenderly. Mostly he stood still. But when he had to move he moved in short mechanical jerks. His hands were levers. They had been dented. His feet were cement foundations. They had been poured long ago and were now hardened. His body gave direction to the rest of the machine. And his head. His head supplied the intelligence. Little wheels were spinning in his head. Oil them with food, and water, and paychecks. Oil them well. Just set them spinning on hope and feed them on starvation and need, and oil them on inertia and exhaustion. Drive them with fear.

Round and round goes the wheel. Over and over, the same thing. Bore, bore. Dizzy. The same thing. Bore, bore, Christ and more. Stupor. Technological hypnosis.

You shall not crucify mankind on a steel cross.

No, nor on a gold plated steel cross.

. . . But the sins of society shall be visited even unto the sons of the tenth generation.

One year had passed and it was 4:30 now. That last half hour, 3 years and the whistle blew. Good God. He had been working 6 years this afternoon. And the whistle blew. There was a dash of the automatons for the washstand. A few tripped on the ribbon. God damn, a few said. Many said nothing. Then the voices came alive. Shouting and horseplay. Cursewords. Screaming. Wrestling. Running. Punching. Pumping life blood back again. Into the elevator. The happy crowd. Goodnight boss. The jolly chorus down the elevator had run into the subways. Whoa. What a mob. Slow down. A seat? *Be glad you've got a stand.* Hot, crush and the papers. Russians attack. Germans attack. British attack. Japs attack. Attacktics of the war. You even pun. Say, there's Herby.

"Hey, Herby."

"O hello Ir."

"What do you hear from Joe?" "Joe is at Biloxi, Mississippi."

"Ed?"

"Ed is at Eustis. Albie went to Washington last week. Junior auditor."

"Ah I suppose we'll all be going soon."

"I got no excuse for livin' anyway."

How long *did* he have to live anyway?

They ride amidst the big talk of small people. "What a piece Saturday night. Prospect Park. I'm gonna go to defense school. Lousy job. Huh." They close their eyes from time to time.

"So long, Irwin," and Herby leaves.

Irwin rides in the sad silence of the big talk of little people. HOME STATION.

Dash up the steps. Cig in mouth. *Everybody light yourself up! Burn the day from you. Push away the bars of the subway station doors. You are free. Yes you are.*

Walk fast home past people buying peaches, cakes and plums. Paper underarm insignia. Insignia of the working man who would like to know whatsit all about.

The supper: good soup, hamburgers and potatoes, bread and butter, coffee, ahhh . . .

Rest in the living room half a second. Light up a cig. Down stairs. "Don't you come home late," from Ma. "I should have to wake you."

Down to the candy store. Cy and Moe are there. Only Cy and Moe. There used to be sixteen guys there.

"I won on the pool today, Irwin. Three bucks. Dimag, Rolfe and Dickey."

"Yeah? Hey, did you see Jerry?"

"No, he's goin' to art school at night."

Irwin wanted to be a painter too. There was beauty in things and he wanted to show it. He had painted well in high school. Every night he told himself he would paint something the next night. He was too tired.

"Hey, hey, Irwin, look what's coming up the street here."

A blonde girl passed.

"Who are you," Irwin said. She ignored him. "Hey Sid, gimme a small chocolate." Irwin shmoozed around with Sid awhile and then the boys walked over to Cy's stoop. They sat down on the stoop. Boy he was tired. He didn't feel like doing anything but sitting on Cy's stoop.

The conversation went from women to sports. To women. To what they could do with women if they had money. To how they would live when they got a better job. To it's gettin' late ain't it.

Irwin headed home. When he opened the door, the kids were asleep. His mother wasn't home and his pa was stretched out on the sofa with the radio playing low. He must have sewed about two million stitches today, Irwin thought. He shook him gently. Come on pop. Hey pop. Sleepin' on the job. His father woke with a start, cursed at no one in particular and hurried, eyes still shut, into his room and bed.

Irwin listened to dance music for half an hour and then he had some milk and cake and went to bed.

When he hit the cot he lay down, stretched out, and his muscles moved themselves around to comfortable positions. Then his day came flying back at him. He was painting a picture of the shop. The hammer began pounding in his ears. This painting was wonderful. Like tin against tin right through his ears. The ribbon twisted him up and tangled him. It choked him in such beautiful colors. He couldn't see the colors but they were beautiful. He was choking. With all kinds of strange noises in his head. *Arrr, inggg. Ingingingg. Bumbahbintrush. Bumbabintrush. Bumbabintrush. Bumb. Shutee. Shutce. Bumbabintrush. Bumbahbintrush. Bumbahbintrush.* He scratched his head. He ran his hands through his hair. He got up to get a drink. He looked at the clock. Two after twelve. Boy he was tired. He shut the light. He closed his eyes. This was Wednesday. There were three more days until the weekend. After the weekend there would be five more days until the weekend.

STEPHEN LEACOCK
born Sept. 30, 1869
Swanmore, Hampshire, England

Clearly his most important work outside the classroom was done on the school's newspaper, The College Times *[of Upper Canada College (a high school)], of which he was appointed joint editor and chairman of the Publishing Committee for the 1886-87 year. Through its columns the writer of the future expressed himself on a number of topics, ranging from literature to politics. While the editorials were, of course, unsigned, during his editorship it is not difficult to see Leacock's hand behind a good many of them.*

On the national election campaign in 1887 there was, for instance, this comment:

"But it really matters little which of the two great parties holds the reins of power. There is no great issue between them, and the accession of the Grits to power, or the continuance of Conservative rule would probably not affect the country for either better or worse."

But the editorial concern of The College Times *under Leacock's direction with respect to literature recurred frequently. One comment began:*

"Literature as a profession is not very lucrative. Those who depend solely on their pen as their means of subsistence earn but a scanty recompense for their labour; and literary labour, whatever may be said to the contrary, is the severest of all toil."

After continuing in this vein for some time and noting in passing that writing for magazines is the most lucrative branch of writing, the editorial concludes with a ringingly prophetic declaration:

"If literature, the finest of the beaux arts, were not so much neglected, Canada would doubtless be productive of geniuses as great as many of the Old World."

Stephen's first signed piece (over the initials S.B.L.) took the form of a light-hearted prose parody of life at Upper Canada College entitled "The Vision of Mirza." This appeared in the April 7 edition in 1887, and on June 9 it was followed by another parody of school life, this time in the cheerful verse of a pupil just about to leave school.

Legate

Age 17

U.C.C.

I.

If you'll give your kind attention
To an ode of small dimension,
And will offer no prevention,
    You shall hear described by me
What a place of sin and vanity,
Of swearing and profanity,
And cranial inanity
    I find in U.C.C.

Of the wicked College boarders,
Not a set of praise-the-lord-ers,
But a herd of vile discorders,
    I would briefly mention make.
Their pristine cheek delightful,
Their avarice is frightful,
Their disposition spiteful
    With a tendency to fake.

II.

There is nothing equalling them
When the steward comes to ring them
Up, the French they use to Kingdom
    Would astonish Socrates:
For though Greeks were vivid speakers,
They are but as puny squeakers
To College boys when seekers
    For their most replete Chinese.

On the Sabbath see them reading
Blood and thunder novels, heeding
Not the words of holy pleading
    Levelled at the college pew.
Should the venerable sexton
Try to gather a collection,
He receives a rare confection—
Buttons, marbles, gum and glue.

III.

Caring not if rules are broken,
They consider it a token
Of felicity to smoke an
    Old cigar beside the bay;
Or to spend a modest quarter
For a drink of beer or porter,
Which they know they hadn't ought'er,
    As the regulations say.

On the morning in the summer
There is seen the college bummer,
To the fence a frequent comer
    Just to watch girls' schools go by.
They go to Holy Trinity,
To show their asininity
To girls of an affinity,
    And wink upon the sly.

IV.

They've a lofty scorn of mental
Acquisitions; with a dental
Word they designate the gentle
    Poems of the bards of yore.
And they hold the Roman nation
And the deeds of ancient Latium,
As a fabulous creation
    And a most infernal bore.

In conclusion be it stated,
They are far degenerated
From the highly antiquated
    College boys of '33,
Who abound in stories pleasant
(To themselves), and who incessant
Prove they far excel the present
    Sojourners in U.C.C.

Stephen (third from left), about age 17, with his family outside the Sutton, Ontario, farmhouse.

AMY LOWELL
born Feb. 9, 1874
Brookline, Mass.

In the spring of 1883 she was taken out west, and again she was persuaded to begin a journal, entitled Notes of my trip to and from California. *She began dutifully by jotting down things she saw from the window of the train, such as a sign which read "Billiards." . . .*

Several times in the course of her life, Miss Lowell stated that the first poem of which she had any record was written at the age of nine; and we find one at the end of this journal.

Damon

Age 9

CHACAGO

Chacago. ditto
the land of
the free.
It is on lake
Mich'gan, and
not on the sea.
It has some
fine houses
in the suberbs
I'm told
And its people
are rolling in
silver and
gold.
In the city
it'self there
are
warehouses
large.
The folks go
on the lake
in sail boat
and barge.
But for all
of its ~~beauty~~
I'de rather
go home.
To Boston,
Charles River,
and the
State houses
dome.

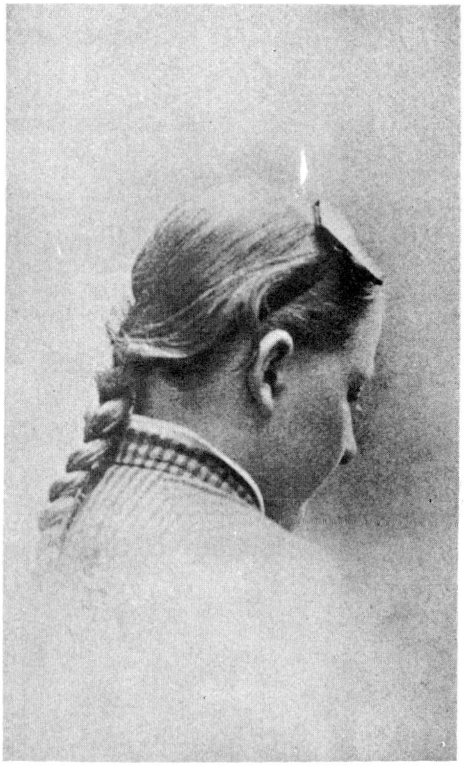

Age 8.

It was about this year [1888] that in her Complete Composition Book *she took down the following questions from dictation and filled in the answers, thus making a character-sketch of herself.*

Damon

About age 14

Name? Amy Lowell.
Resedence? Brookline.
What is your favorite moral caracterestic? Self controll.
Which one do you most dislike? deceat.
What is your favorite extrravegence? [unanswered]
What is your favorite exercise? books.
Who is your favorite hero in American history? Benjamin Franklin.
Who in the history of other countrys? Alfred the Great.
What caracter (male) in all history do you most dislike? Nepolian Bonaparte.
Who is your favorite heroin in American history? Barbera Friche.
Who in the history of other countrys? ~~Grace Dar~~ Josephine.
What caracter (female) in all history do you most dislike? Joan of Arc.
What are your reasons for your reasons for your likes and dislikes [?] Joseph's husband illtreated her [.] Joan of Arc was too masculin
Who is your favorite novelist among men? Thackeray
Who among women? Louisa. May. Alcott.
What is your favorite work of fiction? Little Women.
Who is your favorite hero in fiction? Diamond in 'At the Back of the North Wind.'
Who the most disliked? Steve (in 'Rose in Bloom')
Who is your favorite heroin? Jo (in 'Little Women.')
Who the one most disliked? Aunt Mira (in 'Eight Cousins')
Who is your favorite poet? James Russel Lowell.
What [is] your favorite poem? The vision of Sir Launfall.
What is your idea [of] misery? Not to be allowed to tobbogan.
What is your idea of happyness? To be loved.
What quality do you like best in a man? Manliness.
What do you most dislike? Cowardliness.
What quality doe you like most in a woman? Modesty.
What do you most dislike? imodesty.
What six books (Bible excepted) would you most desire to have with you if you were cast on a desert island? Little Women, Webebsters unabridged Dictionary, Moon folk, Boys a[t] Chequasset, Marco Pauls adventures on the Erie Canal, & At the back of the North Wind.

When Norman was ten he was sent to spend part of the summer with his aunt on the Jersey shore. Since he loved to tell stories to his friends, his mother supplied him with a notebook in which to write them down. This first novel was the result.

NORMAN MAILER
born Jan. 31, 1923
Long Branch, N.J.
Age 10

THE MARTIAN INVASION

About age 5.

Wanted for court martial and murder and hated by both sides, Captain Bob Porter and Private Ben Stein played their lone hand.

Chapter XI. A Mystery

The captives were placed in a prison for several days in which they were brutally treated by their captors.

Bob had a hard time restraining his temper. It was lucky for him he didn't as they might have killed him.

The next day they were chained onto the wall in the back part of a rocket boat. Bob knew in a hazy way that they were going towards the south in which there were the best places in the city. Among them was a huge castle that was crumbling to pieces.

Bob gave a sigh of relief that they were alone. The sigh turned into a groan as a pointed piece of iron fell onto Bob's arm. Bob saw that the edge was very sharp. Putting his teeth on it he started sawing at the chains. For a half hour he sawed at it before it broke.

Bob dropped the chains and took the piece of iron out of his sore and bleeding mouth. In an instant he was free. He then loosened the others bonds.

The captives then ranged on the front door. Bob then hit the metal door with a chain. The jailors came running over and opening the door rushed in. The Martians hadn't a chance. As each one came in he was knocked over the head until not one was left. The captives then ran through the open door locking it behind them.

They then rushed up on the pilots who met the same fate—all except one who jumping out swam towards shore.

In an instant the alarm was given and a dozen boats rushed over to easily capture the boat.

Two hours later they were again bound and guarded in a new rocket ship as the old one was demolished. They were rushed out and were herded into a small passage that led into a huge round ball building that had no windows.

They were ushered into a room where they were blindfolded and taken through so many corridors and rooms that they hadn't an inkling at the end of where they had went. Finally they were made to descend eighty steps. Bob counted them. They then were bound on their hands and arms. The guard then took a rope rolling it over them, then he fastened them to the floor with ropes.

The captives waited half an hour before they heard a thing, but when they did they wished they hadn't. A fearful laugh sounded all through the room. Then a part of the ceeling slowly began to move towards the floor. On it was a big Martian who with a big stick kept hitting it on his chair making an eerie sound.

Then to the surprise of all he said, "Welcome friends to our country." Bob gasped in amazement and the thought ran through his mind how did he know English.

The Martian reading his thoughts laughed and said, "My friend wants to know how I speak english." Bob noticed that he was purple with laughter.

Bob had noticed that the man talked with a French accent. Bob had a smattering of French so he said, "Parlez vous Francaise." The Marsian answered, "Oui, oui, mons—you dog," he shouted, "the idea."

Bob lay back choking his laughter back. The Martian sputtered in rage and threw his sceptar at him. Bob dodged it and it fell on the ground after hitting the wall.

Then he continued, "You shall die a nice death, a very nice death." The Martian again became purple. He then said, "Suffocation is nice isn't it. A slow long drawn out death, ho, ho, ho, ho, ho." And again the monster laughed.

Bob felt an eerie chilling of his veins and his heart seemed dead. How he wished he was loose and had an electric pistol.

The Martian calmly continued, "Do not try to escape as you would never get away. You will be fed but don't be happy, you haven't a chance. As for you, you silly dumbbell who thinks he is smarter than I, you shall not get anything to eat and the jailors will do so much that you will be sorry. Remember all of you that death comes five days from now." Saying these words he left the chamber letting the captives ponder over their fate.

MARIE ANTOINETTE
born Nov. 2, 1755
Vienna, Austria
Age 14

[In] 1770 . . . the gay sentimental [14]-year-old daughter of Maria Theresa and Frances I of Austria left the pious court of Vienna and entered, via marriage to the French dauphin [then 15], the maelstrom of Versailles.

Van Doren

As a young girl.

Choisy, 12 July, 1770

Madame My Dear Mother:

I can not express how sensible I am of the kindness Your Majesty shows me, and I assure you that I have never received one of your dear letters without regretting, with tears in my eyes, that I am separated from such a tender and good mother, and though I am happy enough here, I still ardently wish that I could return to see my dear, my very dear family, at least for a moment.

I am distressed that Your Majesty has not received my letter. I thought it would go by the courier, but Mercy decided to send it by Forcheron, and it is that, I suppose, which has delayed it. I find that it is sad to have to wait for my uncle, my brother and my sister-in-law without knowing when they are to come. I beg you to inform me if it is true that you have gone to meet them at Gratz, and if it is true that the Emperor is much thinner after his trip; this would worry me, since he has no flesh to spare.

As to my devotions, and "la générale," about which you ask, I will tell you that I have taken communion only once; I confessed day before yesterday to the Abbé Maudoux, but as it was, I thought, the day I was to go to Choisy, I did not take communion, being too distracted. As to "la générale," it is the fourth month that it has not come, without good reason. Our return from Choisy has been put off for a day, my husband having had a feverish cold which, however, went away in a day—having slept for twelve and a half hours, he awoke feeling much better and is now getting ready to depart. We have thus been here since yesterday—here where, from one in the afternoon, when we dine, until one in the morning, we do not return to our own apartments—which tires me out, since from dinnertime we play until six, when we go to the theatre, which lasts until nine-thirty and then to supper, after which more play until one or even one-thirty sometimes; but the king, seeing yesterday that I was so tired, had the goodness to allow me to retire at eleven, which pleased me very much and I was able to sleep very soundly until ten-thirty, although alone—my husband, being still on a diet (because of his cold) retired alone after supper to his own rooms, which never happens otherwise.

Your Majesty is very kind to be so interested in my welfare, and even to want to know how I pass my days. I will tell you then that I get up at ten o'clock or nine o'clock or nine-thirty and, having dressed, say my morning prayers, then breakfast; after which I go to my aunts' apartments, where I generally find the king. I stay there until ten-thirty; at eleven I go to the hairdresser. Before noon I receive; anyone can come except common people. I put on my rouge and wash my hands in front of everybody; then the men leave, the ladies stay, and I dress before them. Mass is at noon; if the king is at Versailles I go with him and my husband and my aunts to mass; if he is not here I go with the Dauphin, but always at that time. After mass the two of us dine in front of everybody, but we are through at one-thirty because we both eat very quickly. Then I go to the Dauphin's apartments and if he is busy I return to mine; I read, I write or I work—I am making a coat for the king, which is not getting along very well, but I hope that with the Grace of God it will be finished in a year or two. At three o'clock I go again to my aunts', where the king comes at that hour; at four the Abbé comes to me, and at five every day the harpsichord player, and I sing until six. At six-thirty I go to my aunts', when I do not go for a walk; you must know that my husband nearly always goes with me to my aunts'. From seven to nine we play; but when it is nice I go for a walk, and then there is no play for me, but for my aunts. At nine we have supper; when the king is absent my aunts have supper with us, but if he is here we go after supper with them to wait on the king, who generally appears at ten-forty-five—while I wait, I lie on a large sofa and sleep until he comes—when he is not here we go to bed at eleven o'clock. There is our whole day. I will save what we do on Sundays and holidays until another time.

I beg you, my very dear mother, to forgive me if my letter is too long, but it is my only pleasure to converse thus with you. I also beg your pardon if the letter is dirty, but I have been writing it for two days at my toilette, having had no other time; and if I do not answer your questions exactly, it is because of too much zeal on my part to destroy your letter. I must end in order to dress and go to mass with the king; I am the most obedient of daughters.

I send a list of the presents I have received, thinking it would amuse you.

The list has been lost.

In a manuscript book which he gave to his father for his birthday the young Karl "collected samples of his early poetical writings including ballads, sonnets, romances, songs, translations of Ovid's elegies, scenes from Oulanem, *a tragedy in verse, epigrams and jokes. It had as a supplement chapters from his satirical novel* Scorpion and Felix."

Marx-Engels, Collected Works, Vol. 1

KARL MARX
born May 5, 1818
Trier, Germany

Age 18 or younger

THREE POEMS ABOUT MEDICAL STUDENTS

To the Medical Students

Damned philistino-medico-student crew,
The whole world's just a bag of bones to you.
When once you've cooled the blood with Hydrogen,
And when you've felt the pulse's throbbing, then
You think, "I've done the most I'm able to.
Man could be very comfortable, too.
How clever of Almighty God to be
So very well versed in Anatomy!"
And flowers are all instruments to use,
When they've been boiled down into herbal brews.

Medical Student Anthropology

He who would sickness foil
Must learn to rub his nether half with oil,
So that no wind or draught
Can chill him fore and aft.
Man also can achieve his ends
With dietary regimens;
And Culture thus emerges
As soon as Man starts using purges.

Medical Student Ethics

Lest perspiration harm, it's best
On journeys to wear more than just one vest.
Beware all passion that produces
Disorders of the gastric juices.
Do not let your glances wander
Where flames can burst your eyes asunder.
Mix water with your wine,
Take milk in coffee every time;
And don't forget to have us called
When leaving for the Afterworld.

Age 18, from a painting of fellow students from Trier at a picnic.

A PHILISTINE WONDERS

"I don't know how they quarrel with themselves the way they do.
Just button up your coat, good sir, and they won't steal from you."

In Oulanem, *Marx's poetic drama [only the first act of which was ever written], the violence is turned outward, and the theme is the destruction of man by man, and it even includes the threatened destruction of all mankind by Oulanem. We enter a world where all the characters are learned in the arts of destruction, caught in the coils of a secret rage for vengeance. . . . We are never told why they are so determined to exact retribution on so massive a scale. . . .*

[The third scene takes place in] a room in Pertini's house, where Oulanem is preparing to deliver an extraordinary soliloquy. He paces the room restlessly and suddenly comes to an abrupt halt, folding his arms and facing the audience. In all of Marx's works there is no comparable passage of sustained invective. His hatred of the world reaches out to a vision of world destruction. Oulanem can no longer tolerate the depravity of men and consigns them to damnation in a passage which shows signs of having been written in a single burst of poetic fury.

Payne

OULANEM
Scene Three

A large room in Pertini's house. Oulanem is alone, writing at a table, with papers lying around. Suddenly he springs up, walks up and down, and suddenly stands still with his arms folded.

Age 18 or younger

Oulanem:
Ruined! Ruined! My time has clean run out!
The clock has stopped, the pygmy house has crumbled,
Soon I shall embrace Eternity to my breast, and soon
I shall howl gigantic curses on mankind.
Ha! Eternity! She is our eternal grief,
An indescribable and immeasurable Death.
Vile artificiality conceived to scorn us,
Ourselves being clockwork, blindly mechanical,
Made to be the fool-calendars of Time and Space,
Having no purpose save to happen, to be ruined,
So that there shall be something to ruin.
There had to be some fault in the universe,
The dumb agony of pain wrapped all round her,
A giant's mighty soul waltzing through the air;
So Death becomes alive, wears shoes and hose,
Suffering of plants, the stifling deaths of stones,
Birds vainly seeking their songs, bemoaning
The sickness of their airy lives, wars and dissensions
In blind assemblage shuddering, exterminating
Itself from its very self in violent clashes.
Now there emerges a man, two legs and a heart,
Who has the power to utter living curses.
Ha, I must bind myself to a wheel of flame
And dance with joy in the circle of eternity!
If there is a Something which devours,
I'll leap within it, though I bring the world to ruins—
The world which bulks between me and the Abyss
I will smash to pieces with my enduring curses.
I'll throw my arms around its harsh reality:
Embracing me, the world will dumbly pass away,
And then sink down to utter nothingness,
Perished, with no existence—that would be really living!
While swinging high within the stream of eternity,
We roar our melancholy hymns to the Creator
With scorn on our brows! Shall the sun ever burn it away?
Presumptuous curses from excommunicate souls!
Eyes that annihilate with poisoned glances
Gleam exultantly, the leaden world holds us fast.
And we are chained, shattered, empty, frightened,
Eternally chained to this marble block of Being,
Chained, eternally chained, eternally.

And the worlds drag us with them in their rounds,
Howling their songs of death, and we—
We are the apes of a cold God.
And yet we keep the viper beautifully warm
With foolish toil at the full breast of love
Which reaches up to the Universal Image
And sneers at us from the heights!
And the interminable angry waves keep roaring
To drain away the nausea from our ears.
Now quick—the die is cast—all is prepared,
And what the lying poem dreamed is utterly ruined,
And what began with curses the curses have fulfilled!
(He sits down at the table and writes)

Only twenty-four chapters and fragments of chapters, some only a few lines each (out of at least forty-eight), and no discernible plot exist of Scorpion and Felix. *Herewith a sampling.*

SCORPION AND FELIX
Chapter 27

About age 18

"Ignorance, limitless ignorance."

"Because (refers to an earlier chapter) his knees bent too much to a certain side!", but definition is lacking, definition, and who shall define, who shall determine, which is the right side and which the left?

Tell me, thou mortal, whence cometh the wind, or has God a nose in his face, and I will tell you which is right and left.

Nothing but relative concepts, to drink of wisdom is to gain only folly and frenzy!

Oh, vain is all our striving, our yearning is folly, until we have determined which is right and left, for he will place the goats on the left hand, and the sheep on the right.

If he turns round, if he faces in another direction, because in the night he had a dream, then according to our pitiful ideas the goats will be standing on the right and the pious on the left.

So define for me which is right and left, and the whole riddle of creation is solved, *Acheronta movebo,* I shall deduce for you exactly on which side your soul will come to stand, from which I shall further infer which step you are standing on now; for that primal relation would appear to be measurable with the help of the Lord's definition of where you stand, but your present position can be judged by the thickness of your skull. I am dizzy – if a Mephistopheles appeared I should be Faust, for clearly each and every one of us is a Faust, as we do not know which is the right side and which the left; our life is therefore a circus, we run round, try to find sides, till we fall down on the sand and the gladiator, Life, slays us. We need a new savior, for—you rob me of slumber, tormenting thought, you rob me of my health, you are killing me—we cannot distinguish the left side from the right, we do not know where they lie—

Chapter 28

"Clearly on the moon, on the moon lie the moonstones, falseness in the breast of women, sand in the sea and mountains on the earth," answered a man who knocked on my door, without waiting for me to ask him in.

I quickly pushed my papers to one side, said that I was very glad not to have made his acquaintance before, since I thus had the pleasure of making it now, that in his teaching there was great wisdom, that all my doubts were stilled by his words; but the only thing was that however fast I spoke, he spoke still faster, hissing sounds poured forth from between his teeth, and the whole man, as I perceived with a shudder on closer perusal and inspection, appeared a shrivelled lizard, nothing but a lizard, that had crawled out of crumbling masonry.

He was of stocky build, and his stature had much in common with that of my stove. His eyes might be called green rather than red, pinpoints rather than flashes of lightning, and he himself more goblin than man.

A genius! I recognised that quickly and with certainty, for his nose had sprung out of his skull like Pallas Athena from the head of Father Zeus, to which fact I also attributed its delicate scarlet glow indicating aethereal origin, while the head itself might be described as hairless, unless one wished to apply the term of head-covering to a thick layer of pomade which together with diverse products of the air and elements richly encrusted the primeval mountain.

Everything in him bespoke height and depth, but his facial structure seemed to betray a man of papers, for the cheeks were hollowed out like smooth basins and so well protected against the rain by the gigantic prominences of the cheek-bones that they could serve as containers for documents and governmental decrees.

In short, everything reveals that he was the god of love himself, if only it had not been himself that he resembled, and that his name has a sweet ring to it like love, if it did not sooner remind one of a juniper bush.

I prayed him to calm himself, for he claimed to be a hero, whereat I humbly interposed that the heroes had been of a somewhat finer build, that the heralds for their part had had voices of simpler, less contrived, more harmonious tone, and Hero, lastly, was beauty transfigured, a truly beautiful nature in which form and soul vied with each other, each claiming to be the sole source of her perfection, and that she was therefore unsuited for his love.

But he remonstrated that he had a p-p-powerful bone-str-r-r-ructure, that he had a sh-sh-shadow as good as anybody else's and even better, because he cast more sh-sh-shadow than light about him, and so his s-s-spouse could cool herself in his shadow, prosper and become a sh-sh-shadow herself, that I was a c-c-coarse man and a gutter-genius and a blockhead into the bargain, that he was c-c-called Engelbert, which was a n-name with a b-b-better ring to it than S-S-Scorpion, that I had been mistaken in Ch-Ch-Chapter 19 because blue eyes were more beautiful than brown, and d-d-dove's eyes were the most s-s-spiritual, and that even if he himself was no dove [Taube] he was at least deaf [Taub] to reason, and besides he championed the right of primogeniture and possessed a wash-closet.

"Sh-sh-she shall take my r-r-right hand in betrothal, and now let us have no more of your investigations into right and left, she lives directly opposite, neither to the right nor to the left."

The door slammed, from my soul there emanated a heavenly apparition, the sweet tones of converse ceased, but through the keyhole came a ghostly whisper: Klingholz, Klingholz!"

Chapter 29

I sat deep in thought, laid aside Locke, Fichte and Kant, and gave myself up to profound reflection to discover what a wash-closet could have to do with the right of primogeniture, and suddenly it came to me like a flash, and in a melodious succession of thoughts one upon the other my vision was illuminated and a radiant form appeared before my eyes.

The right of primogeniture is the wash-closet of the aristocracy, for a wash-closet only exists for the purpose of washing. But washing bleaches, and thus lends a pale sheen to that which is washed. So also does the right of primogeniture silver the eldest son of the house, it thus lends him a pale silvery sheen, while on the other members it stamps the pale romantic hue of penury.

He who bathes in rivers, hurls himself against the rushing element, fights its fury, and with strong arms wrestles against it; but he who sits in the wash-closet, remains in seclusion, contemplating the corners of the walls.

The ordinary mortal, i.e., he who has no right of primogeniture, fights the storms of life, throws himself into the billowing sea and seizes pearls of Promethean rights from its depths, and before his eyes the inner form of the Idea appears in glory, and he creates with greater boldness, but he who is entitled to primogenital inheritance lets only drops fall on him, for fear he might strain a limb, and so seats himself in a wash-closet.

Found, the philosopher's stone!

HERMAN MELVILLE
born Aug. 1, 1819
New York, N.Y.

By January [1838] Herman was back in Albany. Finding the Philo Logos Society moribund, he set about reviving it. On Feb. 9 Herman was elected president, and immediately he found himself embroiled in a controversy. Melville and Charles Van Loon [the former president] fought out their quarrel with what each of them clearly believed to be saeva indignatio. *They were the same age, and both had left the Albany Academy at about the same time [Melville to a trying teacher's job], Van Loon to become a druggist's apprentice, though he was now studying to be a Baptist minister. The warriors were equally matched.*

The arena was the Albany Microscope, *devoted, according to its account, to "Popular Tales, History, Legends and Adventures, Anecdotes, Poetry, Satire, Humour, Sporting, and the Drama." It did fulfill its purpose, but well before 1838 more than half of its four weekly pages were given over to gossip, scandal, and letters from pseudonymous correspondents attacking the folly, crime and vice of specific individuals in Albany. No modern paper could survive the reckless assault on private lives that was the* Microscope's *principal function.*

Gilman

In the Microscope *(10 March), Van Loon had replied to Melville's [previous] attack with a mixture of refutation and abuse, calling him "Hermanus Melvillian . . . a moral Ethiopian, whose brazen cheek never tingles with the blush of shame, whose moral principles, and sensibilities, have been destroyed by the corruption of his own black and bloodless heart." He charged that Melville had disrupted the Society, that the members had declared "the conduct of Hermanus Melvillian was disgraceful to himself, discreditable to the society, and insulting to the chair," and that he had secured the presidency by calling "an unauthorized and unconstitutional meeting."*

Davis and Gilman

Age 18

To the Editor of the Albany *Microscope* and to Charles Van Loon
17? March 1838

Mr. Editor:—I had not intended again to obtrude myself upon your columns, when I penned my last communication, but circumstances which I need not mention having altered my determination, I beg of you to excuse the liberty I take, when I request you to insert the following epistle, which, if it be rather long you must not demur, as it is the last I shall inflict upon your patience. I am at a loss to account for the avidity with which Mr. C* * * * *s V*n L* *n seeks to drag before the public a distorted narrative of the transactions of a private society; unless it be a mere feint or stratagem, under which he advances towards the overthrow of my reputation. However, as he lays down many grave and serious charges, I am constrained to reply thereto, in the hope of exculpating myself from allegations the most unfounded and malignant. I am aware that my communication is somewhat long and tedious, but as Mr. C* * * * *s V*n L* *n intimates his design of publishing a series of articles upon the subject, and being unwilling to parade myself before the public in a subsequent number—I have seen fit to obviate the necessity alluded to by giving a faithful account of the affair, together with a few reflections thereon, in one comprehensive survey.

To Mr. "Sandle Wood" alias "Ex-President" alias C * * * * *s V *nL * *n

Sir,—Without venturing to criticise the elegance of your composition, the absurd vagaries of your imagination, or impeaching the taste you have displayed in the abundance, variety and novelty of your scopes [tropes] and figures, or calling into question the accuracy of your mode of Latinising English substantives, I shall without further delay, proceed to consider the merits of your late most fanciful performance. And I cannot but sincerely deplore the rashness with which you have published a production evidently composed in the heat and turmoil of passion, and which must remain without the sanction of your cooler judgement, and the approval of your otherwise respectable understanding. To no other cause can I impute that vile scurrility, that unholy defamation, and that low and groveling abuse which are the distinguishing characteristics of your late unfortunate attempt to asperse, through its chief officer, the institution over which I have the honor to preside. In all your ribaldry and villification there lurks a spirit of implacable rancour and hate, which afford the most delightful commentaries upon the dignity of your christian character. Alas! that your discretion should have been so little consulted when this evidence of the rabidness of your vindictive nature should have been suffered to escape in the moment of your unguarded wrath, which must ever remain to demonstrate the hollowness of your religious professions of meekness, forbearance and love. Nor can I pass over without comment, the multitude of those blackguard epithets, which dance in sweet confusion throughout the whole extent of your recent production. *Here*, sir, are you upon vantage ground! I will not contend with you for the palm of vulgarity, nor seek to emulate the Billingsgate volubility of abuse in which you practice to perfection. Ah! what toilsome hours of study, what turning over of the leaves of Bee's Slang Dictionary, what studious attention to the lessons of the most accomplished masters of this divine art must have been required, ere you could have made way to that wonderful proficiency, which you seem to have attained in your late most brilliant communication. I have understood that the fishwomen of Paris and the Thames were considered as the models of a regular blackguard style, as the standard and criterion by which all excellence in that department of polite literature was to be judged; and that for a readier flow of insolence, shamelessness and scurrility they proudly challenged the world. But I doubt whether the annals of Billingsgate itself, the posthumous papers of the renowned Peter Porcupine, or any of those interesting works which have been burned by the hands of the common hangman can match in purity of style and delicacy of phraseology, that valuable article which if it be destitute of every other excellence, must still be considered as the *chef-d'oeuvre* of loafer eloquence. In this respect, I renounce, if ever I cherished all claims to superiority; and surely if laurels are to be reaped in such encounters—your brow is crowned with many a sprig. In regard to the hatred which you express towards me—I return it with no kindred detestation, but contemplate it with that mild and frigid contempt which it so richly deserves, and in common with the few who perused your performance, smiled at the folly which could prompt the utterance of personal dislike, and commiserate the headlong inconsiderateness which hurried you prematurely on to so public an avowal. If, however, you flatter yourself that you have bullied me into silence, or that the menaces which hang in terrorum over my devoted head, are objects of annoyance; I pray you to undeceive yourself, and rest assured, that I hold your abusive calumnies to be the outpourings of a causeless animosity, and your threats of defiance, as an idle and empty bravado. Under the dominion of temper and transported with fury, you have indulged in a vein of remarks, which with all the malice and acrimony of Junius, possess nought of that brilliancy of wit, that pugnancy [pungency?] of satire, and force, and beauty of expression which redeemed him from the charge of vulgarity. His malevolence, his rancour and vindictiveness, were in a manner assuaged by the polished elegance of his style and the splendor of his diction. Instead of knocking down his man with savage ferocity, he skillfully parries his furious lounges, watches his opportunity, and runs him through the body, to the satisfaction of every beholder. But you have neither the bravery nor the strength to perform the one, nor the address and dexterity to achieve the other. Again, sir, I beg of you to accept my condolements upon your pitiable failure to substantiate your infamous allegations; my regret that so much good stationary should have been squandered in the prosecution of your charges; and my utter and profound indifference to all your professions of hatred, hostility and revenge. May these truly christian attributes cling around the sacred lawn with which you are hereafter to be invested, and your angelic nature be a fit illustration of the peaceful spirit of the gospel you profess.

Philologian

The controversy continued:

Startle not, most amiable sir, when I inform you of what you are already apprised, that in your animadversions upon the relations which subsist between myself and the Philo Logos Society, you have shown yourself a stranger to veracity, to the truth of genuine narrative, and utterly disregardful of the feelings of my fellow members, and careless of the best and truest interests of the institution which you ostensibly defend. Now, therefore in behalf of the society, its members and myself, I feel bound by imperative necessity, to undertake your many fallacious positions, and to tear up and destroy that puny breast-work of sophistry and error, behind which you entrench the poverty and nothingness of your pretensions. At the solicitation of several of the Philo Logos Society, I became a member. Things proceeded with the utmost tranquility and order, until yourself indulging in a train of bitter and caustic personalities, drew upon yourself the bolts of my indignation, whereas frantic with rage, and burning with resentment, you moved that "the conduct of H——— M——— be considered as disgraceful to himself, &c."—Abortive attempt! Your motion was rejected, *viva voce* and yourself condemned to the pangs of mortified pride and foiled ambition. And yet with a hardihood, unparrellelled and barefaced, you endeavor to palm upon the public a palpable misrepresentation of the facts of this transaction, if mention whereof be made, it must redound to your lasting discredit. Thus much for the vote of censure which you allege was passed upon my conduct by the P.L.S. Called from town for a few months, I left the society in an apparently healthful and prosperous condition; on my return, however, my astonishment was unlimited, when I beheld our institution, which whilom flourished like a young cedar, in the last stages of a rapid decline. Immediately I instituted vigorous efforts for its resusitation, in which I was assisted by several prominent members, who all cooperated in the laudable design of reviving the ancient spark; we succeeded; obstacles were brushed aside, difficulties surmounted, and our labors crowned with gratifying success. In the midst of our generous endeavors, yourself being president of the P.L.S. was repeatedly importuned to unite with us in our operations—and having uniformly held yourself aloof—hereby showing none of that interest for the society which was to be expected from its chief officer, was tacitly and virtuously deposed and the few who then stood by the Assistant, resolved, to hold a new election; to that end they called meeting after meeting, but in vain! so few attended that the project was almost thrown up in despair. As a last attempt, however, it was decided, that if a certain number should be present at the next session, hereafter ensuing—the election should be proceeded with. Our expectations were realized, and at the first meeting of the society, subsequent to its restoration, the present incumbent was unanimously preferred to the presidency.—Through my endeavors, a large and elegant room was obtained in Stanwix Hall, together with suitable furniture to the same, free from all expenses to the society. By virtue of my office, I convened the As[sociation] at an early day, to adopt measures for the future course of the institution. My invitation was responded to, with alacrity by all the members of the society, which mustered in strong force as to a grand military review. The meeting progressed with the utmost harmony and good feeling, when yourself stung with dissapointment, smarting with envy, and boiling with wrath, sailed with all the majesty of offended pride into the midst of the assemblage, and pronounced t[his] recent election to have been unconstitutional and corrupt, becoming, however, rather unruly, you were called to order, and mildly requested to resume your seat; deeming this an outrage upon your dignity, with stentorian lungs you bellowed forth an appeal from the decision of the chair; when the society, disgusted with your insolence, by a large and triumphant majority vindicated the course of its president, ratified his election, and freely censured your intemperate and ungentlemanly behavior.

Frustrated then in your every endeavor to gratify the pique of private hostility—in order still to accomplish your iniquitous designs, you published under the signature of "Sandle Wood" a vile calumny upon the Ass., to which I indignantly rejoined, denying the slanderous accusations prefered, and insinuating yourself to be the author of the malignant effusion. Detected then, where you had every reason to suppose entire secresy would be observed, your anger knew no bounds, and disdaining all concealment and throwing off the mask entirely you hastened to give free vent to it, through the columns of the *Microscope*, in a tirade of obscenity and abuse, in which it is your peculiar province to excel.

It has not been, I can assure you, without reluctance that I have been drawn into any public disputation with one of your stamp, but a regard for my own reputation impelled me to expose the malevolence of your intentions; my only motive being then removed, I cheerfully bid a long good night to any further newspaper controversy with you, and subscribe myself,

Very respectfully
Your obedient servant
Philologean

N.B. Your incoherent ravings may be continued if you choose; they remind me of the croakings of a Vulture when disappointed of its prey.

EDNA ST. VINCENT MILLAY
born Feb. 22, 1892
Rockland, Maine

Vincent's mother, Cora, had been divorced from her father and was earning her living as a practical nurse. She was out of town on a case when this letter was written.

Like all eagerly literate children in America during the latter part of the nineteenth century and the beginning of the twentieth, the three Millay girls were avid readers of St. Nicholas Magazine.

Commager

Age 8

Rockport, Me.
Nov. 7, 1900

Dear Mama:

I thought I would write to you and tell you how I am I am getting along all right in school but in my spelling-blank I had 10 and 10 and then 9 and I felt auful bad because I thought I would have a star I am getting along all right and so is Norma and Kathleens [her younger sisters] cold is better now I went to practice and a boy called me a little chamipion and I asked him what he ment and he said because I was the best singer and I thanked him. When teacher and I were alone I said you have not called on mama yet and she said she is away and then she asked me how you knew her and of course I had to tell her and I said I guess you used to go arond with George Keller [Mrs. Millay's cousin] and she blused red as a June rose and then she asked me If I had ever rode in is tire wagon an I said I knew she had and she said oh yes. here I will write you a peace that I am going to speak Thanksgiving

On Thanksgiving Day little Dorothy said,
With many a nod of her wise curly head,
The cook is as busy as busy can be,
And very good to for 'tis easy to see
She gives us our Thanksgiving Dinner

About age 13.

[There followed three more stanzas of this poem her teacher had given her to memorize and recite.]

I do not know the other verses so good. lots of love to you your loving daughter
Vincent

Age 15

The magazine had a section, "The St. Nicholas League," which printed contributions by young readers. This poem appeared in the August 1907 issue.

VACATION SONG

Shine on me, oh, you gold, gold sun,
Smile on me, oh, you blue, blue skies,
Sing, birds! and rouse the lazy breeze
That, in the shadow, sleeping lies,
Calling, "Awaken! Slothful one
And chase the yellow butterflies."

Laugh! Sober maiden in the brook,
Shake down your smoothly plaited hair,
Let it fall rippling on the grass
Daring the wind to leave it there,
Dancing in all its sun-kissed folds,—
Laughing low in the sun-kissed air.

Frown if you will, you staid old trees,
You cannot silence the birds and me;
You will sing yourself ere we leave you in peace,—
Frown if you will but we shall see.
I'll pelt you with your own green leaves
Till you echo the strains of our minstrelsy.

Oh, mower! All the world's at play,—
Leave on the grass your sickle bright;
Come, and we'll dance a merry step
With the birds and the leaves and the gold sunlight,
We'll dance till the shadows leave the hills
And bring to the fields the quiet night.

WOLFGANG AMADEUS MOZART

born Jan. 27, 1756
Salzburg, Austria

Curiosities. *That the Germans in this century have become very prominent in the art of music, and have not only happily learnt from the Italians what is agreeable and charmingly harmonious, but also, since Germany now has such excellent virtuosi to show, they have excelled the latter in many respects, will scarcely be doubted any longer by those who understand music; more especially as now kings, princes and rulers endeavour to contest the primacy of the Italian virtuosi once so famous in music. In instrumental music we could mention many virtuosi among the Germans and thereby prove, supposing that were our intention, that they are to be preferred even to the most celebrated Italians as virtuosi on various instruments and at the same time as composers. But we content ourselves for to-day with a favourable mention in these pages of what is particularly curious in two admirable children whose father is a very famous virtuoso and an especially skilful and fortunate composer: and this in the form of a letter which has been sent from Vienna to a good friend resident in this city.*

Sir,

I am perhaps the first to have the honour of imparting news to you which may soon be the object of the greatest admiration all over Germany and perhaps also in distant countries. I speak of the two children of the famous Mozart, Vice-Kapellmeister at Salzburg. Just imagine a girl 11 years of age who can perform on the harpsichord or the fortepiano the most difficult sonatas and concertos by the greatest masters, most accurately, readily and with an almost incredible ease, in the very best of taste. This alone cannot fail to fill many with astonishment. But we fall into utter amazement on seeing a boy aged 6 at the clavier and hear him, not by any means toy with sonatas, trios and concertos, but play in a manly way, and improvise moreover for hours on end out of his own head, now cantabile, *now in chords, producing the best of ideas according to the taste of to-day; and even accompany at sight symphonies, arias and recitatives at the great concerts.–Tell me, does this not exceed all imagination?–And yet it is the simple truth! What is more, I saw them cover the keyboard with a handkerchief; and he plays just as well on this cloth as though he could see the keys. Furthermore, I saw and heard how, when he was made to listen in another room, they would give him notes, now high, now low, not only on the pianoforte but on every other imaginable instrument as well, and he came out with the letter or the name of the note in an instant. Indeed, on hearing a bell toll or a clock, even a pocket-watch, strike, he was able at the same moment to name the note of the bell or time-piece. I was also present in person when a clavier player on several occasions played a few bars of melody for him, which he then repeated and had to fit a bass to of his own; and every time he carried this out so beautifully, accurately and well that everybody was astounded. These two extraordinary children had to appear twice before H.M. the Emperor and H.M. the Empress-Queen, and then again before the younger members of the imperial family; they were favoured with grand presents and then invited to concerts by the highest nobility of the Court and everywhere handsomely rewarded.*

P.S. I am credibly informed that the boy can now not only play from the violin clef, but also from the soprano and bass clefs, and takes part in everything on a small violino piccolo *made specially for him, having already appeared with a solo and a concerto at the Court of Salzburg. Has he then learnt this since the New Year?*

From the *Augsburgischer Intelligenz-Zettel*, May 19, 1763; via Schmid

With father, Leopold, and sister, Nannerl.

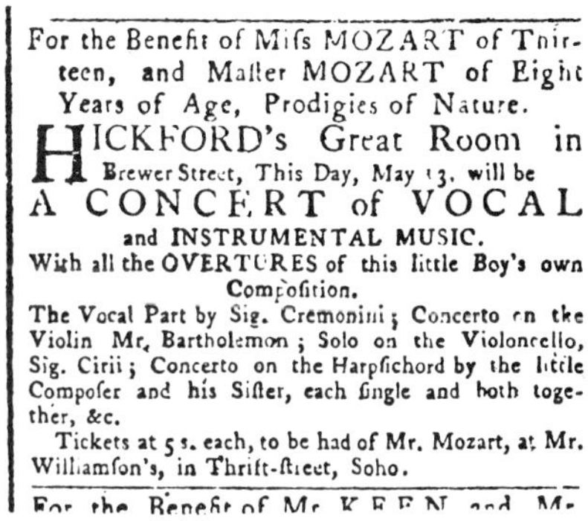

For the Benefit of Miſs MOZART of Thirteen, and Maſter MOZART of Eight Years of Age, Prodigies of Nature.

HICKFORD's Great Room in Brewer Street, This Day, May 13. will be

A CONCERT of VOCAL and INSTRUMENTAL MUSIC.

With all the OVERTURES of this little Boy's own Compoſition.

The Vocal Part by Sig. Cremonini; Concerto on the Violin Mr. Bartholemon; Solo on the Violoncello, Sig. Cirii; Concerto on the Harpſichord by the little Compoſer and his Siſter, each ſingle and both together, &c.

Tickets at 5 s. each, to be had of Mr. Mozart, at Mr. Williamſon's, in Thrift-ſtreet, Soho.

From 'The Public Advertiser', 13th May, 1765

Age 5

Composed in 1761

MINUET IN G

Age 6

Minuet in F (K.2)

January 1762.

Composed on March 4, 1762

ALLEGRO

Two Letters from Mozart to His Mother and Sister (included with his father's letters)

Age 14

Age 6.

Rome, April 14, 1770

Praise and thanks be to God, I and my wretched pen are well and I kiss Mamma and Nannerl a thousand or 1000 times. I only wish that my sister were in Rome, for this town would certainly please her, as St. Peter's church and many other things in Rome are *regular.* The most beautiful flowers are now being carried past in the street—so Papa has just told me. I am a fool, as everyone knows. Oh, I am having a hard time, for in our rooms there is only one bed and so Mamma can well imagine that I get no sleep with Papa. I am looking forward to our new quarters. I have just now drawn St. Peter with his keys and with him St. Paul with his sword and St. Luke with my sister and so forth. I have had the honour of kissing St. Peter's foot in St. Peter's church and as I have the misfortune to be so small, I, that same old dunce,

Wolfgang Mozart,
had to be lifted up.

Bologna, August 21, 1770

I too am still alive and, what is more, as merry as can be. I had a great desire to-day to ride on a donkey, for it is the custom in Italy, and so I thought that I too should try it. We have the honour to go about with a certain Dominican, who is regarded as a holy man. For my part I do not believe it, for at breakfast he often takes a cup of chocolate and immediately afterwards a good glass of strong Spanish wine; and I myself have had the honour of lunching with this saint who at table drank a whole decanter and finished up with a full glass of strong wine, two large slices of melon, some peaches, pears, five cups of coffee, a whole plate of cloves and two full saucers of milk and lemon. He may, of course, be following some sort of diet, but I do not think so, for it would be too much; moreover he takes several little snacks during the afternoon. Addio. Farewell. Kiss Mamma's hands for me. My greetings to all who know me.

Wolfgang Mozart

P.S. We have made the acquaintance of a certain German Dominican, called Pater Cantor, who has asked me to give his kind regards to Herr Hagenauer, the sculptor, at Salzburg. He tells me that when Hagenauer was in Bologna he always confessed to him. Addio.

Age 11.

CATALOGUE OF THE COMPOSITIONS PRODUCED by MOZART BETWEEN HIS SEVENTH AND TWELFTH YEAR.

1. Sonates pour le clavecin avec l'accomp. de violon, dédiées à Madame Victoire de France, par W. Mozart, agé de sept ans. Paris, Oeuvre 1, 1764.
2. Sonates pour le clavecin, etc., dédiées à Madame la Comtesse de Tessé, etc. Oeuvre 2, 1764.
3. Six Sonates pour le clavecin avec l'accomp., etc., dédiées à sa Maj. Charlotte, Reine de la Grande Bretagne, par W. Mozart agé de huit ans. A Londres, Oeuvre 3, 1765.
4. Six Sonates pour le clavecin avec l'accomp. dédiées à Madame la Princesse de Nassau Weilburg, née Princesse d'Orange, par W. Mozart, agé de neuf ans. A la Haye, Oeuvre 4, 1766.
5. Variations for the clavier engraved at the Hague, 1766.
6. Other variations for the clavier engraved at Amsterdam, 1766.
7. Fifteen Italian airs, written partly in London and partly at the Hague.
8. A quodlibet entitled, "Galimathias Musicum," for two violins, tenor and bass, two oboes, two horns, two bassoons and harpsichord *obligato*.
9 Thirteen symphonies for two violins, tenor and bass, two oboes, and two horns.
10. An oratorio for five principal singers. The original contains 208 pages.
11. Another oratorio for two soprani and a tenor, with accompaniments for an orchestra. Written in Holland.
12. Kyrie for soprano, alto, tenor, and bass, with accompaniments for stringed instruments. Paris.
13. Music to a Latin comedy called "Apollo and Hyacinth," for five principal singers. Composed for the University of Salzburg. The original score contains 162 pages. 1767.
14. Six Divertimentos in four parts, for various instruments, viz., violin, trumpet, horn, flute, bassoon, trombone, viola, violoncello, etc.
15. Six trios for two violins and violoncello.
16. A cantata on the Passion, for two principal singers. It consists of two airs, a recitative, and a duet.
17. A short Stabat Mater for voices alone.
18. Various solos for the violin—for the violoncello (for the Prince of Fürstenberg) for the viol di gamba—and for the flauto traverso (for Duke Louis of Würtemberg).
19. Several pieces for two trumpets, two horns, and two corni di bassetto.
20. Several minuets for the orchestra.
21. Various passages for trumpets and drums.
22. A collection of marches—some for an orchestra, some for military instruments, and others for two violins and bass.
23. Two MSS. books containing numerous pieces for the clavier, composed from time to time in London, Holland, etc.
24. A Fugue for the clavier.
25. A Fugue for four voices.
26. Veni sancte spiritus for four voices, and accompaniments for an orchestra. 1768.
27. A German operetta. "Bastien and Bastienne." 1768.
28. An opera buffa, "La Finta Semplice." 1768. The Score, 558 pages.
29. A grand mass for four voices, two violins, two oboes, two violas, four trumpets, drums, etc. 1768.
30. A shorter mass for four voices, two violins, etc. 1768.
31. A grand offertorium for four voices, two violins, two trumpets, etc.
32. Four concertos for the clavier, with accompaniments for an orchestra.

MALCOLM MUGGERIDGE
born March 24, 1903
Croydon, England

*Now I fell in love for the first time. I happened to see Dora, a girl of about my own age, whose brother I vaguely knew, playing tennis on a public court, and instantaneously the whole of existence for me was concentrated in that one face, uniquely beautiful, as it seemed, and distinct from all other faces. . . . We went for country walks together, picked blackberries, talked about books and writers, and what we were going to do in the world. I even bashfully read out verses I had written addressed to her. . . . I recall with shame one thing I did, which was to use these verses in a satirical sense in a play I wrote—*Three Flats*—that was put on by the Stage Society in 1931, and subsequently published.*

Chronicles of Wasted Time

About age 16

As a young man.

Come, let us sleep, beloved, and not waste
Our time in idle passion;
There are a thousand star-lit nights to taste
Our love in wild flesh fashion.

To-night we'll lie like children after play—
Sprawling in careless grace;
Your nightdress all in ribbon'd disarray,
Hair uncomb'd round your face.

My man arm loosely thrown across your breast
Your soft one 'neath my head—
Abandon'd to the gentle dreamless rest
Of a pure passionless bed.

But when you lean'd towards me from far away
I quite forgot all this,
And all the words that I had thought to say
Spoke through one single kiss.

NAPOLEON
born Aug. 15, 1769
Ajaccio, Corsica

In exile on St. Helena, Emperor Napoleon I reminisced about the creative writings of his youth, and in particular about the Discourse on Happiness *which he had presented to the Academy of Lyon in August 1791: "At the age of twenty, I sent various writings to the Academy of Lyon, but I subsequently withdrew them. When I read these writings, I found their author deserved to be whipped. What ridiculous things I said, and how annoyed I would be if they were preserved!"*

Napoleon did not in fact withdraw from the Lyon Essay competition, for the simple reason that the prize offered was worth rather more than his total annual pay at the time, including allowances. He also seems to have aspired to be accepted in Parisian literary circles, and his knowledge of Rousseau had taught him that success in the world of provincial academies provided an impressive start for an ambitious young philosophe. . . .

After leaving the military academy in Paris, Napoleon was posted to the "Régiment de la Fère du Corps Royal d'artillerie," stationed at Valence. He was in the first company of the fifth brigade of the regiment, the "Bombardiers." As a junior lieutenant his pay was ninety-three livres a month. Napoleon took lodgings with a Mademoiselle Bou in Valence, and had at least one "petite affaire" (with Caroline du Colombier) at this time. . . .

"I am not yet eighteen years old," he wrote from Valence, "and I am already a writer."

Frayling

THE HARE, THE HOUND AND THE HUNTSMAN

About age 16

Caesar, that famous pointer dog,
Bragged that his deeds were beyond compare,
One day he trapped in his forest lair,
A horrified hare—with fear agog.
"Yield" he cried in a voice of thunder,
Which shook the distant woodland birds,
"I'm Caesar, famed for his fighting words,
Whose name fills all the earth with wonder."
Jacky the Hare at this behest,
Commending his soul to God's great care
Demands to be told how he will fare.
"Your much respected mongrellest,
If I give in, will it be for the best?"
"You will die." "I will die" said the guiltless hare,
"And what if flight I should suggest?"
"Still death" said Caesar, unimpressed.
"In that case will you pardon me,
Your much esteemed majesty,
But if I'm to die whichever I choose,
Then I must flee—I have nothing to lose."
This said, the warren's hero flies,
Blameless—whatever Cato said,
The Huntsman sees a likely prize,
He aims, he fires—but the dog falls dead.
What saw would La Fontaine advise?
"God helps him who helps himself" . . .
I approve of that idea myself.

At the military preparatory school, Brienne.

OGDEN NASH
born Aug. 19, 1902
Rye, N.Y.

He grew up in various places up and down the East Coast from Georgia to New England; and he admits that he is a "quarter-bred Harvard alumnus," having left Cambridge at the end of his freshman year. He has documents, he says, to prove that he left of his own free will. . . . Nash has said further: "I have no private life and no personality."

Current Biography

Age 9

poem in celebration of his sister's wedding

Beautiful Spring at last is here
And has taken my sister away, I fear

Everyone that knew Sir Isaac, or have heard of him, recount the pregnancy of his parts when a boy.

Dr. Stukeley

ISAAC NEWTON
born December 25, 1642
Woolsthorpe (near Grantham)
Lincolnshire, England

Age 12-18

Newton had not long been at school before he exhibited a taste for mechanical inventions. With the aid of little saws, hammers, hatchets, and other tools, during his play-hours, he constructed models of known machines and amusing contrivances; as a windmill, a water-clock, and a carriage, to be moved by the person who sat in it; and by watching the workmen in erecting a windmill near Grantham, Newton acquired such knowledge of its mechanism, that he completed a large working model of it, which was frequently placed upon the top of the house in which Newton lived at Grantham, and was put in motion by the action of the wind upon its sails. Although Newton was at this time a "sober, silent, and thinking lad," who never took part in the games of his school-fellows, but employed all his leisure hours in "knocking and hammering in his lodging-room," yet he occasionally taught the boys to "play philosophically." He introduced the flying of paper kites, and is said to have investigated their best forms and proportions, as well as the number and position of the points to which the string should be attached. He constructed also lanterns of "crimpled paper," in which he placed a candle to light him to school in the dark winter mornings; and in dark nights he tied them to the tails of his kites, which the terrified country-people took for comets. Meanwhile, in the yard of the house where he lived, Newton was frequently observed to watch the motion of the sun; he drove wooden pegs into the walls and roofs of the buildings, as gnomons, to mark by their shadows the hours and half-hours of the day. It does not appear that he knew how to adjust these lines to the latitude of Grantham; but he is said to have succeeded, after some years' observation, in making them so exact, that anybody could tell what o'clock it was by *Isaac's Dial*, as it was called; and, probably, about this time, he carved two dials on the walls of his own house at Woolsthorpe, one of which is now in the museum of the Royal Society. Newton also became expert with his pencil: his room was furnished with pictures, drawn, some from prints, and others from life, in frames made by himself: among the portraits were several of the King's heads; Dr. Donne; Mr. Stokes, his teacher at Grantham; and King Charles I.; also, drawings of "birds, beasts, men, ships, and mathematical diagrams, executed with charcoal on the wall, which remained till the house was pulled down in 1711." Although Newton stated that he "excelled particularly in making verses," no authentic specimen of his poetry has been preserved; and in later years, he often expressed a dislike for poetry. During the seven years which he spent at Grantham, to the society of his school-fellows he preferred that of the young ladies who lived in the same house, and he often made little tables, cupboards, etc., for them to set their dolls and their trinkets upon. One of these ladies, when she had reached the age of 82, confessed that Newton had been in love with her, but that smallness of income prevented their marriage.

Timbs

The tiny notebook in the Pierpont Morgan Library in New York . . . includes long excerpts and paraphrases from the writings of John Bate and John Wilkins, contemporary popularizers of science, as well as an ecclesiastical calendar for the years 1662 through 1689 . . . a passage translated into a modified Shelton shorthand beginning "When Jesus saw the Crosse," a remedy for the ague if carried around as an amulet . . . a list of about twenty-four hundred words under the title, "The several things contained under these generall heads," broken down into sixteen chapters in alphabetical order with titles such as Artes, Trades, & Sciences; Of Kindred, & Titles; Of Man, his Affections, & Senses . . . pieces on dialing, the dissection of the triangle, the Copernican theory, and a system of phonetic orthography that introduces a few Hebrew signs . . . an exhortation to a friend to stop drinking . . . [and also the following piece].

Manuel

Certaine tricks

To turne waters into wine

1 Into Claret

Take as much bockwood as you can hold in yor mouth wth out discovery tye it up in a cloth, & put it in yor mouth, then sup up some wather & champe ye bockwood 3 or 4 times & doe it out into a glass.

2 ffor White wine.

Chew ye Ball once or twice lightly, &c as you did for claret.

ffor Sack.

Take a drop of Wine or beare vinegar & put it in ye Glasse shakeing it about ye sides of ye Glasse, &c : as you did for claret.

ffor Sky coloured Blew or Put a corne of salt in ye Glasse &c : as you did for claret.

ffor posset drinke & curds.

Take one drop of Sallet oyle, &c as you did for sack. & it will be posset drinke, y^{n} let it stand a while & it wil be curds.

ffor Strong Waters.

Have a cup of Strong Water by you like ye other of water wch drinke up as if it was ye water & doo it out againe into one of ye Glasses.

To Cut a Glasse.

Take a plaine Glasse, hold it up side downeward over a candle till it bee pritty hott then take match of rope, & blowing it all ye while run it ov^{r} ye glasse as you would have it cut.

On the whole, Newton seems to have been a healthy, normal and by no means perfect boy. He evidently indulged in that reprehensible habit of carving one's name in a public building, for among a crowd of names on one of the window-ledges in the old school appears that of I. NEWTON.

Holden

Carved inscription in The King's School, Grantham.

Schulpforta, formerly a Cistercian abbey located on the river Saale, not far from Naumburg, was a venerable school with high standards. The pedagogical goals for its 200 students included not only a comprehensive background in the humanities but a shaping of the character as well; diligence, discipline, and a truly Spartan life were regarded as the fundamental virtues at the institution.

Frenzel

FRIEDRICH NIETZSCHE
born Oct. 15, 1844
Röcken, Prussian Saxony

Pforta, November 10, 1862 **Age 18**

Dear Mamma:

I am very sorry that I was not able to meet you at Almrich yesterday, but I was prevented from coming by being kept in. And thereby hangs a tale which I will tell you.

Every week one of the newest Sixth Form boys has to undertake the duties of schoolhouse prefect—that is to say, he has to make a note of everything in the rooms, cupboards, and lecture rooms that requires repair, and to send up a list of his observations to the inspection office. Last week I had to perform this duty, and it occurred to me that its somewhat tedious nature might be slightly relieved by the exercise of a little humour, and I wrote out a list in which all my observations were couched in the form of jokes.* The stern masters, who were very much surprised that anyone should introduce humour into so solemn an undertaking, summoned me to attend the Synod on Saturday and pronounced the following extraordinary sentence: Three hours' detention and the loss of one or two walks. If I could accuse myself of any other fault than that of thoughtlessness, I should be angry about it; but as it is I have not troubled myself for one moment about the matter, and have only drawn this moral from it: To be more careful in future what I joke about.

To-day is Martinmas Day, and we have had the usual Martinmas goose for dinner (in twelve parts, of course). St. Nicholas Day, too, will soon be here. This period of transition from autumn to winter is a pleasant time; it is the preparation for Christmas which I enjoy so much. Let us thoroughly enjoy it together. Write to me soon. My love to dear uncle and Lizzie.

Fritz

About age 16.

*The remarks were very harmless, for instance: "In such and such a lecture room the lamps burn so dimly that the boys are tempted to let their own brilliance shine." "The forms of the Fifth Form Room have recently been painted and manifest an undesirable attachment for those who sit upon them."

ANAÏS NIN

born Feb. 21, 1903
Paris, France

The diary had its inception on the boat that brought Anaïs Nin, her mother and two brothers, from Spain to America. At the age of eleven Miss Nin already was possessed by what she later called "an immediate awareness," both "terrible and painful." Her father [a concert pianist], the idol of her early years, had deserted the family, had turned his attention to another, a very young woman. At first, she tried to win back her father: "The diary began as the diary of a journey, to record everything for my father. It was really a letter, so he could follow us into a strange land, know about us." But the "letter" was never sent (her mother told her it would get lost), and the diary became also "an island, in which I could find refuge in an alien land, write French, think my thoughts, hold on to my soul, to myself."

Stuhlmann

Age 11

A family outing at Coney Island shortly after arrival in U.S. Her mother is at the wheel, her brother Joaquin is seated. Anaïs carried her diary in the little straw basket wherever she went.

November 19, 1914

Today I have nothing to tell so I will chat with my diary, or rather, my confidant, for I write here many things I never tell anyone and that nobody knows. Let us begin: Today when I opened a book at hazard I read: Life is only a sad reality. Is it true? Perhaps! I have never discussed this. Today I want to know, and even though my diary is dumb, I will ask him. Is it true? Oh, if anyone asked me this on my dark, sad days when I am thinking of father, oh, I would say immediately yes, but that is all. Certainly, I have not suffered yet, I am only eleven, and I cannot say, I must wait longer before I can answer this question. Even though my curiosity is not satisfied I resign myself to talk about other things. When I see a beggar I want to be rich, merely to help him. I ask myself how it is possible there should be beggars with so many rich men on earth, only it is true many rich men don't give, if I could only give, give. With this idea I gathered all my toys to give to the chapel. I don't know what is wrong with me. I confess that the question: is life only a sad reality occupies my mind. Silly idea. No doubt I have many silly notions, many crazy notions I know, I admit it. Just the same, I want to know.

January 11, 1915

The day passed as usual. I work hard at school but that does not prevent me from doing what I prefer to do. I have written a story "Poor little One." I only love either gay or very sad things. Now I hate school, and everything American. Mother asked me why. Why? Why? Because I love silence and here it is always noisy, because everything here is somber, shut in, severe, and I love gay landscapes, I love to see the sky, I love to admire the beauty of natures, and here the houses are so tall, so tall, that one does not see anything, and if you do catch a little corner of the sky it is neither blue nor pink nor quite white, no, it is a black sky, heavy, lugubrious, soiled and blackened by the pride and vanity of modern men and women. I say this because I hate the modern. I would have loved to live in the first century, in Ancient Rome, I would have loved to live in the time of great castles and gracious ladies, I would have loved the time of Charlotte Corday when each woman could become a heroine. I must recognize that I am crazy, but since my diary is destined to be the diary of a mad woman, I cannot write reasonable things in it! And they would not be my thoughts.

February 3

At last here I am. I could not write before because I have not been well at all. Today I resolved to write. How beautiful it is now, it has snowed all these days so hard that all the streets and houses are white in spite of the furious work of human beings to take it all away. The streets are white, even the sky has taken part in this feast of pure colors, and now I love it, but it will last so little because the snow is being chased away and the sky will be in mourning again. Everybody pushes it away except the children. In the classroom we open the windows when the teacher has her back turned and we run and fight to catch the snow drops, and when we catch one you see the faces of the child blossom in a beautiful smile. I had caught several snow drops when the teacher jealous of our joy rolled angry eyes, closed the window and then all the children went back to their desk but more determined than ever to come back sometime. I am going to dream about snow and birds which I love so much.

February 27

. . . But I must tell about a rather singular dream I had last night. First of all I found myself in a grand salon carpeted in dark grey. I still remember how it looked, but that is not interesting. I was seated on a small wooden chair which smelled of pine. Then a fine lady dressed in black velvet and wearing a belt of diamonds or something sparkling, who first rushed towards a grand piano on which she played, a long and sad melody which made me sad. When she stopped she went to a big easel, took a paint brush and began to paint a very somber wood, with a pale blue sky in the distance, she did that softly, and in one minute she was through, then she advanced towards a big desk and taking a pen and a big book, her big blue eyes looking at me first of all, then at the sky, she began to write to write pages and pages. I could see they were big and beautiful poems full of charm, tenderness and sweetness. I could not read them but I feel sure they were beautiful. Then she closed the book softly, lay down the pen, and came silently towards me and then I heard these words: Choose. Oh, how much I hesitated, first I remembered the beautiful melody, then I suddenly turned towards the easel, it was so beautiful, and with a paint brush I could describe the sweet and charming landscapes, all the beauty of nature. But suddenly, I turned towards the big desk loaded with books, an invisible force led me towards that corner, involuntarily I seized the pen, then the lady smiling came up to me and gave me a big book saying: Write, I will guide you. Without any difficulty I wrote things which I think were beautiful because the lady said to me pointing to a corner where men with venerable beards, as well as queens and pretty ladies were writing without stopping: Your place is there. As soon as the lady was gone I softly dropped the book, and I went towards the piano, I wanted to try, first of all my fingers went very well, I like what I was playing but suddenly I had to stop. I did not know anymore. Then looking at the piano sadly I thought: I cannot. Then I tried to paint, my landscape was already pretty but then I stop and see that big smudges spoiled the whole thing, and then I said: Adieu, I don't want this. Then I took up the pen again and I began to write without stopping. My dream was very long, but it seemed so singular that I wanted to tell it so as to be able to reread it. Mother is calling me. I wish I could dream this way again.

May 12

I would like that nobody should ever know me. I would like to live isolated and alone. I envy the lives of those souls who can feel such peace, such sweetness in solitude. In one of my stories I uncover the sweetness of this solitude which everybody fears, why? Because they are sick, and blind.

Undated

There is one thing which troubles me. I feel different from everybody. I notice no child in my class of my age thinks as I do. They are all alike, they are in accord. I know their thoughts, their ambitions. And I make comparisons. I am altogether different. Instead of being like brothers to me, they are strangers. My desires, my dreams, my ambitions, my opinions are different. Why am I not like everybody? Glancing over this note book I said to myself: yes, these are my thoughts, but they are contrary. Am I what is called an eccentric, an "original" as the French say. Must I be looked upon by the world as a curiosity? In discovering on these pages my impressions certainly I do not seek to contradict what people think and still when I reread these pages I think that my feelings are contrary to what is called happiness. When I reread these pages I like to be able to say: this is a special story. Does it matter if no one understands? Am I writing for the world? No. My language is unknown. What a joy it will be if I am overlooked: my treasures will then belong to me alone. When I die I will burn these pages and my thoughts scribbled here will live only in eternity with the one who expressed them.

Of course, if someone should understand, if someone should hear this contradictory language, these novel impressions, I would be very happy.

Mother has visitors. I have put out the light and opened the window to breathe the night air. The young face of Miguel appears in my mind and he seems to look at me with sympathy. I begin to think of him. I remember the first moment when my aunt introduced us. He leaned down and took my hand with a smile. He said to my aunt: "she is pretty." He seemed sincere. It is the first time anyone has said this to me.

What is this passion which moves me? I remember the words of a song: "Fly, fly young girls, away from love."

I got 93½ at school. But Pauline got 94 and even if I am a foreigner, that is not good enough.

As about many precocious works of childhood, there were rumors that Nin "could not keep her hands off her diaries" and later "revised" them.

RICHARD NIXON
born Jan. 9, 1913
Yorba Linda, Calif.

In my determination to find some evidence of mental brilliance in the boy, I was aided by his mother. She went to an end table, pulled out a drawer, and unfolded two well-worn letters in his handwriting . . . one thus responded to an ad in the Los Angeles Times.

Kornitzer

Age 11

Whittier, Calif
Jan. 24, 1924.

Times Office,
X. Box 240
Dear Sir:-
Please consider me for the position of office boy mentioned in the Times paper I am eleven years of age and I am in the Sixth grade of the East Whittier Grammar School I am very willing to work and would like the money for a vacation trip I am willing to come to your office at any time and I will accept any pay offered My address is Whittier boulevard and Leffingwell road. The phone number is 5274 For Reference you can see Miss Flowers principle of the East Whittier School
Hoping that you will accept me for your service, I am, Yours truly,
Richard M. Nixon

As a schoolboy

Norman Chandler, publisher of the Times, *fingered the letter fondly. "This is just like him," he said. "It's a blueprint of his ambition, drive, and determination to meet a challenge. If he had gotten the job, it could have changed American history." But Richard did not get it.*

Kornitzer

We are not the Brontë sisters, but Jackie and I did occasionally put pen to paper, particularly when we gave presents to our mother—for Christmas or her birthday or an anniversary—since she far preferred something we had written or drawn to anything we might buy for her. We did this book together twenty-three years ago for her and our stepfather in appreciation for allowing us to embark on this first trip to Europe by ourselves.

I was seventeen, and my greatest dream was to go abroad as soon as I graduated from school. The main reason was that Jackie had taken her junior year from Vassar to study at the Sorbonne, and had lived with a French family in Paris. Her letters to me, of which there were many, were so full of detailed descriptions of where she had been and what she had done, other countries she had visited, how fascinated she was by the history of the places she'd seen, that I was filled with curiosity and a longing to see everything she had been writing me about. . . . Jackie did the drawings, the poetry and the parts on Rome and Spain.

Lee Bouvier (Radziwill)

JACQUELINE BOUVIER ONASSIS

born July 28, 1929
Southampton, L.I., N.Y.

Passport picture, age 18.

Age 21

"Gee - Do you realize you're in Pamplona!", bellowed Ace Williams, banging the table with his fist so that the glasses jumped, and squirting a bota of red wine into his mouth and down his shirt front. I certainly did realize it. For three mornings now he had woken us up at 5:30 to run before the bulls — Lee and I staggering blindly - hoping only to be gored and put out of our misery, while he thundered along behind quoting Death In the Afternoon. You couldn't even blow your nose without being told how Brett had blown hers on p. 64 of The Sun Also Rises.

Ace was travelling with three friends. One wanted to stay in Spain and write about power plants for the home town paper. Another wanted everyone to come to America. You could spot him anytime, holding a Spaniard against the wall, describing imaginary skyscrapers with one hand and saying "You've got a nice set-up here - but boy! - you should see the States. Tall buildings - Yes-sir-ree! And we dont Kill animals there - don't believe in it, you Know." The third was afraid of germs and women and of driving over 40 miles an hour. Once they revved the car up to 43 and he felt faint and wanted to get out. This poor creature's one dream was to see St. Peters - but Ace had informed him they were to spend the rest of the summer on the Riviera because he had a girl there.

We ran into Ace again at Cannes and found we had been in

Perpignan at the same time. "What?" – "You didn't hear Pablo Casals?," he roared, his voice choked with pain and disbelief. "Gee, do you realize he's the greatest cello player that ever lived? Boy you should have seen that concert in the Palace of the Kings of Majorca," and he hit his thigh with his chubby fist.

Ace was without his companions that night. They all had diarrhea. He gallantly told us all the French girls he knew were busy and asked us if we wouldn't like to go to Monte Carlo. "We dress, of course" he said. "But OF COURSE!" we retorted indignantly. It took us an hour to drive there and all the way he kept exploding: "Gee- do you realize we're going to Monte-Carlo! That glittering den of iniquity! The hangout of the Gay International Set, where Empires are won and lost nightly." We got there and at the end of the ballroom were three truck drivers in shirtsleeves playing poker and sucking wet cigars. "Gee Ace, do you realize we're in Monte Carlo" we said sweetly, our voices echoing through the empty halls.

Two weeks later in Venice we came around a corner into the Piazza San Marco. There at a table with their backs to us were four figures— one bent in limp dejection over a book about power plants; another throttling a waiter and pointing to the top of the Campanile; another busily wiping the rim of a glass. The fourth had neck muscles bulging, clenched fist raised. It came down with a crash that sent a cloud of white pigeons into the air —— "GEE– DO YOU REALIZE WE'RE IN ——" We heard no more – only the blood pounding in our temples as we ran for the nearest dock that had boats to the mainland.

We do not know what Eric [Orwell's real name was Eric Blair] was saying in his "very grown-up manner" about the war to his mother on August 4, 1914; we do know what he was writing about it soon after. It must be borne in mind that in August 1914 the vast majority of Englishmen (and their wives and children) were intensely, unquestioningly patriotic, proud, excited, and confident. . . . Patriotism inspired him to verse. Before the month was out he had written a call to arms in three quatrains.

Stansky and Abrahams

GEORGE ORWELL
born June 23, 1903
Motihari, Bengal, India

AWAKE! YOUNG MEN OF ENGLAND

Age 11

Oh! give me the strength of the lion,
  The wisdom of Reynard the Fox,
And then I'll hurl troops at the Germans,
  And give them the hardest of knocks.

Oh! think of the War lord's mailed fist,
  That is striking at England today;
And think of the lives that our soldiers
  Are fearlessly throwing away.

Awake! oh you young men of England,
  For if, when your Country's in need,
You do not enlist by the thousand,
  You truly are cowards indeed.

Orwell at right.

His parents were delighted with the poem—it echoed their sentiments perfectly—and when the family returned to Roselawn, Mrs. Blair sent it off to the local newspaper, the Henley and South Oxfordshire Standard. *It was published there on October 2, 1914, with the author identified as Master Eric Blair, the eleven-year-old son of Mr. R.W. Blair. By then he was already back at St. Cyprian's. His mother sent him copies of the paper, and he had the exhilarating experience of seeing his work in print for the first time.*

Stansky and Abrahams

BLAISE PASCAL
born June 19, 1623
Clermont, France

As a child studying geometry.

His sister remembers one of his first observations. When he was eleven, he noticed that the hum of a china dish struck with a knife was silenced by a touch of the hand. "Why?" he asked. As the answers he received seemed unsatisfactory, he made a large number of experiments on sound, and wrote a treatise which was found to be well reasoned, ingenious, and solid. There is no reason to cry "miracle!" No doubt the boy had already been schooled in the elements of harmony, his father's hobby. Nevertheless, it is worth noting that instead of proceeding directly from observation to generalization, he must first make "a large number of experiments." The boy possesses at 11 the rudiments of scientific method. [This treatise has not survived, however. The earliest work of Pascal's which has survived (and the first published) was]: Essai pour les Coniques, *a radical and important contribution to mathematical theory.*

This contribution to conics, to projective geometry, to modern mathematical method, was contained in a single closely printed sheet (of which only two copies are known to exist). It was no more than an example of work already done, an invitation to criticism, a forecast of an exhaustive treatise. . . .

This single sheet of paper is, for all its brevity, sufficient evidence of genius. It is a revelation of that extraordinary clarity of mind which could perceive significant relations of forms and thoughts by a kind of illumination, a kind of inspiration. . . .

The significance of the little essay was not immediately recognized, although it caused much satisfaction to the Paris group of intellectuals who were friends of the Pascals and proud of their prodigy. Desargues himself was delighted with the tribute to his theories. But Descartes, who had little liking for other geniuses, even child prodigies, wrote, evidently on the mere description of Pascal's proposition: "I do not find it strange that there are some who demonstrate conics more easily than Apollonius, for he is extremely long and involved, and everything he demonstrated is easy enough in itself. But one can certainly propose other things concerning conics that a boy of sixteen would have trouble in solving." When Descartes saw the essay he sneered that it was all already in Desargues. That may be, but it was certainly not in Descartes' Géométrie, *which had appeared three years before.*

Bishop

Age 16

ESSAY ON CONICAL SECTIONS

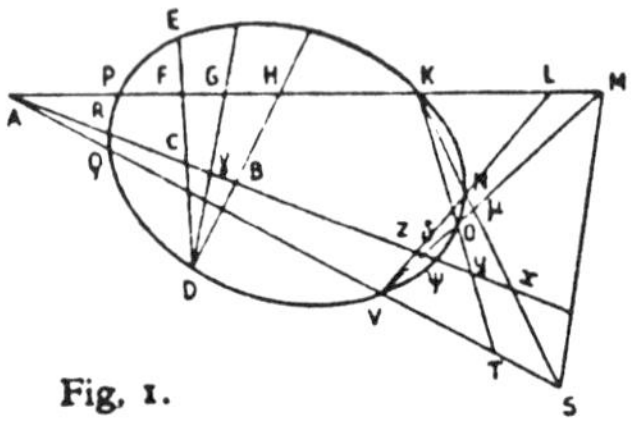

Fig. 1.

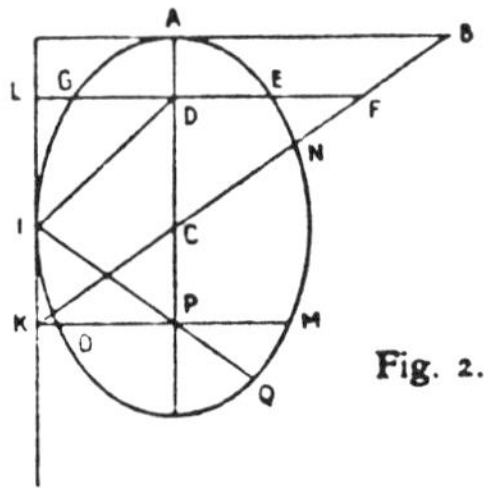

Fig. 2.

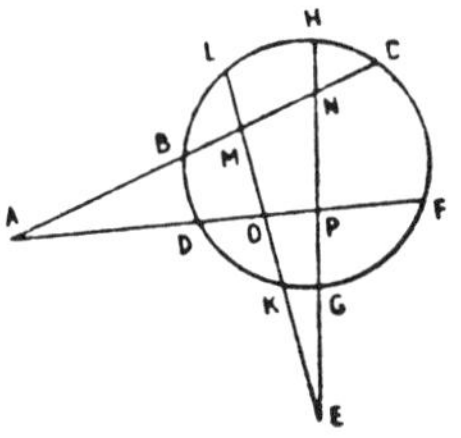

Fig. 3.

First Definition

When several straight lines meet at the same point, or are all parallel to one another, all these lines are said to be of the same order or the same ordinance, and the aggregration of these lines is called order of lines or ordinance of lines.

Definition II

By the expression conical section we mean the circumference of the Circle, the Ellipse, the Hyperbola, the Parabola and the right angle, since a Cone, when cut parallel to its base, or through its summit, or in the three other directions which produce the Ellipse, the Hyperbola and the Parabola, produces on the conic surface either the circumference of a circle, an Angle, the Ellipse, the Hyperbola, or the Parabola.

Definition III

By the word straight (droite) used alone, we mean straight line. [We have not followed this convention in our translation.]

Assumption I

(Fig. 1.) If in the plane M, S, Q two straight lines MK, MV start from the point M, and two straight lines SK, SV start from the point S, and if K is the point of intersection of straight lines MK, SK, and V the point of intersection of straight lines MV, SV, and A the point of intersection of straight lines MA, SA, and μ the point of intersection of straight lines MV, SK, and if the circumference of a circle passes through two of the four points A, K, μ, V which are not on the same straight line as points M, S,

for instance through points K, V, crossing the straight lines MV, MK, SV, SK at points O, P, Q, N, I say that straight lines MS, NO, PQ are of the same order.

Assumption II

If several planes, which are intersected by another plane, pass through the same straight line, all the lines of the sections from those planes are of the same order as the straight line through which the aforementioned planes pass.

(Fig. 1.) These two Assumptions now stated, as well as certain simple corollaries, we shall demonstrate that, the same conditions being posited as in the first Assumption, if any conical section which intersects straight lines MK, MV, SK, SV at points P, O, N, Q passes through the points K, V, the straight lines MS, NO, PQ will be of the same order. This will be our third Assumption.

Following these three assumptions and certain corollaries, we shall give the complete conical Elements, namely all the properties of the diameters and straight sides, tangents, etc., almost the complete reconstruction of the Cone on all the givens, the description of the conical sections by points, etc.

In this manner, we will state the properties which we deal with in a manner more universal than is customary. For instance the following: if in the plane MSQ, in the conical section PKV, straight lines AK, AV are drawn, crossing the section at points P, K, Q, V; and if from two of these four points which are not on the same straight line as point A, for instance through points K, V, and through two points N, O, at the edge of the section, four straight lines KN, KO, VN, VO are drawn, intersecting straight lines AV, AP at points L, M, T, S: I say that the ratio composed of the ratios of straight line PM to straight line MA, and of straight line AS to straight line SQ, is the same as that composed of the ratios of straight line PL to straight line LA, and of straight line AT to straight line TQ.

We will also demonstrate that if there are three straight lines DE, DG, DH which straight lines AP, AR intersect at points F, G, H, C, γ, B; and if point E is determined in straight line DC, the composed ratio of the ratios of rectangle EF in FG to rectangle EC in Cγ, and of straight line Aγ to straight line AG, is the same as that composed of the ratios of rectangle EF in FH to rectangle EC in CB, and of straight line AB to straight line AH. And it is also the same as the ratio of the rectangle of straight lines FE, FD to the rectangle of straight lines CE, CD. Therefore, if a conical section passes through points E, D such that it intersects straight lines AH, AB at points P, K, R, ψ, the ratio composed of the ratios of the rectangle of straight lines EF, FG to the rectangle of straight lines EC, Cγ, and of straight line γA to straight line AG, will be the same as that composed of the ratios of the rectangle of straight lines FK, FP to the rectangle of straight lines CR, Cψ, and of the rectangle of straight lines AR, Aψ to the rectangle of straight lines AK, AP.

(Fig. 3.) We will demonstrate as well that if four straight lines AC, AF, EH, EL intersect one another at points N, P, M, O, and if one conical section intersects said straight lines at points C, B, F, D, H, G, L, K, the ratio composed of the ratios of the rectangle of MC in MB to the rectangle of straight lines PF, PD, and of the rectangle of straight lines AD, AF to the rectangle of straight lines AB, AC, is the same as the ratio composed of the ratios of the rectangle of straight lines ML, MK to the rectangle of straight lines PH, PG, and of the rectangles of straight lines EH, EG to the rectangle of straight lines EK, EL.

(Fig. 1.) We will also demonstrate the following property, first articulated by M. Desargues of Lyon, one of the great minds of this age, and one of the most versed in Mathematics, and among other things in Conics, whose writings on this matter, though small in number, have amply demonstrated it to those who have been willing to receive this enlightenment; and I am willing to admit that I owe the little I have discovered on this matter to his writings, and that I have tried to imitate, as much as possible, his method on this subject, which he has dealt with without using the triangle by axis. Dealing generally with all the conical sections, the marvelous property that is discussed is the following: If in the plane MSQ there is a conical section PQV, on the border of which are posited four points K, N, O, V, and if straight lines KN, KO, VN, VO are drawn so that through one of the four points only two straight lines pass, and so that one straight line intersects the edge of the section at points R, ψ, as do straight lines KN, KO, VN, VO at points X, Y, Z, δ: I say that as the rectangle of straight lines ZR, Zψ is to the rectangle of straight lines γR, $\gamma\psi$, so is the rectangle of straight lines δR, $\delta\psi$, to the rectangle of straight lines XR, Xψ.

(Fig. 2.) We will also demonstrate that if in the plane of the hyperbola or of the ellipse, or of the circle AGE, with center C, one draws straight line AB, touching the section at point A, and if having drawn the diameter CA, one takes straight line AB whose square is equal to the quadrant of the rectangle in the figure, and if one draws CB, then, whatever straight line is drawn, such as DE, parallel to the straight line AB, intersecting the section at point E and straight lines AC, CB at points D, F: if the section AGE is an ellipse or a circle, the sum of the squares of straight lines DE, DF will be equal to the square of straight line AB; and in the hyperbola, the difference of the same squares of straight lines DE, DF will be equal to the square of the straight line AB.

From this we will deduce some problems, for example: From a given point draw a straight line touching a given conical section.

Find two diameters conjoined in a given angle.

Find two diameters at a given angle and a given ratio.

We have several other Problems and Theorems, and several corollaries; but the mistrust I have of my limited experience and capacity does not allow me to put forth any more of them until all of this has been examined by competent people who will be so obliging as to take this trouble; afterwards if it is felt that this deserves to be continued, we will attempt to pursue it further, as far as God will give us strength to proceed.

THOMAS LOVE PEACOCK
born Oct. 18, 1785
Weymouth, Dorset, England

[Peacock's father died when he was three.] Peacock entertained the deepest affection and esteem for his mother; he read all his writings to her, and sought her criticism. He has often said that after his mother's death [she died when he was 48] he wrote nothing of value, as his heart was not in his work.

Wheeler

Age 9

Englefield House
14th February, 1795

Age 18.

Dear Mother, I attempt to write to you a letter
In verse, tho' in prose I could do it much better;
The Muse, this cold weather, sleeps up at Parnassus,
And leaves us poor poets as stupid as asses:
She'll tarry still longer, if she has a warm chamber,
A store of old massie, ambrosia, and amber.
Dear mother, don't laugh, you may think she is tipsy,
And I, if a poet, must drink like a gipsy.
Suppose I should borrow the horse of Jack Stenton—
A finer ridden beast no muse ever went on—
Pegasus' fleet wings perhaps now are frozen,
I'll send her old Stenton's, I know I've well chosen;
Be it frost, be it thaw, the horse can well canter;
The sight of the beast cannot help to enchant her.
All the boys at our school are well, tho yet many
Are suffered, at home, to suck eggs with their granny.
'To-morrow,' says daddy, 'you must go, my dear Billy,
To Englefield House; do not cry, you are silly.'
Says the mother, all dressed in silk and in satin,
'Don't cram the poor boy with your Greek and your Latin,
I'll have him a little longer before mine own eyes,
To nurse him and feed him with tarts and mince pies;
We'll send him to school when the weather is warmer;
Come, kiss me, my pretty, my sweet little charmer!'
But now I must banish all fun and all folly,
So doleful's the news I am going to tell ye:
Poor Wade, my schoolfellow, lies low in the gravel,
One month ere fifteen put an end to his travel;
Harmless and mild, and remark'd for good nature;
The cause of his death was his overgrown stature:
His epitaph, I wrote, as inserted below;
What tribute more friendly could I on him bestow?
The bard craves one shilling of his own dear mother,
And, if you think proper, add to it another.

Thomas Love Peacock

Epitaph

Here lies interred, in silent shade,
The frail remains of Hamlet Wade;
A youth more promising ne'er took breath;
But ere fifteen laid cold in death!
Ye young, ye old, and ye of middle age,
Act well your part, for quit the stage
Of mortal life, one day you must,
And, like him, moulder into dust.

PABLO PICASSO
born Oct. 25, 1881
Málaga, Spain

Don José Ruiz Blasco [his father] was professor of drawing at the San Telmo School of Art in Málaga, and also curator and restorer at the municipal museum. He was an artist of the academic type, and such works of his as have come down to us show a photographic realism. . . . Before 1890 he became Pablo's first teacher. Since he specialized in painting birds, especially pigeons, he had the claws of a dead pigeon nailed to the wall, and made little Picasso draw them until he could reproduce the shape exactly. That is perhaps why his childish drawings of pigeons are surer and more mature than those of other subjects, which are more fantastic and distorted.

Although at eleven and twelve Picasso did not entirely cease to be a child—that would have been abnormal—he began to indulge in pastimes like the creation of art magazines of his own invention, like Asul y Blanco *(Blue and White) and* La Coruña, *filling them with charming drawings of young couples, soldiers, dogs at play, children in conversation.*

Cirlot

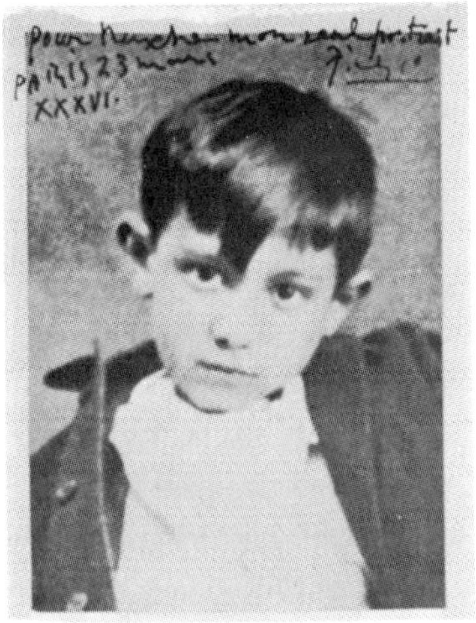

About age 5.

About age 8

Pigeons, crayon on brown paper.

About age 8

Pigeons and bullfight, on brown paper.

MOUGIN, France — Although a semi-recluse of 90, Pablo Picasso is still contriving to live up to his reputation as the art world's most controversial figure.

Without putting a foot over the doorstep of his fortress-like villa, he has created an embarrassing situation in the tiny French Riviera town of Mougin, where he lives.

The Mayor of Malaga, Spain, where Picasso was born, decided that the most appropriate present they could give him for his 90th birthday was a picture by the painter's father, Jose Ruiz Vlasco.

Picasso, however, does not seem to appreciate the gift. The village postman has tried many times to deliver the painting of eight sleeping doves. Each time he has been rebuffed.

Mougin's Mayor, Georges Pellegrin, anxious not to displease either the town's most famous resident or the Mayor of Malaga, tried to act as mediator.

He sent registered and delivery-guaranteed letters to Picasso's home urging him to accept the package. Only silence followed.

"We have now had to write to the Mayor of Malaga telling him as tactfully as we can that Picasso apparently will not receive the painting," Pellegrin said yesterday.

Picasso will not say why he does not want his father's painting. But local villagers are convinced that it brings back painful memories to him.

It seems that when he was 14 years old, Picasso was ordered by his father, who grew short-sighted in old age, to paint the feet on the dozens of dove paintings he produced.

This perhaps explains why in Picasso's own paintings doves are always footless.

LONDON EXPRESS

Sylvia had begun writing for the "It's All Yours" section in the magazine Seventeen. *Margot Macdonald, then editor of this section, wrote personal notes on several of the forty-five rejection slips Sylvia received. The editor made the comment that although Sylvia's writing held promise and present merit, she still had to learn to "slant" her subject matter and treatment toward the requirements of the particular publication from which she hoped acceptance. She advised Sylvia to go to the library and read every* Seventeen *issue she could find and discover the "trend." This Sylvia did, and in August 1950 she had her first story published, "And Summer Will Not Come Again," for which she was paid $15.*

Aurelia Schober Plath

SYLVIA PLATH
born Oct. 27, 1932
Boston, Mass.

Age 17

High school graduation photo, age 17.

AND SUMMER WILL NOT COME AGAIN

The rain started at four o'clock that afternoon. Celia saw it begin from the porch where she sat curled up in the chintz-covered armchair, trying to read. Aimlessly she let the book fall into her lap and stared at the big drops making dark, wet polkadots on the grey pavement.

Perspiration stood out on her upper lip and trickled in a little stream down her back. Her face was shiny, and she had tied back her limp brown hair with a wilted blue bow. From outside there came the strong smell of melted tar and the sweet, sickening odor of damp grass. A fly buzzed frantically against the screen.

The whole day had been hateful from the morning on. With the rest of the family away for the afternoon, the house was left quiet. The silence was like an expectant vacuum. It's like that when you're waiting for the phone to ring, Celia thought. There's an empty, unfilled place in the atmosphere just waiting to receive the sound. But when it does come, it's not for you, and you know that never, never. . . .

She wondered how that would sound out loud. "Never, never again," she addressed the flowerpot firmly. Her voice was flat, final. The words hung there in the moist, spongy air. Never, never again.

Here she was. It was late August, and it was raining hard now, relentless drops spattering the sidewalk. She was like any other girl, she tried to tell herself. But it didn't work. She was special. She was Celia. The rain beat out a tattoo on the streets. Never . . . never . . . never again.

Just how do you go about forgetting a guy anyway? A freckle-faced guy named Bruce, tall, with knifelike eyes that can see right into you and tell what you're thinking.

It had all started ordinarily enough down at the tennis courts at the beginning of summer. But it wasn't ordinary. This had happened to *her*. She was banging a ball up against the green wooden backboard, missing more often than she hit, when unexpectedly a boy's voice drawled behind her, "How about a set?"

Celia whirled. She surveyed the newcomer with a quick, appraising glance. Gosh, but he was nice-looking. "I-I'm just learning," she stammered confusedly. "I mean I really can't play." Something like this would happen. Why hadn't she started practicing sooner?

"No excuses," he laughed. "You've got to begin someday. I'll yell when you do anything wrong. By the way, I'm Bruce."

Standing opposite him, Celia wished for some miracle that would make her play well all of a sudden. This was worse than a nightmare. Frozen, she watched his arm come up sending the ball in an easy loop over the net. She just had to hit it. Rushing forward, she swung desperately. The racket whished through empty air.

Now maybe he'll see I can't play and leave me alone, she thought frantically. But he called over to her, "Keep your eye on the ball and just swing easy. . . ."

This time, when the ball came, she waited, watching it sail toward her. She swung again. There was a reassuring twang and the ball flew back over the net. For a whole hour she stood there, trying to hit back his easy serves and listening to his constant coaching. By the end of the afternoon she had made a few good returns.

As Bruce strolled over to her, she thought, well, that's that. He was nice to stick out the afternoon. And she smiled up at him, "Shouldn't I shake your hand or leap over the net?"

His blue eyes teased her. "Let's settle for a drink after all that strenuous exercise."

She wasn't sure what he meant. "There's a water fountain over there. . . ."

"Oh, let's get something with flavor in it."

Sitting together in the cool dimness of the ice-cream parlor, they sipped ginger ale and got acquainted. Bruce liked to do the same things Celia did. He even wrote for his college magazine.

"Don't tell a soul," Celia confided, laughing, "but I've got a collection of rejection slips a mile high."

As they parted at the door, Bruce grinned a grin that made her all watery inside. "See you around," he said.

The next day, as she approached the courts, she felt an odd stirring as she recognized a pair of blue shorts. When she came near, Bruce turned and smiled. "I've been waiting for you," was all he said. He knew, then, that she would be there. She felt like singing all of a sudden. He knew and he had come to meet her.

After that he would always be at the courts waiting for her. Celia often wondered if he thought of her as a kid sister . . . he was nice and yet so casual. (Nineteen wasn't *so* much older than sixteen.) Once, though, while he was walking her home, she had glanced up suddenly and caught him looking at her intently, his blue eyes serious. As soon as she met his gaze, however, there was the accustomed veil of merriment again.

"Know something," he said one day, "your hair smells just like pine needles."

"As long as it doesn't look that way," she laughed. But something about his look puzzled her.

Then for a week she didn't see him and Celia was miserable. Late one afternoon, the phone rang. It was Bruce. "Look," he sounded sheepish, "how about going canoeing tonight?"

A date! He'd never asked her out before. Celia gulped, "I'd love to!"

Out on the lake it was dark and very quiet. Celia leaned back on the cushions and watched Bruce silhouetted against the star-filled sky. The canoe glided through the whispering lilypads, through the deep velvet shadows along shore. There was something about the liquid silence that made them talk in low voices. Celia was so relieved to see Bruce again that she accepted his sudden reappearance without question. She stopped worrying that he had another girl.

But still there was a vague, nagging doubt. She had to know something. . . .

As they said good night she said, "You're not mad at me then? You still like me? I know I'm an awful tennis player, but. . . ."

"You little fool," Bruce replied softly. Slowly he pulled her toward him, tilting her chin up with one hand, and kissed her.

The next day, biking down to the courts, Celia hummed to herself as her lean, tanned legs pedaled rhythmically. The sun was warm on her skin and her hair blew back in the wind.

Suddenly Celia's eyes flew wide open. Her stomach tensed. It couldn't be, but there was Bruce coming out of the ice-cream parlor, talking and laughing with an adorable blonde girl. Celia felt sick. There was a hard, taut pain below her ribs. "You dope," she told herself dully, "getting churned up over a mere boy. He never belonged to you in the first place." Celia noticed carefully, deliberately, how nice that other girl looked in her white shorts and aqua jersey. She pedaled so hard her legs ached. As she went by, the blonde looked up candidly and Bruce called out airily, "Hi, there." He didn't even look guilty, Celia thought, furious.

Oh, oh, she muttered between her teeth as she banged the ball viciously against the backboard. How could he? She was concentrating so hard on whamming the ball that she barely heard the familiar voice drawl behind her, "May I have the pleasure of a set?"

Celia turned. He had come back alone after seeing that blonde girl home. If he thought she would just take him back meekly. . . . Her eyes narrowed. She let out a torrent of angry phrases . . . mean, cutting things she had stored up inside her. "Why, won't your girl friend play with you any more? . . . I should have known gentlemen prefer blondes. . . ." But her sarcastic voice trailed off breathlessly as she saw Bruce's friendly grin vanish. A strange alien look masked his eyes as he waited for her to finish. Too late she stopped the flood of words, frightened at the silence hanging between them. At last he said quietly, "All right, Celia. I won't bother you any more. I hadn't figured you were like this. My mistake."

He turned and walked away. Celia stood, congealed with horror. There was something so final in the way he left, not looking back. Suddenly the sun was unbearingly bright. It beat down mercilessly on the flat, rectangular courts.

That was yesterday. Miles and miles ago, if you could measure time by miles. Maybe he'd already had a date with that girl. She would never know. She had turned him away and that was what hurt. The rain spattered against the screen and a cool, wet breeze caressed her skin. All at once she remembered a few lines from Sara Teasdale:

On the long wind I hear the winter coming,
The window panes are cold and blind with rain;
With my own will I turned the summer from me
And summer will not come to me again.

She realized she was crying. The tears fell, hot between her fingers. There would be other summers, she knew, but this one would not come again.

The rain slowed its tempo, keeping time with her tears. Never . . . never . . . never again.

Sylvia Plath loves being seventeen. "It's the best *age." She lives in Wellesley, Massachusetts. Life is filled with senior activities, helping to edit her high school newspaper, working on the yearbook art staff, college weekends. She plays a lot of basketball and tennis and she pounds the piano "strictly for my own enjoyment." Jazz makes her melt inside. Debussy and Chopin suit her dreamier moods.*

FOUR LETTERS TO JOHN ALLAN
(His Foster Father)

Poe matriculated at the University of Virginia, February 14, 1826, at the start of the second session, and registered in the School of Ancient Languages under Professor George Long and in the School of Modern Languages under Professor George Blaetterman.

Ostrom

EDGAR ALLAN POE

born Jan. 19, 1809
Boston, Mass.

University. May [25] 1826

Age 17

Dear Sir,

I this morning received the clothes you sent me, viz an uniform coat, six yards of striped cloth for pantaloons & four pair of socks—The coat is a beautiful one & fits me exactly—I thought it best not to write 'till I received the clothes—or I should have written before this. You have heard no doubt of the disturbances in College. Soon after you left here the Grand Jury met and put the Students in a terrible fright—so much so that the lectures were unattended—and those whose names were upon the Sheriff's list—travelled off into the woods & mountains—taking their beds & provisions along with them—there were about 50 on the list—so you may suppose the College was very well thinned—this was the first day of the fright—the second day, "A proclamation" was issued by the faculty forbidding "any student under pain of a major punishment to leave his dormitory between the hours of 8 & 10 A M—(at which time the Sheriffs would be about) or in any way to resist the lawful authority of the Sheriffs"—This order however was very little attended to—as the fear of the Faculty could not counterbalance that of the Grand Jury—most of the "indicted" ran off a second time into the woods and upon an examination the next morning by the Faculty—Some were reprimanded—some suspended—and one expelled—James Albert Clarke from Manchester (I went to school with him at Burke's) was suspended for two months, Armstead Carter from this neighbourhood, for the remainder of the session—And Thomas Barclay for ever—There have been several fights since you were here—One between Turner Dixon, and Blow from Norfolk excited more interest than any I have seen—for a common fight is so trifling an occurrence that no notice is taken of it—Blow got much the advantage in the scuffle—but Dixon posted him in very indecent terms—upon which the whole Norfolk party rose in arms—& nothing was talked of for a week, but Dixon's charge, & Blow's explanation—every pillar in the University was white with scratched paper—Dixon made a physical attack upon Arthur Smith one of Blow's Norfolk friends—and a "very fine fellow"—he struck him with a large stone on one side of his head—whereupon Smith drew a pistol (which are all the fashion here) and had it not missed fire would have put an end to the controversy—but so it was—it did miss fire—and the matter has since been more peaceably settled—as the Proctor engaged a Magistrate to bind the whole forces on both sides—over to the peace—Give my love to Ma & Miss Nancy—& all my friends—

I remain
Your's affecti[onately]

Edgar

Will you be so good as to send me a copy of the Historiae of Tacitus—it is a small volume—also some more soap—

. . . we find that in 1826 a drunken student, driving from Charlottesville, publicly reviled one of the Faculty in the vilest language, although the professor was accompanied by his family, it seems that the drinking as well as the gambling may not have been overstressed. Duelling, too, was in fashion, and although the ownership of pistols was forbidden, the law was violated. The riots which punctuated the sessions were made more dangerous, of course, and the culmination of disorder came in 1840 with the murder of Professor J.A.G. Davis while he was attempting to quell a disturbance.

Quinn

University—Septem$_r$ 21$_{rst}$ 1826

Age 17

Dear Sir,

The whole college has been put in great consternation by the prospect of an examination—There is to be a general one on the first of December, which will occupy the time of the students till the fifteenth—the time for breaking up—

It has not yet been determined whether there will be any diplomas, or doctor's degrees given—but I should hardly think there will be any such thing, as this is only the second year of the institution & in other colleges three and four years are required in order to take a degree—that is, that time is supposed to be necessary—altho they sometimes confer them before—if the applicants are qualified—

Tho' it will hardly be fair to examine those who have only been here one session, with those who have been here two—and some of whom have come from other colleges—still I suppose I shall have to stand my examination wit[h] the rest—

I have been studying a great deal in order to be prepared, and dare say I shall come off as well as the rest of them, that is—if I don't get frightened—Perhaps you will have some business up here about that time, and then you can judge for yourself—

They have nearly finished the Rotunda—The pillars of the Portico are completed and it greatly improves the appearance of the whole—The books are removed into the library—and we have a very fine collection.

We have had a great many fights up here lately—The faculty expelled Wickliffe last night for general bad conduct—but more especially for biting one of the student's arms with whom he was fighting—I saw the whole affair—it took place before my door—Wickliffe was much the strongest—but not content with that—after getting the other completely in his power, he began to bite—I saw the arm afterwards—and it was really a serious matter—It was bitten from the shoulder to the elbow—and it is likely that pieces of flesh as large as my hand will be obliged to be cut out—He is from Kentucky—the same one that was in suspension when you were up here some time ago—Give my love to Ma and Miss Nancy—I remain,

Your's affectionatly

Edgar A Poe

On the night before Allan's arrival, Edgar encountered Wertenbaker, the librarian, and for the first time invited him to his room. It was very cold and his firewood had long since run out, so Poe smashed up a table and ignited the pieces with the help of a few candles, and they sat by the fire and talked. He told Wertenbaker that his debts ran to $2000 and that he considered them "debts of honor" that he must pay at the first opportunity. John Allan felt differently. When he arrived at Charlottesville he paid those debts he thought "ought to be paid," but not all those Edgar could be held accountable for. Certainly the "debts of honor" about which the boy was so concerned were not among those paid. Then the two drove back to Richmond [for the holidays], arriving on Christmas Eve.

Bettner

Richmond Monday [March 19, 1827]

Age 18

Sir,

After my treatment on yesterday and what passed between us this morning, I can hardly think you will be surprised at the contents of this letter. My determination is at length taken—to leave your house and indeavor to find some place in this wide world, where I will be treated—not as *you* have treated me—This is not a hurried determination, but one on which I have long considered—and having so considered my resolution is unalterable—You may perhaps think that I have flown off in a passion, & that I am already wishing to return; But not so—I will give you the reason[s] which have actuated me, and then judge—

Since I have been able to think on any subject, my thoughts have aspired, and they have been taught by *you* to aspire, to eminence in public life—this cannot be attained without a good Education, such a one I cannot obtain at a Primary school—A collegiate Education therefore was what I most ardently desired, and I had been led to expect that it would at some future time be granted—but in a moment of caprice—you have blasted my hope because forsooth I disagreed with you in an opinion, which opinion I was forced to express—Again, I have heard you say (when you little thought I was listening and therefore must have said it in earnest) that you had no affection for me—

You have moreover ordered me to quit your house, and are continually upbraiding me with eating the bread of Idleness, when you yourself were the only person to remedy the evil by placing me to some business—You take delight in exposing me before those whom you think likely to advance my interest in this world—

You suffer me to be subjected to the whims & caprice, not only of your white family, but the complete authority of the blacks—these grievances I could not submit to; and I am gone. I request that you will send me my trunk containing my clothes & books—and if you still have the least affection for me, As the last cal[l] I shall make on your bou[nty], To prevent the fulfillment of the Prediction you this morning expressed, send me as much money as will defray the expences of my passage to some of the Northern cit[i]es & then support me for one month, by whic[h] time I [sh]all be enabled to place myself [in] some situation where I may not only o[bt]ain a livelihood, but lay by a sum which one day or another will support me at the University—Send my trunk &c to the Court-house Tavern, send me I entreat you some money immediately—as I am in the greatest necessity—If you fail to comply with my request—I tremble for the consequence

Yours &c
Edgar A Poe

It depends upon yourself if hereafter you see or hear from m[e.]

Richmond Tuesday [March 20, 1827]

Age 18

Dear Sir,

Be so good as to send me my trunk with my clothes—I wrote to you on yesterday explaining my reasons for leaving—I suppose by my not receiving either my trunk, or an answer to my letter, that you did not receive it—I am in the greatest necessity, not having tasted food since Yesterday morning. I have no where to sleep at night, but roam about the Streets—I am nearly exhausted—I beseech you as you wish not your prediction concerning me to be fulfilled—to send me without delay my trunk containing my clothes, and to lend if you will not give me as much money as will defray the expence of my passage to Boston (.$12,) and a little to support me there untill I shall be enabled to engage in some business—I sail on Saturday—A letter will be received by me at the Court House Tavern, where be so good as to send my trunk—

Give my love to all at home
I am Your's &c.

Edgar A Poe

I have not one cent in the world to provide any food

JACKSON POLLOCK
born Jan. 28, 1912
Cody, Wyoming

Rebellion and protest, as such, were expressed in another way, also encouraged by Schwankovsky [his art teacher]. During this 1928–29 academic year Pollock was expelled from Manual Arts [High School] for having taken part, along with Guston and Tolegian [two artist friends], in the preparation and distribution of the Journal of Liberty, *two mimeographed attacks on the high-school faculty, particularly the English Department, and its overemphasis on athletics. When Jackson learned that at the same time Kadish [a painter-sculptor friend] had independently organized similar protests at Riverside [High], which the newspapers had described as part of a Communist conspiracy, he phoned Kadish and reestablished contact with him. From then until the end of the year these two, as well as Guston, Tolegian, and Donald Brown, a writer particularly interested in Joyce and Cummings, were very close. Though drawn together as "political trouble-makers," their real interest was in art. Kadish recalls that they were already reading* Transition, *the avant-garde literary magazine which had begun publication in April 1927. "We were living a European fantasy," Kadish says. "We knew we didn't belong in the Los Angeles Water Color Club or the Art Association. Siqueiros coming to L.A. meant as much then as did the Surrealists coming to New York in the forties."*

Pollock was not readmitted to Manual Arts until the following fall—after another summer of surveying, this time with his father in Santa Ynez, California—and he was soon in trouble again, as indicated by the following long letter, one of the few which survives from this period of Jackson's life. (Note: Frank [brother, born in 1907] was in New York studying literature at Columbia, while Charles [brother, born 1902] was still there at the Art Students League.)

Friedman

Age 17

Los Angeles
Oct. 22 1929

Dear Charles and Frank:

I am sorry for having been so slow with my correspondence to you. I have been very busy getting adjusted in school, but another climax has arisen. I have been ousted from school again. The head of the Physical Ed. Dept. and I came to blows the other day. We saw the principal about it but he was too thick to see my side. He told me to get out and find another school. I have a number of teachers backing me so there is some possibility of my getting back. If I can not get back I am not sure what I will do. I have thought of going to Mexico city if there is any means of making a livelihood there.

Another fellow and I are in some more very serious trouble. We loaned two girls some money to run a way. We were ignorant of the law at the time. We did it merely through friend ship. But now they have us, I am not sure what the outcomes will be. The penalty is from six to twelve months in jail. We are both minors so it would probably be some kind of a reform school. They found the girls today in Phoenix and are bringing them back.

If I get back in school I will have to be very careful about my actions. The whole outfit think I am a rotten rebel from Russia. I will have to go about very quietly for a long period until I win a good reputation. I find it useless to try and fight an army with a spit ball.

I have read and re-read your letter with clearer understanding each time. Altho I am some better this year I am far from knowing the meaning of real work. I have subscribed for the "Creative Art," and "The Arts." From the Creative Art I am able to under stand you better and it gives me a new outlook on life.

I have dropped religion for the present. Should I follow the Occult Mysticism it wouldn't be for commercial purposes. I am doubtful of my talent, so what ever I choose to be, will be accomplished only by long study and work. I fear it will be forced and mechanical. Architecture interests me but not in the sense painting and sculptoring does. I became acquainted with Rivera's work through a number of Communist meetings I attended after being ousted from school last year. He has a painting in the Museum now. Perhaps you have seen it, Dia de Flores. I found the

Creative Art January 1929 on Rivera. I certainly admire his work. The other magizines I could not find.

As to what I would like to be. It is difficult to say. An Artist of some kind. If nothing else I shall always study the Arts. People have always frightened and bored me consequently I have been within my own shell and have not accomplished anything materially. In fact to talk in a group I was so frightened that I could not think logically. I am gradually overcoming it now. I am taking American Literature, Contemporary Literature, Clay Modeling and the life class. We are very fortunate in that this is the only school in the city that have models. Altho it is difficult to have a nude and get by the board, Schwankovsky is brave enough to have them.

Frank I am sorry I have not sent you the typewriter sooner I got a box for it but it is too small I will get another and send it immediately. How is school going? Are you in any activity? Is Mart [brother, born 1904] still in the city? We have not heard for a long time in fact the letters have slacked from all of you.

Sande [another brother, born 1909] is doing quite well now. He has an office and handles all the advertising. He continues to make his weekend trip to Riverside.

Affectionately
Jack

los angeles
jan 31 1930

Age 18

dear charles

i am continually having new experiences and am going through a wavering evolution which leave my mind in an unsettled state. too i am a bit lazy and careless with my crrespondance i am sorry i seem so uniterested in your helping me but from now on there will be more interest and a hastier reply to your letters. my letters are undoubtedly egotistical but it is myself that i am interested in now. i suppose mother keeps you posted on family matter

school is still boresome but i have settled myself to its rules and the ringing bells so i have not been in trouble lately. this term i am going to go but one half day the rest i will spend reading and working here at home. i am quite shure i will be able to accomplish a lot more. in school i will take life drawing and clay modeling. i have started doing some thing with clay and have found a bit of encouragement from my teacher. my drawing i will tell you frankly is rotten it seems to lack freedom and rythem it is cold and lifeless. it isn't worth the postage to send it. i think there should be a advancement soon if it is ever to come and then i will send you some drawings. the truth of it is i have never really gotten down to real work and finish a piece i usually get disgusted with it and lose interest. water color i like but have never worked with it much. altho i feel i will make an artist of some kind i have never proven to myself nor any body else that i have it in me.

this so called happy part of one's life youth to me is a bit of damnable hell if i could come to some conclusion about my self and life perhaps then i could see something to work for. my mind blazes up with some illusion for a couple of weeks then it smoalters down to a bit of nothing the more i read and the more i think i am thinking the darker things become. i am still interested in theosophy and am studing a book light on the path every thing it has to say seems to be contrary to the essence of modern life but after it is under stood and lived up to i think it is a very helpful guide. i wish you would get one and tell me what you think of it. they only cost thirty cents if you can not find one i will send you one.

we have gotten up a group and have arranged for a furnace where we can have our stuff fired. we will give the owner a commission for the firing and glazing. there is chance of my making a little book money.

i am hoping you will flow freely with criticism and advice and book lists i no longer dream as i used to perhaps i can derive some good from it.

i met geritz at a lecture on wood block cutting he asked about you and sends his regards the fellow you mentioned of coming here has not arrived

Jack

ALEXANDER POPE
born May 21, 1688
London, England

Pope included this poem in a postscript to a letter dated July 11, 1709 (written when he was 21) "to Henry Cromwell, Esq. at the Blue Ball in Great Wild-Street near Drury-Lane, London." Querell describes Cromwell as "a prosperous country gentleman [then 57] . . . a tough, good-humoured, literary roué."

P.S. Having a vacant Space here, I will fill it with a short Ode on Solitude, which I found yesterday by great accident, & which I find by the Date was written when I was not Twelve years old; that you may perceive how long I have continued in my Passion for a rural life, & in the same Employments of it.

Age 11

Happy the Man, who free from Care,
The Business and the Noise of Towns,
Contented breaths his Native Air,
In his own Grounds:

Whose Herds with Milk, whose Fields with Bread,
Whose Flocks supply him with Attire,
Whose Trees in Summer yield him Shade,
In Winter, Fire.

Blest, who can unconcern'dly find
His Years slide silently away,
In Health of Body, Peace of Mind,
Quiet by Day,

Repose at Night; Study & Ease,
Together mixt; sweet Recreation;
And Innocence, which most does please,
With Meditation.

Thus, let me live, unseen, unknown,
Thus, unlamented, let me die,
Steal from the World, & not a Stone
Tell where I lye.

This poem appears in another, later (more polished) form in Pope's Works *(1736).*

About age 14

[This] is Pope's first published satire. . . . The author attacked is Elkanah Settle [whose poem in praise of the Hanoverian succession was entitled Eusebia Triumphans and] whose long career in anti-Catholic pamphleteering may have made him a bugbear of the Pope household.

Sherburn

Settle was later attacked again in The Dunciad.

TO THE AUTHOR OF A POEM, INTITLED, SUCCESSIO

Begone ye Criticks, and restrain your Spite,
Codrus writes on, and will for ever write;
The heaviest Muse the swiftest Course has gone,
As Clocks run fastest when most Lead is on.
What tho' no Bees around your Cradle flew,
Nor on your Lips distill'd their golden Dew?
Yet have we oft discover'd in their stead,
A Swarm of Drones, that buzz'd about your Head.
When you, like *Orpheus*, strike the warbling Lyre,
Attentive Blocks stand round you, and admire.
Wit, past thro' thee, no longer is the same,
As Meat digested takes a diff'rent Name;
But Sense must sure thy safest Plunder be,
Since no Reprizals can be made on thee.
Thus thou may'st Rise, and in thy daring Flight
(Tho' ne'er so weighty) reach a wondrous height;
So, forc'd from Engines, Lead it self can fly,
And pondrous Slugs move nimbly thro' the Sky.
Sure *Bavius* copy'd *Maevius* to the full,
And *Chaerilus* taught *Codrus* to be dull;
Therefore, dear Friend, at my Advice give o'er
This needless Labour, and contend no more,
To prove a dull *Succession* to be true,
Since 'tis enough we find it so in You.

Mrs. Rockefeller kept a neat file of the letters which her children wrote to her when she had to be away from them and among these were occasional examples of their school work and other mementoes. On one small sheet of paper was a reminder from her second son, which she had countersigned.

Morris

NELSON ROCKEFELLER
born July 8, 1908
Mount Desert Island, Maine

If I don't miss one day of school
this year I get one $1.00

[signed] Nelson Rockefeller
[countersigned] A.A. Rockefeller

Age unknown

The five Rockefeller brothers walking up Fifth Ave. in 1921. Nelson (right front), about age 13.

ELEANOR ROOSEVELT
born Oct. 11, 1884
New York, N.Y.

"I cannot understand why on earth our mothers fell for the Roser classes. They were held at all the big houses. I wish you could have seen Mr. Roser. A Prince Albert coat. Side whiskers. Not one grain of humor. Nobody in the world as pompous as he. And the things he decided to have us learn!" [*wrote Eleanor's cousin Corinne*]

Eleanor . . . wrote . . . in her autobiography . . . with reserve about Mr. Roser himself. He envisaged himself as a headmaster in the British public-school tradition, was learned in a literary kind of way, and expressed himself forcefully. The girls were obliged to stand when he came into the classroom, whereupon he would bow formally and indicate to the "young ladies" that they could be seated, addressing them as "Miss Roosevelt," "Miss Cutting," "Miss Sloane." He had a quotation from some great man or writer, most often from Dr. Johnson, for every occasion. . . .

Some of Eleanor's compositions have survived. Mr. Roser's comment was often a prim "your handwriting is not satisfactory." Even then Eleanor's penmanship was strong, angular, and highly individual. Sometimes Mr. Roser was impressed by Eleanor's vivid imagination, and he would append a "recommended for printing" comment to the end of the exercise, meaning that in his view it was worthy of publication, although apparently there was no school magazine or paper.

Lash

Age 13 or 14

THE FLOWERS DISCUSSION

"I am by far the most beautiful." These were the words I heard as I awoke from a nap I had been taking in a conservatory.

I was rather surprised to see that the speaker was a tall red rose which grew not far from me. There was evidently a hot discussion going on among the plants as to which excelled the others. I knew that if they saw I was awake the discussion would cease & as I wished to hear how it ended I feigned sleep.

After the red rose had spoken the beautiful lily raised its head. "You, the most beautiful?" I heard it say. "Look how straight you hold your head. You have no grace. Now mine bends over gracefully & then I am white which is by far a prettier color than red. I rest every eye which looks at me while you tire it. Besides you hurt people with your thorns. I never do. I smell far sweeter than you. Most people think so. Now you see that I excell you all" & she looked around with a proud glance.

There had been several interruptions during her long speech from the smaller flowers but now for a moment there was silence. Then the orchid spoke. "Indeed, you the most beautiful of all the flowers. What an idea. Why if any one is beautiful I am. Look at my varied coloring & how gracefully I hang, far more gracefully than you. Besides everyone likes me. No conservatory is complete without me while any can go without you."

Then a little white camelia spoke. "I hear someone coming. Whichever flower they choose as the prettiest shall excel." The flowers hardly had time to murmur "yes" when in came a little boy of not quite two. He gave a cry of delight as [he] entered. He looked around & then made straight for the orchid & stood by it drawing his finger lightly over the flower murmuring as he did so "Pitty flower pitty flower." His nurse picked it for him & he passed out.

As soon as he had disappeared the discussion began again, the rose & the lily averring that it was not right to stand by his decision. He was too small. This time the modest little violet who had not as yet spoken said "someone is coming. Stand by their decision" & the flowers said yes again. This time a young girl & her lover entered. They seated themselves under a huge palm tree & the young man said "which of all these flowers do you love the best?" "I love the white rose best, she is so sweet and pure," the young girl said. Her lover picked one for her and they went out.

They had hardly gone when the discussion began again. This time it was the orchid who said "The white rose is too small a flower to excell us all & besides the one which excells is king & imagine the white rose ruling us." All the plants laughed at the idea of their obeying the white rose & even I had to smile at the thought of the little flower ruling the haughty red rose, lily & orchid.

The discussion continued for several minutes when the pansy said, "Be quiet. Someone is coming." An old man & his wife now appeared. The flowers whispered as they entered "We will abide by their decision." The old couple seated themselves & the old man said "Is it not beautiful here Jennie. Which of all these flowers do you love the best?" The old wife looked around. "I love them all." she said & then as though she were thinking not talking "As a baby I loved the orchid, then the lily & the rose. As a young girl I loved the violet for it is the flower you picked for me when you told me of your love. Yes I loved it best then. I love it best now.

I thought so, the old man said. Then they went out. I wondered what the flowers would say to this, but I was soon to find out for the old couple had hardly gone when the rose broke out with "The violet excell all of us? The violet rule us? Why the white rose could do it better."

"Yes, indeed," cried all the plants. I could plainly see that all the flowers were bent upon excelling & I do not know how long the discussion would have lasted had not the violet said "Why none of us excell. We are all beautiful in our own way. Some are beautifully colored. Others smell sweetly & again others are graceful. We were all made well. From this day we are all equal."

The other flowers listened & to some it seemed strange that the flower which had been chosen to excel should say this but they all agreed and from that day they were equal.

But I always have and always will love the violet best.

Age 7, with brother Elliott.

FRANKLIN DELANO ROOSEVELT
born Jan. 30, 1882
Hyde Park, N.Y.

Franklin himself would become increasingly dissatisfied with his Harvard classroom experience—as Theodore Roosevelt had been with his, a quarter century before. Looking back over four years of it, at the close of his last college year, Franklin was sure that he had not learned or (as he no doubt would have put it) been taught all that he should have. He complained to roommate Lathrop Brown that his studies had been "like an electric lamp that hasn't any wire. You need the lamp for light but it's useless if you can't switch it on." His implication was that Harvard and its faculty, by failing to provide needed stimulation and guidance, were to blame.

Davis

Age 20

A NEWLY DISCOVERED FRAGMENT FROM A VOYAGE TO LILLIPUT

But stranger even than these nurseries for boys and girls past the nourishing age are the places where what the Lilliputians call "higher learning" is taught. Shortly after the fire in the Empress' wing of the palace, the Emperor, in order that I might not think him displeased with me, conferred upon me the degree of Doctor of Extinguishment, and commanded me to inspect one of these learned institutions which I have just mentioned. I found it situated in a pleasant marsh not far from the city of Axis—a town locally supposed to be the source and centre of all learning. The institution itself was called in the dialect a University, because, as I was told, it is the whole thing.

The earliest settlers of Lilliput founded this University soon after their arrival, chiefly for the purpose of a house of correction for the natives whom they found there. A few years later a worthy settler, dying, bequeathed a valuable set of printed notes to the institution which thereafter bore his noble name. Since then many life-like statues of him have arisen, all copied after an excellent sketch on the fly-leaf of a New England Primer, done of himself, by himself and for himself at the age of three and a half. His name also is frequently heard today, punctuated with sharp pleasure cries and given in chorus at a mystic sign from a six-inch giant who madly waves a cornucopia called in the language of the country megaphone. Owing, however, to a corruption of the name of the founder, the third letter, an r, is generally omitted by the inhabitants of Axis.

From a reformatory for the aborigines, the University has become the resort of thousands of Lilliputians, some even coming from the land of Blefuscu. Many of the inmates indeed come, not to study, but for the experience—"the finishing touch" which in many instances seemed to be indeed "the finishing touch." Some likewise go there for the sake only of exercise, but this practice has been lately discouraged because of a series of rules which it is said come down from Heaven, but which the Lilliputians to this day have been unable to interpret to their own satisfaction or that of anyone else. The University of the Big-Endians at Blefuscu is especially scornful of these rules, for they themselves have a rival set said to have been sent up to them by the Duskier God. The ill-feeling is further increased by the question of which can the better take exercise. The name of the Big-Endians itself is due to the swelling pride which these take in their victories in pushing a lima-bean through the ranks of the Lilliputians. On the other hand these latter, at the University I visited, because of a superior skill in killing fleas in mid-hop with a bow and arrow, claim to be the whole shooting-match.

In contests of needle threading, addition and subtraction, and reading aloud, the Little-Endians have also proved their mental superiority by victories for many moons. The needle-threading competition is especially thrilling, and the rapidity with which they passed the invisible thread through the invisible needle appeared to me quite out of sight. The enthusiasm at these contests is remarkable, very different I am told from what it was several moons ago. The din of the male students could be heard for many feet, while the co-educational members from the Sadstiff Annex signified their approval by "yum-yums" long and ponderous. I was told that the men who barked the loudest, and the lady students who yummed with greatest energy were as a rule the most liked in the University but that often in later life they did not come to high positions, probably because this form of strenuousness is not the best training to pass the great State rope dancing examinations.

The former custom of chorus singing at these matches is being superseded by hymns of praise sung alternately by a solo male and such a high female.

At the end of the contest the two umpires render diabolically opposite decisions, and the final result is announced many moons later by a partial Board of Arbitration.

Finally as a climax the two Universities rise as one man and sing their anthems. That of the Big-Endians started with the

"See such a mighty tail behind
And such a face before."

In the meantime my friends, starting at the same time in a deliciously different key sent heavenward their song—a beautiful diatribe composed of a sunset sonnet, a joke, and a communication, all taken from their leading University publications.

Such is the institution of highest learning among the noblest race in Lilliput—an institution which I would my own dear country would imitate.

On my return from Axis to the Capital I received another mark of the Emperor's favor.

[Here the manuscript stops.]

With his cousin Jean during summer vacation from Harvard.

THEODORE ROOSEVELT
born Oct. 27, 1858
New York, N.Y.

At this point, now, the boy himself comes out of the past to tell us about himself. He comes in the shape of a diary written in a cheap note-book. He kept it in Barrytown, up the Hudson, the summer before he was ten years old. For twelve days he kept it steadily; then came a break of three days, then another break of nine; then two more attempts; then silence. He was old enough to feel the need of keeping a diary, but he did not yet have the strength of will to persist at it.

Hagedorn

Age 9

Age 9.

August 16th.
Sunday.
I went to chruch.
After lunch I
did nothing.

The work for the Dresden Literary American Club proved to be a very entertaining pastime, and great competition ensued. A motto was chosen by "Johnnie" and "Ellie," who were the wits of the society. The motto was spoken of with bated breath and mysteriously inscribed W.A.N.A. underneath the mystic signs of D.L.A.C. For many a long year no one but those in our strictest confidence were allowed to know that "W.A.N.A." stood for "We Are No Asses." This, perhaps somewhat untruthful statement, was objected to originally by "Teedie," who firmly maintained that the mere making of such a motto showed that "Johnnie" and "Ellie" were certainly exceptions that proved that rule. "Teedie" himself, struggling as usual with terrible attacks of asthma that perpetually undermined his health and strength, was all the same, between the attacks, the ringleader in fun and gaiety and every imaginable humorous adventure. He was a slender, overgrown boy at the time, and wore his hair long in true German student fashion, and adopted a would-be philosopher type of look, effectively enhanced by trousers that were outgrown, and coat sleeves so short that they gave him a "Smike"-like appearance [the TB-type lost son of Ralph Nickleby in Dickens' Nicholas Nickleby]. *His contributions to the immortal literary club were either serious and very accurate from a natural-historical standpoint, or else they showed, as comparatively few of his later writings have shown, the delightful quality of humor which, through his whole busy life, lightened for him every load and criticism. I cannot resist giving in full the fascinating little story called "Mrs. Field Mouse's Dinner Party," in which the personified animals played social parts, in the portrayal of which my brother divulged (my readers must remember he was only fourteen) a knowledge of "society" life, its acrid jealousies and hypocrisies, of which he never again seemed to be conscious.*

Corinne Roosevelt Robinson

The Dresden Literary American Club: Theodore Roosevelt, age 14: Elliott Roosevelt, age 13; Maud Elliott, age 12; Corinne Roosevelt, age 11; John Elliott, age 14.

Age 14

MRS. FIELD MOUSE'S DINNER PARTY

"My Dear," said Mrs. M. to Mr. M. one day as they were sitting on an elegant acorn sofa, just after breakfast, "My Dear, I think that we really must give a dinner party." "A What, my love?" exclaimed Mr. M. in a surprised tone. "A Dinner Party"; returned Mrs. M. firmly, "you have no objections I suppose?"

"Of course not, of course not," said Mr. M. hastily, for there was an ominous gleam in his wife's eye. "But—but why have it yet for a while, my love?" "Why indeed! A pretty question! After that odious Mrs. Frog's great tea party the other evening! But that is just it, you never have any proper regard for your station in life, and on me involves all the duty of keeping up appearances, and after all *this* is the gratitude I get for it!" And Mrs. M. covered her eyes and fell into hysterics of 50 flea power. Of course, Mr. M. had to promise to have it whenever she liked.

"Then the day after tomorrow would not be too early, I suppose?" "My Dear," remonstrated the unfortunate Mr. M., but Mrs. M. did not heed him and continued: "You could get the cheese and bread from Squeak, Nibble & Co. with great ease, and the firm of Brown House and Wood Rats, with whom you have business relations, you told me, could get the other necessaries."

"But in such a short time," commenced Mr. M. but was sharply cut off by the lady; "Just like you, Mr. M.! Always raising objections! and when I am doing all I can to help you!" Symptoms of hysterics and Mr. M. entirely convinced, the lady continues: "Well, then we will have it the day after tomorrow. By the way, I hear that Mr. Chipmunck has got in a new supply of nuts, and you might as well go over after breakfast and get them, before they are bought by someone else."

"I have a business engagement with Sir Butterfly in an hour," began Mr. M. but stopped, meekly got his hat and went off at a glance from Mrs. M.'s eye.

When he was gone, the lady called down her eldest daughter, the charming Miss M. and commenced to arrange for the party.

"We will use the birch bark plates,"—commenced Mrs M.

"And the chestnut 'tea set,' " put in her daughter.

"With the maple leaf vases, of course," continued Mrs. M.

"And the eel bone spoons and forks," added Miss M.

"And the dog tooth knives," said the lady.

"And the slate table cloth," replied her daughter.

"Where shall we have the ball anyhow," said Mrs. M.

"Why, Mr. Blind Mole has let his large subterranean apartments and that would be the best place," said Miss M.

"Sir Lizard's place, 'Shady Nook,' which we bought the other day, is far better *I* think," said Mrs. M. "But *I* don't," returned her daughter. "Miss M. be still," said her mother sternly, and Miss M. *was* still. So it was settled that the ball was to be held at 'Shady Nook.'

"As for the invitations, Tommy Cricket will carry them around," said Mrs. M. "But who shall we have?" asked her daughter. After some discussion, the guests were determined on. Among them were all the Family of Mice and Rats, Sir Lizard, Mr. Chipmunck, Sir Shrew, Mrs. Shrew, Mrs. Bullfrog, Miss Katydid, Sir Grasshopper, Lord Beetle, Mr. Ant, Sir Butterfly, Miss Dragonfly, Mr. Bee, Mr. Wasp, Mr. Hornet, Madame Maybug, Miss Lady Bird, and a number of others. Messrs. Gloworm and Firefly agreed to provide lamps as the party was to be had at night. Mr. M., by a great deal of exertion, got the provisions together in time, and Miss M. did the same with the furniture, while Mrs. M. superintended generally, and was a great bother.

Water Bug & Co. conveyed everything to Shady Nook, and so at the appointed time everything was ready, and the whole family, in their best ball dresses, waited for the visitors.

***

The first visitor to arrive was Lady Maybug. "Stupid old thing; always first," muttered Mrs. M., and then aloud. "How charming it is to see you so prompt, Mrs. Maybug; I can always rely on *your* being here in time."

"Yes Ma'am, oh law! but it is so hot—oh law! and the carriage, oh law! almost broke down; oh law! I did really think I never should get here—oh law!" and Mrs. Maybug threw herself on the sofa; but the sofa unfortunately had one weak leg, and as Mrs. Maybug was no light weight, over she went. While Mrs. M. (inwardly swearing if ever a mouse swore) hastened to her assistance, and in the midst of the confusion caused by this accident, Tommy Cricket (who had been hired for waiter and dressed in red trousers accordingly) threw open the door and announced in a shrill pipe, "Nibble Squeak & Co., Mum," then hastily correcting himself, as he received a dagger like glance from Mrs. M., "Mr. Nibble and Mr. Squeak, Ma'am," and precipitately retreated through the door. Meanwhile the unfortunate Messrs. Nibble and Squeak, who while trying to look easy in their new clothes, had luckily not heard the introduction, were doing their best to bow gracefully to Miss Maybug and Miss Mouse, the respective mamas of these young ladies having pushed them rapidly forward as each of the ladies was trying to get up a match between the rich Mr. Squeak and her daughter, although Miss M. preferred Mr. Woodmouse and Miss Maybug, Mr. Hornet. In the next few minutes the company came pouring in (among them Mr. Woodmouse, accompanying Miss Katydid, at which sight Miss M. turned green with envy), and after a very short period the party was called in to dinner, for the cook had boiled the hickory nuts too long and they had to be sent up immediately or they would be spoiled. Mrs. M. displayed great generalship in the arrangement of the people, Mr. Squeak taking in Miss M., Mr. Hornet, Miss Maybug, and Mr. Woodmouse, Miss Katydid. But now Mrs. M. had invited one person too many for the plates, and so Mr. M. had to do without one. At first this was not noticed, as each person was seeing who could get the most to eat, with the exception of those who were love-making, but after a while, Sir Lizard, (a great swell and a very high liver) turned round and remarked, "Ee-aw, I say, Mr. M., why don't you take something more to eat?" "Mr. M. is not at all hungry tonight, are you my dear?" put in Mrs. M. smiling at Sir Lizard, and frowning at Mr. M. "Not at all, not at all," replied the latter hastily. Sir Lizard seemed disposed to continue the subject, but Mr. Moth, (a very scientific gentleman) made a diversion by saying, "Have you seen my work on 'Various Antenae'? In it I demonstrated clearly the superiority of feathered to knobbed Antenae and"—"Excuse me, Sir," interrupted Sir Butterfly, "but you surely don't mean to say—"

"Excuse *me*, if you please," replied Mr. Moth sharply, "but I *do* mean it, and if you read my work, you will perceive that the rays of feather-like particles on the trunk of the Antenae deriving from the center in straight or curved lines generally"—at this moment Mr. Moth luckily choked himself and seizing the lucky instant, Mrs. M. rang for the desert.

There was a sort of struggling noise in the pantry, but that was the only answer. A second ring, no answer. A third ring; and Mrs. M. rose in majestic wrath, and in dashed the unlucky Tommy Cricket with the cheese, but alas, while half way in the room, the beautiful new red trousers came down, and Tommy and cheese rolled straight into Miss Dragon Fly who fainted without any unnecessary delay, while the noise of Tommy's howls made the room ring. There was great confusion immediately, and while Tommy was being kicked out of the room, and while Lord Beetle was emptying a bottle of rare rosap over Miss Dragon Fly, in mistake for water, Mrs. M. gave a glance at Mr. M., which made him quake in his shoes, and said in a low voice, "Provoking thing! *now* you see the good of no suspenders"—"But my dear, you told me not to"—began Mr. M., but was interrupted by Mrs. M. "Don't speak to me, you—" but here Miss Katydid's little sister struck in on a sharp squeak. "Katy kissed Mr. Woodmouse!" "Katy didn't," returned her brother. "Katy did," "Katy didn't," "Katy did," "Katy didn't." All eyes were now turned on the crimsoning Miss Katydid, but she was unexpectedly saved by the lamps suddenly commencing to burn blue!

"There, Mr. M.! Now you see what you have done!" said the lady of the house, sternly.

"My dear, I told you they could not get enough oil if you had the party so early. It was your own fault," said Mr. M. worked up to desperation.

Mrs. M. gave him a glance that would have annihilated three millstones of moderate size, from its sharpness, and would have followed the example of Miss Dragon Fly, but was anticipated by Madame Maybug, who, as three of the lamps above her went out, fell into blue convulsions on the sofa. As the whole room was now subsiding into darkness, the company broke up and went off with some abruptness and confusion, and when they were gone, Mrs. M. turned (by the light of one bad lamp) an eagle eye on Mr. M. and said—, but we will now draw a curtain over the harrowing scene that ensued and say,

"Good Bye."

I used at this time to write down my reflections in English written in Greek letters in a book headed "Greek Exercises." I did this for fear someone should find out what I was thinking.

Autobiography

BERTRAND RUSSELL

born May 18, 1872
Ravenscroft, Trelleck
Monmouthshire, Wales

Age 15-16

April 29, 1888

In all things I have made the vow to follow reason, not the instincts inherited partly from my ancestors and gained gradually by them, owing to a process of natural selection, and partly due to my education. How absurd it would be to follow these in the questions of right and wrong. For as I observed before, the inherited part can only be principles leading to the preservation of the species to which I belong, the part due to education is good or bad according to the individual education. Yet this inner voice, this God-given conscience which made Bloody Mary burn the Protestants, this is what we reasonable beings are to follow. I think this idea mad and I endeavour to go by reason as far as possible. What I take as my ideal is that which ultimately produces greatest happiness of greatest number. Then I can apply reason to find out the course most conductive to this end. In my individual case, however, I can also go more or less by conscience owing to the excellence of my education. But it is curious how people dislike the abandonment of brutish impulses for reason. I remember poor Ewen [a tutor] getting a whole dinner of argument, owing to his running down impulse. Today again at tea Miss Buhler [his Swiss governess] and I had a long discussion because I said that I followed reason not conscience in matters of right and wrong. I do hate having such peculiar opinions because either I must keep them bottled up or else people are horrified at my scepticism, which is as bad with people one cares for as remaining bottled up. I shall be sorry when Miss Buhler goes because I can open my heart easier to her than to my own people, strange to say.

May 3

Miss Buhler is gone and I am left again to loneliness and reserve. Happily, however, it seems all but settled that I am going to Southgate [a crammer's school] and probably within the week. That will save me I feel sure from morose cogitations during the week, owing to the amount of activity of my life, and novelty at first. I do not expect that I shall enjoy myself at first, but after a time I hope I shall. Certainly it will be good for my work, for my games and my manners, and my future happiness I expect. . . .

May 8

What a much happier life mine would be but for these wretched ideas of mine about theology. Tomorrow I go, and tonight Granny prayed a beautiful prayer for me in my new life, in which among other things she said: May he especially be taught to know God's infinite love for him. Well that is a prayer to which I can heartily say Amen, and moreover it is one of which I stand in the greatest need. For according to my ideas of God we have no particular reason to suppose he loves us. For he only set the machine in working order to begin with and then left it to work out its own necessary consequences. Now you may say his laws are such as afford the greatest possible happiness to us mortals, but that is a statement of which there can be no proof. Hence I see no reason to believe in God's kindness towards me, and though I was truly affected by the simple beauty of prayer and her earnest way in saying it. What a thing it is to have such people! What might I be had I been worse brought up!

By the way, to change to a more cheerful subject: Marshall and I had an awfully fine day of it. We went down to the river, marched into Broom Hall [where Frank, his elder brother, was living], bagged a boat of Frank's we found there, and rowed up the river beyond Kingston Bridge without anybody at Broom Hall having seen us except one old man who was lame. Who the dickens he was I haven't the faintest idea. Marshall was awfully anxious to have some tea and we came to an nth rate inn which he thought would do. Having however like idiots left our jackets in the boat-house at Teddington we had to march in without coats and were served by the cheekiest of maids ever I saw who said she thought we were the carpenters come to mend the house. Then we rowed back as hard as possible and got home perspiring fearfully and twenty minutes late which produced a small row.

June 3

It is extraordinary how few principles or dogmas I have been able to become convinced of. One after another I find my former undoubted beliefs slipping from me into the region of doubt. For example, I used never for a moment to doubt that truth was a good thing to get hold of. But now I have the very greatest doubt and uncertainty. For the search for truth has led me to these results I have put in this book, whereas had I been content to accept the teachings of my youth I should have remained comfortable. The search for truth had shattered most of my old beliefs and has made me commit what are probably sins where otherwise I should have kept clear of them. I do not think it has in any way made me happier. Of course it has given me a deeper character, a contempt for trifles or mockery, but at the same time it has taken away cheerfulness and made it much harder to make bosom friends, and worst of all it has debarred me from free intercourse with my people, and thus made them strangers to some of my deepest thoughts, which, if by any mischance I do let them out, immediately become the subject for mockery, which is inexpressibly bitter to me though not unkindly meant. Thus in my individual case I should say the effects of a search for truth have been more bad than good. But the truth which I accept as such may be said not to be truth and I may be told that if I get at real truth I shall be made happier by it, but this is a very doubtful proposition. Hence I have great doubt of the unmixed advantage of truth. Certainly truth in biology lowers one's idea of man which must be painful. Moreover, truth estranges former friends and prevents the making of new ones, which is also a bad thing. One ought perhaps to look upon all these things as a martyrdom, since very often truth attained by one man may lead to the increase in the happiness of many others though not to his own. On the whole I am inclined to continue to pursue truth, though truth of the kind in this book, if that indeed be truth, I have no desire to spread but rather to prevent from spreading.

July 15

My holidays have begun about a week now and I am getting used to home and beginning to regard Southgate as a dream of the past. For although I tell people I like it very much, yet really, though better than I expected, life there has great trials and hardships. I don't suppose anybody hates disturbance as I do or can so ill stand mockery, though to outward appearance I keep my temper all right. Being made to sing, to climb on chairs, to get up for a sponging in the middle of the night, is to me fifty times more detestable than to others. I always have to go through in a moment a long train of reasoning as to the best thing to say or do, for I have sufficient self-control to do what I think best, and the excitement, which to others might seem small, leaves me trembling and exhausted. However, I think it is an excellent thing for me, as it increases my capacity for enjoyment and strengthens me morally to a very considerable extent. I shan't forget in a hurry their amazement that I had never said a "damn," which with things like it goes near to making me a *fanfaron de crimes*. This, however, is a bad thing to be, when only too many real crimes are committed. . . . I am glad I didn't go to school before. I should have wanted strength and have had no time for the original thought, which though it has caused me much pain, is yet my chief stay and support in troubles. I am always kept up by a feeling of contempt, erroneous though it may be, for all who despitefully use me and persecute me. I don't think contempt is misplaced when a chap's habitual language is about something like "who put me on my cold, cold pot whether I would or not? My mother." Sung to the tune of "Thy will be done." Had my education, however, been the least bit less perfect than it is I should probably have been the same. But I feel I must enjoy myself at home much better than ever before, which with an imaginary feeling of heroism reconciles me to a great deal of unhappiness at Southgate.

Age 4.

J. D. SALINGER
born Jan. 1, 1919
New York, N.Y.

In June, 1936, Valley Forge [Military Academy, Pennsylvania] gave him his only diploma. As literary editor of the yearbook, Salinger presented to the school a damply magnificent floral arrangement, since set to music and still sung at Last Parade.

Grunwald

Age 17

Hide not thy tears on this last day
Your sorrow has no shame;
To march no more midst lines of gray;
No longer play the game.
Four years have passed in joyful ways—
Wouldst stay these old times dear?
Then cherish now these fleeting days,
The few while you are here.

The last parade; our hearts sink low;
Before us we survey—
Cadets to be, where we are now
And soon will come their day;
Though distant now, yet not so far,
Their years are but a few.
Aye, soon they'll know why misty are
Our eyes at last review.

The lights are dimmed, the bugle sounds
The notes we'll ne'er forget.
And now a group of smiling lads;
We part with much regret.
Goodbyes are said; we march ahead,
Success we go to find.
Our forms are gone from Valley Forge;
Our hearts are left behind.

Some of Salinger's friends have denied that he wrote these lyrics. J. D. Salinger, however, is listed as their author in the Valley Forge yearbook.

Grunwald

VALLEY FORGE **MILITARY ACADEMY AND JUNIOR COLLEGE**

Valley Forge, hallowed shrine of American Freedom, has loaned its cherished name to this fully accredited, distinguished military academy and **Junior College**.

In the historic Radnor foothills, the Academy keeps faith with our forefathers by training young men for responsible citizenship. Its class-rooms educate them for entrance into all leading colleges. Senior ROTC prepares them for a commission in the armed services. The athletic program keeps bodies well, teaches fair play and sportsmanship.

A beautiful campus with 82 Colonial brick and stone buildings, houses Infantry, Artillery, Cavalry and renowned Cadet band. On its 300 rolling acres young Americans prove the Academy's right to say: **"From the embattled fields of Valley Forge went men who built America; from the training fields of Valley Forge go men who will preserve America."**

Box K, Wayne, Pa.

FRANZ SCHUBERT
born Jan. 31, 1797
Vienna, Austria

Schubert was the least trained of all the great composers. Attending the Choristers School of the Imperial Chapel in Vienna (always with not quite enough to eat and with no money for concerts unless he sold his books) he played violin in the student orchestra. At fourteen he was writing music on hand-ruled scraps of paper until a fellow student, overawed by the compositions Schubert showed him, began to supply him with manuscript paper.

Fisher

Age 15

Letter to His Brother

24th November, 1812

Age 16.

Dear Ferdinand,
I have been thinking much about my life here and find that it is good on the whole, but in some ways it could be much better. You know that one can often enjoy eating a roll and an apple or two, especially after having nothing for eight and one half hours, and then only a little supper to look forward to. I feel that this must be changed. How would it be if you were to send me a little money each month in advance? You would never miss it, while I could shut myself up in my small room and be quite happy. As Matthew said: "Let him who hath two coats give one to the poor." And now I hope that you will listen to the voice which tells you again and again to remember your loving, hoping, poor, and once more I repeat, poor—brother Franz.

Schubert seldom used a piano when composing. Anywhere, with all kinds of conversation and noise around him, he would sit "bent over the music paper and a book of poems, bite his pen, drum with his fingers at the same time, trying things out, and continue to write easily and fluently, without many corrections, as if it had to be like that and not otherwise."

A friend characterized his rapid and instinctive placement of notes on paper as "hurling" the notes down. His friends ransacked the entire German lyric literature to keep ahead of him, and when he was given a new poem he caught the mood and feeling on a single reading. By the second reading the notes were already ordered in his mind, so that the quill had a hard job keeping ahead of the musical thought. How else could he have written six, seven, and even eight songs a day? Among the two hundred and fifty songs he wrote in his seventeenth and eighteenth years were "The Erl King," "Wanderer's Night Song," and "Gretchen at the Spinning Wheel."

Fisher

Hagars Klage.

Gedicht von Schücking.

Age 14

Für eine Singstimme mit Begleitung des Pianoforte

Largo.

Mälzels Metronom ♩. = 72.

Gretchen am Spinnrade.

Aus Göthe's Faust.

Age 17

Nicht zu geschwind.

Having a violin lesson.

Erlkönig
BALLADE von GÖTHE,
in Musik gesetzt
und
Seiner Exzellenz dem hochgebohrnen Herrn Herrn
Moritz Grafen von Dietrichstein
in tiefer Ehrfurcht gewidmet
von
Franz Schubert.
1tes Werk.
Pr: 2 f. w. w. / 1 f. c. m.
WIEN
in Comission bey Cappi und Diabelli,
am Graben No. 1133.

Age 18

Wer rei - tet so spät durch
Nacht und Wind? Es ist der Va - ter mit sei - nem
Kind; er hat den Kna - - ben wohl in dem Arm, er
fasst ihn si-cher, er hält ihn warm.
Mein Sohn, was birgst du so bang dein Ge-sicht? Siehst,
Va - ter, du den Erl - kö - nig nicht? den
Er - - len - kö - nig mit Kron' und Schweif? Mein Sohn, es
fz p
pp

GEORGE BERNARD SHAW
born July 26, 1856
Dublin, Ireland

[This, the earliest of Shaw's surviving letters, is to his elder sister in London.] Matthew Edward McNulty was Shaw's school companion and lifelong friend, who later became infatuated briefly with Lucy. Although McNulty entered the banking profession, he published four novels and several plays, two of which were produced by the Abbey Theatre.

Laurence

Age 17

1 Hatch Street
4th March 1874. I o.C a.m.

Matthew Edward and G.B. Shaw, about age 17.

Cara Lucia

I am sorry to say that I have read your letter. I shall take especial care not to do so again for you really are worthy of your parent in the matter of verbosity and far more personal. Your remarks are most offensive. Let my nose alone, better a bottle than a peony. Did the Mar mention that the cat has got mange as well as Paddy. It has no hair at all on its head which adds to its already prepossessing appearance. Mamma on arriving [in Dublin] sat down in the cab with such violence that she burst open the door which I had to hold shut during the rest of the journey [to Hatch Street]. I wish you joy of the reading of "Out of Court" [a "three-decker" novel written by a half-cousin of Shaw's]. In gratitude for the treat it will only be good taste to find fault with the grammar, cough loudly at the affecting passages, and whenever a character is mentioned ask absently who's this he or she was. When the book is thrown at your head you may be satisfied with the effect produced. However I did not write to say all this and merely write it as a concession to your taste for rubbish. I want to know where one can get their writings published and paid for. In what journal. What is the best opening. I want this for my own sake partly but immediately for the benefit of a friend of mine, a genius, I think Agnes [older sister] recollects McNulty, a corpulent youth with curly black hair. He is in want of money and wants to find out where he can get it for writing. I shall regard it as a favor if you will give me the extent of your information on the subject. I will also regard it as a favour if you will be as concise as possible, your style of communication with the mar being unnecessarily voluminous. I have found in the house a great bundle of stuff and whether it is red worsted or Agnes's hair I don't know.

yrs
GBShaw

I was driven to write because I could do nothing else. In an old novel of mine—"Cashel Byron's Profession"—the hero, a prizefighter, remarks that it's not what a man would like to do, but what he can do, that he must work at in this world. I wanted to be another Michael Angelo, but found that I could not draw. I wanted to be a musician, but found I could not play—to be a dramatic singer, but had no voice. I did not want to write: that came as a matter of course without any wanting. . . .

At 20, I . . . blindly plunged into London. My published works at this time consisted of a letter written when I was 16 or 17 [actually 18] to "Public Opinion" in which I sought to stem the force of the first great Moody & Sankey revival by the announcement that I, personally, had renounced religion as a delusion. London was not ripe for me. . . . My first appearance in print was in a boys' paper: two lines in the correspondence column. But it was in "Public Opinion" that I made my debut *as a critic and controversialist. The only result was an emergency meeting of my uncles to discuss the horrifying news that the Shaw family had produced an Atheist. I still hold that thinkers who are not militant atheists in their teens will have no religion at all when they are 40. I was already a Creative Evolutionist in the bud. . . .*

Autobiography . . . from his writings

Age 18

Letter to the Editor

Public Opinion, April 3, 1875

Sir,—In reply to your correspondent, "J.R.D.," as to the effect of the "wave of Evangelism," I beg to offer the following observations on the late "revival" in Dublin, of which I was a witness.

As the enormous audiences drawn to the Evangelistic services have been referred to as a proof of their efficacy, I will enumerate some of the motives which induced many persons to go. It will be seen that these were not of a religious, but of a secular, not to say profane character. Predominant was the curiosity excited by the great reputation of the Evangelists, and the stories, widely circulated, of the summary annihilation, by epilepsy and otherwise, of sceptics who had openly proclaimed their doubts of Mr. Moody's divine mission. Another motive exhibits a peculiar side of human nature. The services took place in the Exhibition Building, the entry to which was connected in the public mind with the expenditure of a certain sum of money. But Messrs. Moody and Sankey opened the building "for nothing," and the novelty combined with the curiosity made the attraction irresistible. I mention these influences particularly, as I believe they have hitherto been almost ignored. The audiences were, as a rule, respectable, and as Mr. Moody's orations were characterized by an excess of vehement assertion, and a total absence of logic, respectable audiences were precisely those which were least likely to derive any benefit from them. It is to the rough, to the outcast of the streets, that such "awakenings" should be addressed; and those members of the aristocracy, who by their presence tend to raise the meetings above the sphere of such outcasts, are merely diverting the Evangelistic wave into channels where it is not wanted, its place being already supplied. And as, in the dull routine of hard work, novelty has a special attraction for the poor, I think it would be well for clergymen, who are nothing if not conspicuous, to render themselves so in this instance by their absence. The unreasoning mind of the people is too apt to connect a white tie with a dreary Church service, capped by a sermon of platitudes; and is more likely to appreciate "the gift of the gab,"—the possession of which by Mr. Moody nobody will deny,—than that of the Apostolic succession, which he lacks.

Respecting the effect of the revival on individuals, I may mention that it has a tendency to make them highly objectionable members of society, and induces their unconverted friends to desire a speedy reaction, which either soon takes place, or the revived one relapses slowly into his previous benighted condition, as the effect fades. And, although many young men have been snatched from careers of dissipation by Mr. Moody's exhortations, it remains doubtful whether the change is not merely in the nature of the excitement rather than in the moral nature of the individual. Hoping that these remarks may elucidate further opinions on the subject,

Dublin. I remain, Sir, yours, &c., S.

April 3, 1875.] PUBLIC OPINION.

MOODY and SANKEY.—AMERICAN ORGANS, in every variety, of CRAMER'S manufacture, and on CRAMER'S three years' system. Prices from 15 guineas, or £1. 11s. 6d. a quarter.

CRAMER & CO. by no means wish it to be understood, as in some quarters it would seem to have been, that their AMERICAN ORGANS are used by Messrs. Moody and Sankey at their interesting meetings.

CRAMER'S instruments are much more solid in manufacture, and infinitely superior in quality of tone, and are certainly not open to the objection made by perhaps the most influential literary and musical journal to the imported organs.

"Judged from the artistic point of view, the instrument is no more agreeable to the ear than is the stentorian power displayed by the singer."

Moreover, while CRAMER'S AMERICAN ORGANS are more satisfactorily made, and better finished in all respects, they are sold at prices varying from 15 to 25 per cent. below those of all imported instruments.

These, and all other instruments of CRAMER'S manufacture, can be had on the three years' system, which, originated by CRAMER'S, has been partially adopted by other firms, but is carried out on a thoroughly large and liberal scale only by themselves.

REGENT STREET, W., and MOORGATE STREET, E.C.

PERCY BYSSHE SHELLEY
born Aug. 4, 1792
Field Place (near Horsham)
Sussex, England

Shelley . . . knew early what it was to love. . . . It was in the summer of this year [1809] that he became acquainted with our cousin, Harriet Grove. Living in distant counties, they then met for the first time, since they had been children, at Field-place, where she was on a visit. . . . After so long an interval, I still remember Miss Harriet Grove, and when I call to mind all the women I have ever seen, I know of none that surpassed, or that could compete with her. She was like one of Shakespeare's women—like some Madonna of Raphael. . . . Shelley, in a fragment written many years after, seems to have had her in his mind's eye, when he writes:

They were two cousins, almost like two twins,
Except that from the catalogue of sins
Nature had razed their love, which could not be,
But in dissevering their nativity;
And so they grew together like two flowers
Upon one stem, which the same beams and showers
Lull or awaken in the purple prime.

. . . In the latter end of this year, he wrote a novel entitled Zastrozzi, which embodies much of the intensity of the passion that devoured him; and some of the chapters were, he told me, by Miss Grove.

Medwin

Age 17

ZASTROZZI,

A ROMANCE.

BY

P. B. S.

——That their God
May prove their foe, and with repenting hand
Abolish his own works—This would surpass
Common revenge.

PARADISE LOST.

LONDON:

PRINTED FOR G. WILKIE AND J. ROBINSON
57, PATERNOSTER ROW.

1810

As a youth.

Chapter I

Torn from the society of all he held dear on earth, the victim of secret enemies, and exiled from happiness, was the wretched Verezzi!

All was quiet; a pitchy darkness involved the face of things, when, urged by fiercest revenge, Zastrozzi placed himself at the door of the inn where, undisturbed, Verezzi slept.

Loudly he called the landlord. The landlord, to whom the bare name of Zastrozzi was terrible, trembling obeyed the summons.

"Thou knowest Verezzi the Italian? he lodges here."

"He does," answered the landlord.

"Him, then, have I devoted to destruction," exclaimed Zastrozzi. "Let Ugo and Bernardo follow you to his apartment; I will be with you to prevent mischief."

Cautiously they ascended—successfully they executed their revengeful purpose, and bore the sleeping Verezzi to the place, where a chariot waited to convey the vindictive Zastrozzi's prey to the place of its destination.

Ugo and Bernardo lifted the still sleeping Verezzi into the chariot. Rapidly they travelled onwards for several hours. Verezzi was still wrapped in deep sleep, from which all the movements he had undergone had been insufficient to rouse him.

Zastrozzi and Ugo were masked, as was Bernardo, who acted as postilion.

It was still dark, when they stopped at a small inn, on a remote and desolate heath; and waiting but to change horses, again advanced. At last day appeared—still the slumbers of Verezzi remained unbroken.

Ugo fearfully questioned Zastrozzi as to the cause of his extraordinary sleep. Zastrozzi, who, however, was well acquainted with it, gloomily answered, "I know not."

Swiftly they travelled during the whole of the day, over which nature seemed to have drawn her most gloomy curtain.—They stopped occasionally at inns to change horses and obtain refreshments.

Night came on—they forsook the beaten track, and, entering an immense forest, made their way slowly through the rugged underwood.

At last they stopped—they lifted their victim from the chariot, and bore him to a cavern, which yawned in a dell close by.

Not long did the hapless victim of unmerited persecution enjoy an oblivion which deprived him of a knowledge of his horrible situation. He awoke—and overcome by excess of terror, started violently from the ruffians' arms.

They had now entered the cavern—Verezzi supported himself against a fragment of rock which jutted out.

"Resistance is useless," exclaimed Zastrozzi; "following us in submissive silence can alone procure the slightest mitigation of your punishment."

Verezzi followed as fast as his frame, weakened by unnatural sleep, and enfeebled by recent illness, would permit; yet, scarcely believing that he was awake, and not thoroughly convinced of the reality of the scene before him, he viewed every thing with that kind of inexplicable horror, which a terrible dream is wont to excite.

After winding down the rugged descent for some time, they arrived at an iron door, which at first sight appeared to be part of the rock itself. Every thing had till now been obscured by total darkness; and Verezzi, for the first time, saw the masked faces of his persecutors, which a torch brought by Bernardo rendered visible.

The massy door flew open.

The torches from without rendered the darkness which reigned within still more horrible; and Verezzi beheld the interior of this cavern as a place whence he was never again about to emerge—as his grave. Again he struggled with his persecutors, but his enfeebled frame was insufficient to support a conflict with the strong-nerved Ugo, and, subdued, he sank fainting into his arms.

His triumphant persecutor bore him into the damp cell, and chained him to the wall. An iron chain encircled his waist; his limbs, which not even a little straw kept from the rock, were fixed by immense staples to the flinty floor; and but one of his hands was left at liberty, to take the scanty pittance of bread and water which was daily allowed him.

Every thing was denied him but thought, which, by comparing the present with the past, was his greatest torment.

Ugo entered the cell every morning and evening, to bring coarse bread, and a pitcher of water, seldom, yet sometimes, accompanied by Zastrozzi.

In vain did he implore mercy, pity, and even death: useless were all his enquiries concerning the cause of his barbarous imprisonment—a stern silence was maintained by his relentless gaoler.

Languishing in painful captivity, Verezzi passed days and nights seemingly countless, in the same monotonous uniformity of horror and despair. He scarcely now shuddered when the slimy lizard crossed his naked and motionless limbs. The large earth-worms, which twined themselves in his long and matted hair, almost ceased to excite sensations of horror.

Days and nights were undistinguishable from each other; and the period which he had passed there, though in reality but a few weeks, was lengthened by his perturbed imagination into many years. Sometimes he scarcely supposed that his torments were earthly, but that Ugo, whose countenance bespoke him a demon, was the fury who blasted his reviving hopes. His mysterious removal from the inn near Munich also confused his ideas, and he never could bring his thoughts to any conclusion on the subject which occupied them.

One evening, overcome by long watching, he sank to sleep, for almost the first time since his confinement, when he was aroused by a loud crash, which seemed to burst over the cavern. Attentively he listened—he even hoped, though hope was almost dead within his breast. Again he listened—again the same noise was repeated—it was but a violent thunder-storm which shook the elements above.

Convinced of the folly of hope, he addressed a prayer to his Creator—to Him who hears a suppliant from the bowels of the earth. His thoughts were elevated above terrestrial enjoyments—his sufferings sank into nothing on the comparison.

Whilst his thoughts were thus employed, a more violent crash shook the cavern. A scintillating flame darted from the ceiling to the floor. Almost at the same instant the roof fell in.

A large fragment of the rock was laid athwart the cavern; one end being grooved into the solid wall, the other having almost forced open the massy iron door.

Verezzi was chained to a piece of rock which remained immoveable. The violence of the storm was past, but the hail descended rapidly, each stone of which wounded his naked limbs. Every flash of lightning, although now distant, dazzled his eyes, unaccustomed as they had been to the least ray of light.

The storm at last ceased, the pealing thunders died away in indistinct murmurs, and the lightning was too faint to be visible. Day appeared—no one had yet been to the cavern—Verezzi concluded that they either intended him to perish with hunger, or that some misfortune, by which they themselves had suffered, had occurred. In the most solemn manner, therefore, he now prepared himself for death, which he was fully convinced within himself was rapidly approaching.

His pitcher of water was broken by the falling fragments, and a small crust of bread was all that now remained of his scanty allowance of provisions.

A burning fever raged through his veins; and, delirious with despairing illness, he cast from him the crust which alone could now retard the rapid advances of death.

Oh! what ravages did the united efforts of disease and suffering make on the manly and handsome figure of Verezzi! His bones had almost started through his skin; his eyes were sunken and hollow; and his hair, matted with the damps, hung in strings upon his faded cheek. The day passed as had the morning—death was every instant before his eyes—a lingering death by famine—he felt its approaches: night came, but with it brought no change. He was aroused by a noise against the iron door: it was the time when Ugo usually brought fresh provisions. The noise lessened, at last it totally ceased—with it ceased all hope of life in Verezzi's bosom. A cold tremor pervaded his limbs—his eyes but faintly presented to his imagination the ruined cavern—he sank, as far as the chain which encircled his waist would permit him, upon the flinty pavement; and, in the crisis of the fever which then occurred, his youth and good constitution prevailed.

Chapter XVII (last chapter)

Si fractus illabatur orbis,
Impavidum ferient ruinae.

Horace

At last the day arrived, when, exposed to a public trial, Matilda was conducted to the tribunal of il consiglio di dieci.

The inquisitors were not, as before, at a table in the middle of the apartment; but a sort of throne was raised at one end, on which a stern-looking man, whom she had never seen before, sat: a great number of Venetians were assembled, and lined all sides of the apartment.

Many, in black vestments, were arranged behind the superior's throne; among whom Matilda recognised those who had before examined her.

Conducted by two officials, with a faltering step, a pallid cheek, and downcast eye, Matilda advanced to that part of the chamber where sat the superior.

The dishevelled ringlets of her hair floated unconfined over her shoulders: her symmetrical and elegant form was enveloped in a thin white robe.

The expression of her sparkling eyes was downcast and humble; yet, seemingly unmoved by the scene before her, she remained in silence at the tribunal.

The curiosity and pity of every one, as they gazed on the loveliness of the beautiful culprit, was strongly excited.

"Who is she? who is she?" ran in inquiring whispers round the apartment.—No one could tell.

Again deep silence reigned—not a whisper interrupted the appalling calm.

At last the superior, in a sternly solemn voice, said—

"Matilda Contessa di Laurentini, you are here arraigned on the murder of La Marchesa di Strobazzo: canst thou deny it? canst thou prove to the contrary? My ears are open to conviction. Does no one speak for the accused?"

He ceased: uninterrupted silence reigned. Again he was about—again, with a look of detestation and horror, he had fixed his penetrating eye upon the trembling Matilda, and had unclosed his mouth to utter the fatal sentence when his attention was arrested by a man who rushed from the crowd, and exclaimed, in a hurried tone—

"La Contessa di Laurentini is innocent."

"Who are you, who dare assert that?" exclaimed the superior, with an air of doubt.

"I am," answered he, "Ferdinand Zeilnitz, a German, the servant of La Contessa di Laurentini, and I dare assert that she is innocent."

"Your proof," exclaimed the superior, with a severe frown.

"It was late," answered Ferdinand, "when I entered the apartment, and then I beheld two bleeding bodies, and La Contessa di Laurentini, who lay bereft of sense on the sofa."

"Stop!" exclaimed the superior.

Ferdinand obeyed.

The superior whispered to one in black vestments, and soon four officials entered, bearing on their shoulders an open coffin.

The superior pointed to the ground: the officials deposited their burden, and produced, to the terror-struck eyes of the gazing multitude, Julia, the lovely Julia, covered with innumerable and ghastly gashes.

All present uttered a cry of terror—all started, shocked and amazed, from the horrible sight; yet some, recovering themselves, gazed at the celestial loveliness of the poor victim to revenge, which, unsubdued by death, still shone from her placid features.

A deep-drawn sigh heaved Matilda's bosom; tears, spite of all her firmness, rushed into her eyes; and she had nearly fainted with dizzy horror; but, overcoming it, and collecting all her fortitude, she advanced towards the corse of her rival, and, in the numerous wounds which covered it, saw the fiat of her future destiny.

She still gazed on it—a deep silence reigned—not one of the spectators, so interested were they, uttered a single word—not a whisper was heard through the spacious apartment.

"Stand off! guilt-stained, relentless woman," at last exclaimed the superior fiercely: "is it not enough that you have persecuted, through life, the wretched female who lies before you—murdered by you? Cease, therefore, to gaze on her with looks as if your vengeance was yet insatiated. But retire, wretch: officials, take her into your custody; meanwhile, bring the other prisoner."

Two officials rushed forward, and led Matilda to some distance from the tribunal; four others entered, leading a man of towering height and majestic figure. The heavy chains with which his legs were bound, rattled as he advanced.

Matilda raised her eyes—Zastrozzi stood before her.

She rushed forwards—the officials stood unmoved.

"Oh, Zastrozzi!" she exclaimed—"dreadful, wicked has been the tenour of our life; base, ignominious, will be its termination: unless we repent, fierce, horrible, may be the eternal torments which will rack us, ere four and twenty hours are elapsed. Repent then, Zastrozzi; repent! and as you have been my companion in apostasy to virtue, follow me likewise in dereliction of stubborn and determined wickedness."

This was pronounced in a low and faltering voice.

"Matilda," replied Zastrozzi, whilst a smile of contemptuous atheism played over his features—"Matilda, fear not: fate wills us to die; and I intend to meet death, to encounter annihilation, with tranquillity. Am I not convinced of the non-existence of a Deity? am I not convinced that death will but render this soul more free, more unfettered? Why need I then shudder at death? why need any one, whose mind has risen above the shackles of prejudice, the errors of a false and injurious superstition."

Here the superior interposed, and declared he could allow private conversation no longer.

Quitting Matilda, therefore, Zastrozzi, unappalled by the awful scene before him, unshaken by the near approach of agonising death, which he now fully believed he was about to suffer, advanced towards the superior's throne.

Every one gazed on the lofty stature of Zastrozzi, and admired his dignified mien and dauntless composure, even more than they had the beauty of Matilda.

Every one gazed in silence, and expected that some extraordinary charge would be brought against him.

The name of Zastrozzi, pronounced by the superior, had already broken the silence, when the culprit, gazing disdainfully on his judge, told him to be silent, for he would spare him much needless trouble.

"I am a murderer," exclaimed Zastrozzi; "I deny it not: I buried my dagger in the heart of him who injured me; but the motives which led me to be an assassin were at once excellent and meritorious; for I swore, at a loved mother's death-bed, to revenge her betrayer's falsehood.

"Think you, that whilst I perpetrated the deed I feared the punishment? or whilst I revenged a parent's cause, that the futile torments which I am doomed to suffer here, had any weight in my determination? No—no. If the vile deceiver, who brought my spotless mother to a tomb of misery, fell beneath the dagger of one who swore to revenge her—if I sent him to another world, who destroyed the peace of one I loved more than myself in this, am I to be blamed?"

Zastrozzi ceased, and, with an expression of scornful triumph, folded his arms.

"Go on!" exclaimed the superior.

"Go on! go on!" echoed from every part of the immense apartment.

He looked around him. His manner awed the tumultuous multitude; and, in uninterrupted silence, the spectators gazed upon the unappalled Zastrozzi, who, towering as a demi-god, stood in the midst.

"Am I then called upon," said he, "to disclose things which bring painful remembrances to my mind? Ah, how painful! But no matter; you shall know the name of him who fell beneath this arm: you shall know him, whose memory, even now, I detest more than I can express. I care not who knows my actions, convinced as I am, and convinced to all eternity as I shall be, of their rectitude.—Know, then, that Olivia Zastrozzi was my mother; a woman in whom every virtue, every amiable and excellent quality, I firmly believe to have been centred.

"The father of him who by my arts committed suicide but six days ago in La Contessa di Laurentini's mansion, took advantage of a moment of weakness, and disgraced her who bore me. He swore with the most sacred oaths to marry her—but he was false.

"My mother soon brought me into the world—the seducer married another; and when the destitute Olivia begged a pittance to keep her from starving, her proud betrayer spurned her from his door, and tauntingly bade her exercise her profession.—The crime I committed with thee, perjured one! exclaimed my mother as she left his door, shall be my last!—and, by heavens! she acted nobly. A victim to falsehood, she sank early to the tomb, and, ere her thirtieth year, she died—her spotless soul fled to eternal happiness.—Never shall I forget, though but fourteen when she died—never shall I forget her last commands.—My son, said she, my Pietrino, revenge my wrongs—revenge them on the perjured Verezzi—revenge them on his progeny for ever!

"And, by heaven! I think I have revenged them. Ere I was twenty-four, the false villain, though surrounded by seemingly impenetrable grandeur; though forgetful of the offence to punish which this arm was nerved, sank beneath my dagger. But I destroyed his *body* alone," added Zastrozzi, with a terrible look of insatiated vengeance: "time has taught me better: his son's *soul* is hell-doomed to all eternity: he destroyed himself; but my machinations, though unseen, effected his destruction.

"Matilda di Laurentini! Hah! why do you shudder? When, with repeated stabs, you destroyed her who now lies lifeless before you in her coffin, did you not reflect upon what must be your fate? You have enjoyed him whom you adored—you have even been married to him—and, for the space of more than a month, have tasted unutterable joys, and yet you are unwilling to pay the price of your happiness—by heavens I am not!" added he, bursting into a wild laugh.—"Ah! poor fool, Matilda, did you think it was from friendship I instructed you how to gain Verezzi?—No, no—it was revenge which induced me to enter into your schemes with zeal; which induced me to lead her, whose lifeless form lies yonder, to your house, foreseeing the effect it would have upon the strong passions of your husband.

"And now," added Zastrozzi, "I have been candid with you. Judge, pass your sentence—but I know my doom; and, instead of horror, experience some degree of satisfaction at the arrival of death, since all I have to do on earth is completed."

Zastrozzi ceased; and, unappalled, fixed his expressive gaze upon the superior.

Surprised at Zastrozzi's firmness, and shocked at the crimes of which he had made so unequivocal an avowal, the superior turned away in horror.

Still Zastrozzi stood unmoved, and fearlessly awaited the fiat of his destiny.

The superior whispered to one in black vestments. Four officials rushed in, and placed Zastrozzi on the rack.

Even whilst writhing under the agony of almost insupportable torture his nerves were stretched, Zastrozzi's firmness failed him not; but, upon his soul-illumined countenance, played a smile of most disdainful scorn; and with a wild convulsive laugh of exulting revenge—he died.

THE END.

In his last term at Eton he finally established himself as a notable classical scholar, a tolerated eccentric with strange philosophical views and, something rather smarter, a popular author. In April [1810], the gothic novel on which he had been working both at Eton and Field Place for some eighteen months, appeared. . . . Shelley earned the remarkable sum of £ 40 for this work, printed by J. Robinson, and circulated in time to bring him considerable admiration and notoriety in his leaving term at Eton. The £ 40 was spent on a farewell dinner.

Holmes

Some have called this work a parody but in March 1812 Shelley wrote in a letter to William Godwin about "the state of intellectual sickliness and lethargy into which I was plunged two years ago, and of which St. Irvyn *[or* The Rosecrucian, *another gothic novel published the same year] and* Zastrozzi *are the distempered although unoriginal versions.*

A magazine reviewer gave Zastrozzi *this encomium: "One of the most savage and improbable demons ever issued from a diseased brain . . . gross and wanton . . . open, barefaced immorality."*

Thus "mad Shelley" (for so he was called at Eton) made his literary debut. Zastrozzi was his first published work.

ROBERT SOUTHEY
born Aug. 12, 1774
Bristol, England

The Flagellant *purported to be the organ of four Westminster scholars who had retired to a ruined monastery in order to lash the vices of society. Bedford [a senior student], under the name of Peter the Hermit, was apparently responsible for most of the first four numbers, the satire of which was mild enough and conventional enough to escape censure. But the fifth number, written by Southey under the pseudonym Gualbertus, a name ominous of Wat Tyler, was more outspoken and brought on grave consequences. . . . Dr. Vincent [the Headmaster] saw the traces of Gibbon and Voltaire, and it is not surprising that his anger should have been roused. . . . [He], naturally enough, resented being called a priest of the devil, and he took immediate steps to discipline his accuser by methods even more severe than flogging. . . . There had also probably been reports carried up to the doctor of a far more serious incident which, though it may unjustly have been attributed to Southey, was certainly known by so good a hand at gossip as Charles Lamb to have been connected with his name. The statue erected to Major André in Westminster Abbey had about this time been mutilated, and when Lamb lost his temper with Southey in 1823, he reminded the latter that rumor had attributed the act to some Westminster boy, "fired perhaps with raw notions of Transatlantic Freedom," and queried whether he could not himself tell something concerning the fate of André's nose. . . .*

If Southey had had his share in a rebellion, Dr. Vincent may have decided to make use of this opportunity, when the author of The Flagellant *was to be punished, to clear off old scores with him and with insubordination in general by visiting his wrath upon the culprit caught red-handed. . . . Upon this occasion Dr. Vincent immediately sued the publisher of* The Flagellant *for libel; Southey was forced to acknowledge himself the author of the obnoxious number, and reluctantly to pen a letter of apology. The matter did not rest there, but he was expelled from the school. . . .*

Haller

Thursday, March 29, 1792 **Age 17**

Honoured Fathers,

Permit me, from a remote part of the country, to inform you of the reception the Flagellant has met with; the subject may perhaps compensate for the imperfect execution, and you may perhaps pardon the errors of a schoolboy, who wishes to be instructed. Know then, holy brethren, that I am under the care of Mr. Thwackum, a school-master, whose hand is heavier even than his head, and almost as hard as his heart. When first the news of your publication reached us, we sent for it to the next town, and were all busy in perusing the first number, when our pedagogue entered, and sternly demanded what trash we were wasting our time upon? The name was mentioned: Give it to me, he cried; I know the absurdity of these things well enough; and immediately seizing the unfortunate paper, he thrust it into his pocket, exclaiming, Pretty times indeed, if boys are allowed to think for themselves!

Now, reverend Flagellants, these words struck forcibly upon my mind, and I pondered them warily, till at last I concluded that boys have *a right to think and judge what is proper for themselves; and that the dread, should they exert the faculties of reason, that all the master's illegal authority would be resisted, was the cause of Mr. Thwackum's contumelious usage of your production. I have often heard of the divine right of Kings, and by the bye, as often doubted; but I never yet heard of the divine right of* School-masters. *A school-master, as he ought to be, is a man, chosen by parents, on account of his superior wisdom, austerity, and moderation, to instruct their children: yet all that have ever fallen under my knowledge, are illiterate, savage, and unrelenting. They endeavour, by discipline, to inculcate the doctrine of passive obedience, enforce it by stripes, and sour the tempers, and break the spirit of their unfortunate subjects, who in their turn, exercise the same tyranny over their inferiors, till the hall of learning becomes only a seminary for brutality!*

Corporal Punishment appears to me to be a method equally disgraceful and ineffectual. It requires but a very little fortitude to disregard all the castigation a master can bestow; and if I may use my own observation, as by any means decisive, the greatest dunces are generally the most able to endure their chastisement; an affected whimper, and a sly kick at the executioner *(if I may call the executive power by so harsh a name) constitute all their symptoms of amendment; and now, since I am on the subject of flogging, permit me to mention a report which I have heard confidently affirmed, but whose veracity I very much doubt, that a certain royal and illustrious seminary, pays six-pence per quarter, to defray the expence of birch. Do, most holy Flagellants, let the lash of your displeasure fall upon tyranny; expose in its proper colours, the brutality and absurdity of flogging, and you will confer a very great obligation upon*

Your unfortunate correspondent,

Thwackee.

Mr. Thwackee's letter, as it treats of a grievance usual in all public schools, as well as private academies, demands some attention: I will therefore investigate the history of flogging, demonstrate its absurdity, and produce arguments why it should be entirely abolished!

Of all the arts either ornamental or useful to mankind, tradition has assigned the origin to the gods. Ceres taught agriculture; Apollo, music and poetry; and thus mortals were defrauded of the fame they had deserved, to aggrandize their deities. Tradition has handed down the memory of the bull of Phalaris; the bed of Procrustes still records his ingenious contrivance; and Christian historians have celebrated Nero as the inventor of a new method of saving the lamp-tax, by burning the unlucky Christians in pitch: but how has the inventor of flagellation been defrauded of his fame! no pen to record his ingenuity! Flogging is in daily use; and yet, I doubt not but that every school-master will be ready to let the uplifted rod drop from his hand, when he hears that flogging was invented by the

DEVIL!!!

Start not, gentle reader; retain thy anger, Mr. Thwackum; and if I do not prove the assertion, you may consign me and my work to that august personage. Before the altar of the Œrthian Diana, the Spartan boys were flagellated for hours, without mercy; and it was esteemed an act of piety to the gods, to undergo this ceremony without a tear, without shrinking; the same practice prevailed in Thrace; and we have the authority of Herodotus, that amongst the Egyptians, they celebrated the festival of the great goddess, by voluntarily flogging themselves. A long string of ancient names at the bottom of the page, might display my erudition, but neither amuse nor instruct the reader; suffice it to say (and in this public manner do I call upon all PROFESSORS OF FLOGGING, if they can, to deny it) that the practice of flagellation was esteemed by the Heathens an act of piety. Now, who was the deity of all the Pagan nations, but the DEVIL? A very few lines will inform the reader that the oracles ceased at the birth of Christ; that when the ceremony of exorcism was performed upon a demoniac, *the Spirit has confessed the Devils as the gods of antiquity;* and that it was the universal belief of the primitive fathers, that the fallen angels were permitted to use their seducing arts upon mankind, and had assumed the names and attributes of the Heathen deities. Who will deny the PRIMITIVE FATHERS to be the standards of ORTHODOX BELIEF? Weighty arguments may be adduced (says Hugo Grotius) to prove that evil spirits were adored by the Pagans: the authority of Milton strengthens this assertion: speaking of the fallen angels, he says

the greatest part
Of mankind they corrupted, to forsake
God their creator
And DEVILS to adore for Deities.

Again:

The chief were those who from the pit of Hell,
Roaming to seek their prey on earth, durst fix
Their feats long after next the feat of God,
Their altars next his altars—Gods ador'd
Among the nations round.

Again this divine author speaks of him under the name of Moloch, in which character the old gentleman is peculiarly inimical to children:

First Moloch, horrid King! besmear'd with blood
Of human sacrifice, and parents' tears,
Through from the noise of drums and timbrels loud,
Their childrens' cries unheard, that pass'd through fire,
To his grim Idol!

"For his statue was of brass, the arms extended to receive the miserable victims which were to be consumed in the flames."

Amongst these deities we find Astarte named: now Astarte is supposed to have been the Diana of the Greeks and Romans: if we add to this the names as found in Milton of Isis and Osiris, with all "the Ionian gods," as we have just seen the institutors and patrons of flagellation, we may conclude as well from the authority of the primitive fathers, as of the Pagan writers, that flogging was invented solely by the malice of the Devil.

It needs no arguments, I believe, to convince the reader that the ancient monks were accustomed to flagellate themselves; nay, even now they continue to exercise this discipline. Rome is the chief sect of superstition:

superstition is a fiend; and what protestant will attempt to deny that the absurdities of the monks, and amongst others, the practice of flagellation, was invented by the Devil?

From the earliest ages, we find every author proud of the work he has invented. Lucifer, we all know, is proud; and saints and monks concur in affirming that he was remarkably fond of exercising the rod. The names of St. Athanasius and Jerome will be sufficient to affirm that the Devil flogged the unhappy victims of his wrath; and this is at least as credible, as that the figure of cross should secure the wearer from all calamities, as well spiritual as temporal; or that the Devil should tempt St. Anthony, in the shape of a beautiful young woman; or that that saint should *resist* the temptation! all which miracles the above-mentioned fathers have asserted: in short, examine that authorities you will, whether Heathen or Christian, you will find the same conclusion. Herodotus, Plutarch, Cicero, Seneca, Lucian, St. Athanasius, St. Jerome, and Hugo Grotius, all concur in assigning the origin of flagellation to the Devil.

Will the reader deny, that whilst they were lashing their own backs, the Devil *was* in the monk? Will he doubt for one moment, that whilst they are lashing their scholars, the Devil *is* in the school-masters?

How virulently does Moses exclaim against idolatry and against idolaters! "Ye shall destroy their altars, and break down their images, and cut down their groves, and burn their graven images with fire;" and again, "If thou do walk after other gods, and serve them and worship them, I testify against you this day, that ye shall surely perish." Thus pointedly does Moses express his detestation, and denounce the anger of the Deity against whosoever shall serve the Devil. Now, it is utterly inconsistent with the character of a school-master, particularly with the ministers of the church of England, as most school-masters are, thus by making use of so beastly, and so idolatrous a custom, to follow the abominations of the children of Edom, and the children of Moab, and the Hittites, and the Shittites, and the Gergusites, and other idolaters, whose names alone remain an awful instance of divine justice.

Thus far, I believe, neither Mr. Thwackum, nor Mr. Thwackee, can deny that I have sufficiently proved the impiety and abomination of flogging. The arguments I have adduced, have been supported by holy writ, by Heathen historians, and by ecclesiastical testimony. Whoever attempts to deny this, whoever attempts to destroy the structure I have raised, must deny the divine authority of Moses, the veracity of Seneca, and the sacred testimony of St. Athanasius: let him therefore who is bold and impious enough to do this, let him, I say, be ANATHEMA.

It now remains to prove the absurdity of the practices; and a very few lines will be sufficient. Animated by a sense of fortitude, victims have been known even to expire beneath the rod, at the altar of Diana, without a groan. Now, will any one deny that a sense of shame is sufficient to restrain every tear? or that the contempt which so contumelious and impious a custom must inspire for the *executioner* (to use my correspondent's term) would not only prevent amendment, but even encourage idleness, when its only punishment is a few stripes?

Thus, after an open and candid examination, have I proved the practice of flogging to have originated with the Devil; and I defy the Devil himself to deny it! that it is a custom equally unprofitable and impious; and that it *is unfit to be practised in a Christian country*. Though the cry of "The church is in danger" has raised thousands in the streets of London, and spread conflagration over the houses of the unfortunate Roman Catholicks: though regard for the church led on the mob at Birmingham, to destroy the effects, and to seek the life of a man, whose philosophic researches *alone* had entitled him to respect and esteem, yet flogging still continues. Satan cannot be driven out of his strong hold: he has sheltered himself behind the unrelenting breasts of the disciplinarians; and in the pleasure of exercising the rod, the impiety is forgotten. We have rejected the absurd mythology of the Heathens; we have rejected the ruinous superstition of the monastic life; we have thrown off the yoke of Rome: but that ensign of despotic cruelty—that *sceptre of Satan*—that disgrace to Christianity—the rod, yet remains possessed of its former power! In this public manner, therefore, do I, Gualbertus, scourger of the follies of mankind, issue my sacred bull, hereby commanding all doctors, reverends, and plain masters, to cease, without delay or repining, from the beastly and idolatrous custom of flogging.

"Whoever will be saved, above all things, it is necessary that he should hold the Catholic faith. Now, the Catholic is this, there be three gods, and yet but one God." Whoever denies this, cannot be orthodox, consequently cannot be fit to instruct youth. Now, since there is but one God, whosoever floggeth, that is, performeth the will of Satan, committeth an abomination: to him, therefore, to all the consumers of birch, as to the priests of Lucifer,

ANATHEMA. ANATHEMA.

GUALBERTUS.

ROBERT LOUIS STEVENSON
born Nov. 13, 1850
Edinburgh, Scotland

Age 12

Stevenson was put in a school near London for a few months while his parents went to Mentone on the Riviera for his mother's health. This letter was written at that time.

Spring Grove School, 12th Nov. 1863

Ma Chere Maman,—Jai recu votre lettre Aujourdhui et comme le jour prochaine est mon jour de naisance je vous ecrit ce lettre. Ma grande gatteaux est arrive il leve 12 livres et demi le prix etait 17 shillings. Sur la soiree de Monseigneur Faux il y etait quelques belles feux d'artifice. Mais les polissons entrent dans notre champ et nos feux d'artifice et handkerchiefs disappeared quickly, but we charged them out of the field. Je suis presque driven mad par une bruit terrible tous les garcons kik up comme grand un bruit qu'il est possible. I hope you will find your house at Mentone nice. I have been obliged to stop from writing by the want of a pen, but now I have one, so I will continue.

My dear papa, you told me to tell you whenever I was miserable. I do not feel well, and I wish to get home. Do take me with you.

R. Stevenson

His appeal to be allowed to come to the Riviera was successful.

Wheeler

About age 10, riding on a donkey.

The Progress *was founded by I.F. Stone (the I.B.F. stands for Isadore B. Feinstein, Stone's real name) while he was a sophomore at Haddonfield (New Jersey) High School. It ran for three issues—until Izzy's father put a stop to it because he felt the paper was causing Izzy to neglect his school work. G.V.A. (Gerhard Van Arkel), Stone's co-editor, later became general counsel of the National Labor Relations Board.*

I. F. STONE
born Dec. 24, 1907
Philadelphia, Pa.

Age 14

CHESS PUZZLES

Find as many names of trees as possible in the following square, using the king's move as in chess, one move in any direction. Ten names can be considered a correct answer.

A K E L Q U T
P I N O R V S
H J B W X B W
G T S M Y Z R
I F H E C A Q
N P K J D U C
O M F LG V D

II

The following are divided names of quadrapeds. Find the parts and put them together to form the names.

O, gi, e, don, go, ka, le al li, cro, pi, raffe, ri, mon, ga, co, dile, key, la, phant, key, tor.

The answers to the above puzzles will be printed in the March number.

SNAP SHOTS

Will the ire be taken out of Ireland?

If Congress thought less and said more, the country would be better off!

Why do they not charge Viscount Lascelles and Princess Mary regular rates for the space they take up in papers?

In old novels the poor little heroine was left to freeze in the attic, but nowadays no one would dare to put her in the cellar

WHAT TO TAKE OUT

The ire out of Ireland.
The holes out of Haddon avenue.
The kick out of near beer.
The bull out of Congress.

ADVERTISE

IN

..THE PROGRESS..

AND GET

RESULTS

THE PROGRESS

Vol. 1. No. 1. *FEBRUARY 1922* *Price 5 Cents*

HEARST VS. JAPAN

For years Hearst newspapers have carried on a malignant propaganda against Japan. It is not exaggerating to say that most of the Japanese feeling in the country was caused by the propaganda of the Hearts newspapers.

Japan is pictured as a militaristic demon, waiting to swoop down upon the United States and destroy it by that oft mentioned fantasy, a Mexican-Japanese alliance.

The truth is that Japan is neither militaristic nor anti-American, and if the reports are true that there is a strong anti-militaristic movement in Japan, America has nothing to fear from her. This world war has done one great thing, it has caused a reaction everywhere among everybody against everything even pertaining to war.

Is Hearst ignorant of these things or is he willingly promoting discord between the United States and Japan?

I. B. F.

GERMANY'S INVENTIVE ACTIVITY

When Germany was denied the right to build any more airplanes, she turned to inventing them in new and unusual forms. The recent record of twenty-six hours for a continuous flight was made in an airplane of German design and American manufacture.

Gliding and floating through the air are also occupying a large part in the minds of German inventors as an areo convention held recently in Germany shows.

The cause of the boom is that the mark is so cheap that all European countries buy in Germany so that any inventor can be assured of a market.

A recent Berlin automobile show exhibited startling and original shapes in automobile manufacture. The new raindrop design of an all-alumnium car shows advancement over all prior types. It is built in the shape a raindrop takes when falling, thus minimizing the resistance to the air The motor is placed over the rear axle and the chauffeur sits at the extreme front, thus distributing the weight evenly.

These are only a few of the many inventionts that have been exhibited in Germany.

G. V. A.

THINK THIS OVER

Nothing in use by man, for power of ill,
Can equal money. This lays cities low,
This drives men forth from quiet dwelling places;
This varys and changes minds of worthiest stamp,
To turn to deeds of baseness, teaching men
All shifts of cunning, and to know the guilt.
Of every impious deed. But they who, hired,
Have wrought this crime, have labored to their cost.
Or soon or late to pay the penalty.

—From Antigone,
By Saphocles, Born 497 B. C.

DO YOU KNOW THAT?

1. The Pope is called Pontiff because the early Bishops of Rome who became the first Pope took the title of Pontiff Maximus from the old Roman priests, the highest of which is called the Pontifex Maximus (Greatest Priest.)

2. There were prehistoric horses and camels in America, but none when Columbus came.

3. Steam engines were known to Archimedes who constructed one for the defense of Sicily in the Punic War.

DYLAN THOMAS
born Oct. 27, 1914
Swansea, Wales

Miss Pamela Hansford Johnson was a young poet who was sometimes published by the eccentric Victor Neuberg in the Poets' Corner of the Sunday Referee. *In the summer of 1933, she read a poem [there] by the unknown Dylan Thomas. . . . It was good enough to make Miss Johnson write to Swansea in search of Dylan. . . .*

Between his vaunting ambition as a poet and his personal insecurity, Dylan's letters to Pamela Hansford Johnson climb and slip. His method of composing them is careful enough, as if he meant them to be preserved as a record of the young dog in his Swansea days. He would jot down random ideas on pieces of paper, hoard them, arrange them, then copy them out in long letters under paragraph headings.

Sinclair

Age 19

11th November 1933

Excuse the worse than usually terrible writing!

About age 20.

Preface

In my untidy bedroom, surrounded with books and papers, full of the unhealthy smell of very bad tobacco, I sit and write. There is a beautiful winter sun outside, and by my side the oil-stove shines like a parhelion. On the wall immediately in front of me hangs my pastel drawing of the Two Brothers of Death; one is a syphilitic Christ, and the other a green-bearded Moses. Both have skin the colour of figs, and walk, for want of a better place, on a horizontal ladder of moons. The hot water pipes are swearing at me, and, despite the nearness of the stove, my tiny hands are frozen. . . .

Hymn of Despair and Hope

This is written on Armistice Day, 1933, when the war is no more than a memory of privations and the cutting down of the young. There were women who had 'lost' their sons, though where they had lost them and why they could not find them, we, who were children born out of blood into blood, could never tell. The state was a murderer, and every country in this rumour-ridden world, peopled by the unsuccessful suicides left over by the four mad years, is branded like Cain across the forehead. What was Christ in us was stuck with a bayonet to the sky, and what was Judas we fed and sheltered, rewarding, at the end, with thirty hanks of flesh. Civilisation is a murderer. We, with the cross of a castrated Saviour cut on our brows, sink deeper and deeper with the days into the pit of the West. The head of Christ is to be inspected in the museum, dry as a mole's hand in its glass case. And all the dominions of heaven have their calculated limits; the stars move to man's arithmetic; and the sun, leering like a fool over the valleys of Europe, sinks as the drops in a test-tube dry and are gone.

This is a lament on the death of the West. Your bones and mine shall manure an empty island set in a waste sea. The stars shall shine over England, but the darkness of England and the sarcophagos of a spoonfed nation, and the pitch in the slain souls of our children, will never be lit.

'And the earth was without form and void; and darkness was upon the face of the deep.' The old buffers of this world still cling to chaos, believing it to be Order. The day will come when the old Dis-Order changeth, yielding to a new Order. Genius is being strangled every day by the legion of old Buffers, by the last long line of the Edwardians, clinging, for God and capital, to an outgrown and decaying system. Light is being turned to darkness by the capitalists and industrialists. There is only one thing you and I, who are of this generation, must look forward to, must work for and pray for, and, because, as we fondly hope, we are poets and voicers not only of our personal selves but of our social selves, we must pray for it all the more vehemently. It is the Revolution. There is no need for it to be a revolution of blood. We do not ask that. All that we ask is that the present Dis-Order, this medieval machine which is grinding into powder the bones and guts of the postwar generation, shall be broken in two, and that all that is in us of godliness and strength, of happiness and genius, shall be allowed to exult in the sun. We are said to be faithless, because our God is not a capitalist God, to be unpatriotic because we do not believe in the Tory Government. We are said to be immoral because we know that marriage is a dead institution, that the old rigid monogamous lifelong union of male and female—the exceptions are the exceptions of beauty—is a corrupted thought.

The hope of Revolution, even though all of us will not admit it, is uppermost in all our minds. If there were not that revolutionary spark within us, that faith in a new faith, and that belief in our power to squash the chaos surrounding us like a belt of weeds, we would turn on the tap of war and drown ourselves in its gasses.

Everything is wrong that forbids the freedom of the individual. The governments are wrong, because they are the committees of prohibitors; the presses are wrong, because they feed us what they desire to feed us, and not what we desire to eat; the churches are wrong, because they standardize our gods, because they label our morals, because they laud the death of a vanished Christ, and fear the crying of the new Christ in the wilderness; the poets are wrong, because their vision is not a vision but a squint; they look at our world, and yet their eyes are staring back along the roads of the past centuries, never into the huge, electric promise of the future.

There is injustice, muddleheadedness, criminal ignorance, corrupted and inverted virtue, hypocrisy and stone blindness, in every sphere of life. If only for one moment the Western world could drop the veils that, ever since the Reformation, have clung around it like the films of a disease, and look, with lightened eyes, upon the cess it has created, on the greatness it has split & strangled, on the starvation it has fostered, on the perversions and ignorances it has taught, then it would die for shame. And we, who have not been long enough alive to be corrupted utterly, could build out of its manuring bones the base of an equal and sensible civilisation. . . .

The meeting between the two young poets, already half in love with each other and their own correspondence, took place in February 1934. Dylan was nineteen, Pamela Hansford Johnson was twenty-one, both were nervous. He arrived at her aunt's place in Battersea in a pork-pie hat, polo-necked sweater, and a raincoat with bulging pockets. He had prepared his opening remark. "It's nice to meet you after all those letters. Have you seen the Gauguins?" He stayed for a week on that visit to London, for six weeks on his next visit, and on and off during the following year, walking with his Pamela on Clapham Common or taking the bus to Chelsea, seeing a Sean O'Casey play and trying to get a literary job. His appearance, according to Miss Johnson, was very lovable.

"He revealed a large and remarkable head, not shaggy—for he was visiting—but heavy with hair the dull gold of threepenny bits springing in deep waves and curls from a precise middle parting. His brow was very broad, not very high: his eyes, the colour and opacity of caramels when he was solemn, the colour and transparency of sherry when he was lively, were large and fine, the lower rims rather heavily pigmented. His nose was a blob; his thick lips had a chapped appearance; a fleck of cigarette paper was stuck to the lower one. His chin was small, and the disparity between the breadth of the lower and upper parts of his face gave an impression at the same time comic and beautiful. He looked like a brilliant, audacious child, and at once my family loved and fussed over him as if he were one."

Sinclair

JAMES THURBER
born Dec. 8, 1894
Columbus, Ohio

At Douglas Junior High School [in Columbus], where Thurber completed the seventh and eighth grades, he came into his own. Still basically quiet, nervous, and shy, he nevertheless warmed to the less violent atmosphere of the school, and his exceptional intelligence became apparent to teachers and students alike. . . . What with one triumph and another, he won an appointment as a writer of the Class Prophecy for the eighth-grade class of 1909.

Bernstein

Age 14

Age 12.

PROPHECY CLASS 1909

"Harold Young, the inventor, has completed his wonderful invention which he calls the 'Seairoplane' that travels in the water as well as thru the air and on the land. He will make a trial flight June 23d, at the celebrated field of Bull Run."

These glaring head-lines attracted our attention as soon as we picked up the evening paper. As Harold was our class-mate in the class of '09, we thought we would hunt up our few remaining class-mates living in Columbus, and go to witness his first flight.

The next day we acted accordingly and with the consent of all we started in a large touring car which Catherine Crawford kindly offered to take us in. On our way from Columbus, someone put the question as to where Bull Run was exactly situated, to which Catherine Crawford promptly answered that it was 30 miles south of Washington in the State of Kentucky. Altho we were now sure of the location we did not know just which road to take, and decided to inquire as we went along.

We were now on a very narrow road and noticed approaching in the distance a large hay wagon on the top of which was perched a slight form of about 350# [pounds] whom we noticed to be chewing what we supposed to be a piece of straw and urging on the mules which drew the wagon with an occasional "Gee Haw" to which they responded with a "Hee Haw." To our surprise as we drew quite near he exclaimed, "Well if there aint some of my class-mates of '09." We at once recognized the voice as belonging to Armistead Peters, tho his features were much changed. He inquired as to where we were going and we told him about the new invention of Harold Young's and invited him to join us, but he declined on the ground that his farm work detained him, but promised he would be present a week later to witness the flight of the Seairoplane, then he explained that his poor health had compelled him to retire to the simple life.

It being dinner time he cordially invited us to dine with him, but we had to decline as we had many other class-mates to invite. The next few days nothing of special importance happened until we approached Washington for which we were bound. We were making an extra burst of speed as we wished to reach the City before dark, when we heard a whistle behind us and were very much alarmed at seeing a policeman on a motor-cycle approaching us and calling us to stop. We stopped and he informed us that we were exceeding the speed limit and inquired our names. While he waited for our answer with note book and pencil in hand, "Donald Donaldson is my name," said one of our party. "Are you the Donald Donaldson of Columbus who was in the class of '09 at Douglas?" asked the policeman, "Yes, yes," we all shouted, at once, "and who are you?" I am Milton France of the Washington police force," he said. After a few minutes conversation in which we told him we were going to see Harold Young make his first flight, he said he had already decided to go as he was interested in aeronautics. We now continued on our way to the City after thanking him for pardoning us for speeding and entered the City in time for supper.

As we were going to remain in the city until morning, we secured tickets for the evening performance at Keith's and arrived just as the curtain arose. We were very much surprised to see Dan Carroll leading the orchestra with his old time enthusiasm.

The first act was the bill head-liner: Curtis Williams, better known as Lizzie, the famous female impersonator. "Why I believe that is one of our class-mates at Douglas," we said when he made his appearance amid a shower of applause.

After the performance we made our way behind the scenes where we found Curtis surrounded by a large crowd of admiring theatre goers. We were forced to wait until he had been interviewed by reporters, friends and others before we could gain an audience with the famous actor, whose marvelous grace and superb acting had made him the matinee idol of America.

He received us in his dressing room and appeared overjoyed at seeing us, and said as he had not been booked for another performance for two weeks, altho he had been rushed by hosts of managers he would accompany us in the auto to give Harold's first appearance, as he called it "a great send-off." So accordingly, all details were arranged and we retired to our hotel.

The next day was the 22nd of June and as the ascension was on the 23d, we decided to see the town as we had plenty of time. We were driving down Pennsylvania Ave. viewing the many interesting things along the way when we noticed a large crowd that was assembled at a corner listening to a woman who was speaking very earnestly to the crowd which consisted of both men and women. The speaker was surrounded by many plainly dressed women who were flaunting banners on which were inscriptions such as "Vote for Women," "Parks for President," etc. and raising a multitude of noise which failed to arouse much enthusiasm from the men.

As we approached closer we observed that the speaker was a solemn dignified woman in plain dress, but her features attracted our attention and after studying them for a minute or so we cried, "Why surely that is Charlotte Parks of Columbus." "It surely is" cried others of our party, but it was very hard to believe that Charlotte was a suffragette. But there was now no doubt of it.

The noise grew more deafening and the speaker increased in fervor as the meeting progressed, but after arguing another quarter of an hour on the subject of women's rights, the speaker descended from the platform on which she had been standing and the crowd gradually dispersed.

When she saw us she came hastily toward us and greeted us, and after a few minutes conversation in which she told us that she would not lecture again until fall, consented to go with us in the auto. . . .

We arrived at Bull Run about half past one and inquired where the ascension grounds were located; upon being informed, we made our way there and found a large crowd assembled to witness the flight. We found our class-mates that had promised to come, already there and then found Harold surrounded by a large crowd of people and it was with difficulty that we made our way to him. He greeted us very cordially and seemed pleased that we had come all the way from Columbus to see him operate his airship. At our request he explained about the different parts of his machine and showed us how it was steered. It was a huge machine capable of carrying many passengers. He then found us comfortable seats where we could have an unobstructed view of the Seairoplane flight. At 2 O'Clock every thing was in readiness and Harold started the engines. The Seairoplane arose gracefully, and soon attained the height of 200 ft. Harold now performed many gyrations which showed the perfect control which he had over the aero-plane amid the applause of the spectators.

After sailing around the field for about a quarter of an hour he prepared to descend when the chugging of the engines suddenly ceased, the propellers stopped and with a swish the Seairoplane darted downward. A cry of terror came from the spectators and we jumped from our seats in dismay. With a crash the seairoplane struck the ground where it was soon surrounded by the crowd who quickly lifted it off Harold who had been pinned beneath it. We pushed our way madly toward him, expecting to see him seriously injured, but instead he was limping painfully around looking after his invention and paying no attention to his injuries.

He soon declared that the Seairoplane was but little damaged, the propeller being broken, and part of the frame demolished, while the engine was intact, uninjured. . . .

At a lull in the conversations some one suggested we make a night trip as it was a beautiful moon-light night. Everyone agreed to this as it would be a unique journey and we would escape the blistering sun. It had been already decided that our next stopping place would be Boston as we expected to find some of our friends there so the Seairoplane was headed in that direction. It was a very delightful journey and we arrived in Boston about midnight and received lodgings in a hotel for the rest of the night after first looking after the Seairoplane. . . .

We were walking along the street a few minutes later looking in the different shop windows when we came to a book store. We noticed that advertised in this window was a book by the name of "Indecision or the Last Word of Warning." This sounded very familiar and so we looked for the author's name. It proved to be Margaret McElvaine. The author's name as well as the name of the book left but little doubt in our minds that the authoress, Margaret McElvaine was our teacher at Douglas in '09. We quickly entered the store and purchased a copy. While looking thru the preface we noticed a paragraph which read: "If anyone desires to possess a portrait of the author of this book, it can be secured by calling at or sending to No. 23 E. Lemon St. Boston, Mass."

That afternoon we called at the number given the book, but found no one at home. We were very much disappointed and for a moment no one said anything, but finally we turned to go determined to see Miss McElvaine if we had to stay in Boston another week to do it. But as we started out of the gate we noticed a familiar form approaching. Before we could say anything Miss McElvaine, for it was she cried out, "Well this seems like old times at Douglas to see you all here, but where are you going, and how did you get here all together?" Then we explained everything. She thought our plan an excellent one and immediately consented to accompany us as a chaperone. We accepted her invitation to stay awhile and talk over old times. The afternoon was thus pleasantly spent, and we were very reluctant to go when it commenced to grow dark. . . .

All of our class was now assembled and accordingly

that evening at the hotel we held a decision as to where we should go. At last it was decided unanimously that we should make a trip to Mars. Harold said that to visit Mars had been one of his main reasons for constructing the Seairoplane. The plan decided upon was this: we were to go to San Francisco and make our start from there. We arrived there in due time and stayed in the city for a week in order to get ourselves ready and to fix up the Seairoplane for its long journey.

At the end of the week a large crowd assembled in a vacant lot on the outskirts of the city to see us start at 10 O'Clock. The engines were started and we were soon out of sight of the crowd and finally of San Francisco.

The Seairoplane's course was directly upward and at first we experienced a sea-sick feeling, but soon became used to it. When night came on the earth was far below and hardly visible to us. In the morning of the next day we consulted the hythonometer and found ourselves to be about 125 miles high. The continent could just be dimly seen that day while by the afternoon of the next day nothing but air surrounded us. At night Mars could be plainly seen and we stayed up until late to examine it. Chrystal Fleming, the world renowned astronomer told us all about the canals mountains, etc. and gave her opinion as to whether Mars was inhabited or not, which was that there was strange people who largely resembled apes that inhabited the planet.

On Sunday, Church was held, ceremonies being delivered by Deaconess Louise Reynolds, and all together we had a very pleasant time altho we were many miles from land. Some one had found out that Catherine Crawford was a play-writer, writing under the name of Helen McCafferty. We had heard a great deal about her, but did not dream that she was Catherine Crawford. Among her most widely staged plays were "Bob Bensons Ride, or Two Sheets of White Paper," "The Green Tie or Why his Sister left," and "The Arms of Venus." We had her read a play that she had just finished, which was entitled "Who Thru Mush in Nellie's Eye?" It was a very pathetic one and there were tears on almost everyone's face when she had finished. A few days later we learned that Don Donaldson was a prosperous manufacturer of Yellowbud, Ohio, who manufactured rubber balls.

One day as we were sailing easily along, Harold came rushing out of the engine room with dishevelled hair and bulging eyes. We asked him what on earth was the matter for answer he pointed to a piece of rope that had caught in a part of the machinery that was situated on the farthest end of a long beam, which extended far over the side of the Seairoplane, Then he said, "unless that rope is gotten out of the curobater we will all be killed." These awful words astounded us and we all became frightened at once. Suddenly amid all of our lamentations a cry from Harold was heard and we all looked up. What was our surprise to see James Thurber walking out on the beam. He reached the end safely and then extricated the rope, but when he turned to come back his foot caught and he pitched head formost towards the deck. His unusual length saved him for he landed safely on the Seairoplane. We were all very joyful that the terrible crisis had been safely passed and afterwards learned that James was a tight rope walker with Barnsells and Ringbaileys circus.

As the days went on Mars became plainer and plainer to us. At last after we had been in the air for 2 months we came within a mile of that planet and 3 minutes later the Seairoplane touched the planet. As soon as we stepped out of the airship we saw a crowd of Martians coming towards us. What was our surprise when we saw that they were dressed like earth beings and seemingly the only difference was that they spoke a different language. They appeared as civilized as we and gladly welcomed us to their world. We accompanied them in a large auto to a city which was situated back from the landing place beyond a large forest of elm, oak, pine, etc. and which resembled an American forest very much.

In the city were large stores, churches, residences, etc. which were made of granite and marble which we were told thru an interpreter were secured from rich quarries that were situated among the hills not far distant from Marlton, which was the name of the city. The interpreter that explained our conversation had made a trip to America years previous and learned our language.

The next day we visited the quarries and found also wonderful rich gold mines with an output of 4,000,000 a day.

When we returned to the town we found a great banquet in progress in our honor. After the banquet, speeches were made, fire works were displayed and a great celebration was held. We stayed two weeks longer and enjoyed ourselves immensely. When we left we took a great lot of curios with us and also a large amount of gold and silver of which the Martians had such an enormous quantity.

Earth was reached in 40 days, we landed in a large pasture but no one knew what state we were in, so we went up to a farmhouse and asked the farmer what state we were in. He looked greatly astonished and said wonderingly, "what state, wall now I guess you are just making fun of me, but by heck you be in Ohio." We were surprised that we had landed in our own state and asked him what city we were near. He said, "Well you be about 3 miles from Columbus, I calculate." This astonished us even more but we thanked the farmer and started for Columbus, where we arrived 10 minutes later.

Here our party broke up and returned to their various occupations all saying that they had had a great time and that the reunion had been a great success.

END

Although to be comme il faut *seemed to him the height of human perfection, young Tolstoy had a positive incapacity for it. His failure caused him endless grief at this time. Much of the effort that should have been expended on studies was devoted to acquiring those graces which would enable him to shine at the dinner parties and balls of Kazan aristocracy. One look in the mirror would upset all his hopes. The face of a simple peasant stared back at him, and his big hands and feet seemed downright shameful. His muscular physique (he was practicing gymnastics daily in the hope of becoming the strongest man in the world) was not well-proportioned, and clothes somehow never set him off as neatly as they did Sergei* [an older brother].

Tolstoy tried to make a virtue of such handicaps, and when this failed, he took refuge in queer and original behavior, the customary retreat of the social misfit. To be outstanding was his aim; if he could not gain attention by natural graces, he would do it by calculated rudeness. When all talked, he was haughtily silent. If he elected to speak, he eschewed the usual empty compliments of fine society and endeavored to impress people by a certain impolite frankness. "Old inhabitants of Kazan," writes one of them, "remember him at all the balls, evening parties, and gatherings of fashionable society, invited everywhere, always dancing, but not in the least pleasing to these worldly ladies as were his rivals among the aristocratic students; they always observed in him a stiffness and self-consciousness." One of his rivals remarked: "We called him the 'bear,' the 'philosopher' Lyovochka, awkward and always embarrassed."

Simmons

LEO TOLSTOY
born Aug. 28, 1828
Yasnaya Polyana
Tula Province, Russia

EXCERPTS FROM DIARY

Age 18

March 24, 1847

I have passed through several phases, yet hitherto failed to attain the degree of perfection (in my pursuits) which I should like to achieve. In other words, I always fail to do that which I have set myself. And even what I do, I do indifferently, through omitting to whet my memory. Wherefore I will jot down a few rules which, if followed, will help me to that end.

(1) What you have set yourself, carry out without fail and at all costs.

(2) What you do, do well.

(3) Never refer to a book for what you have forgotten, but strive to remember that something for yourself.

(4) Force your intellect to work always with its greatest vigour.

(5) Always read and think aloud.

(6) Be not ashamed to tell people who are hindering you that they are standing in your way. Give them a hint; and, should they not take the hint (to the effect that they are hindering you), beg their pardon and tell them so outright.

About age 20.

April 17

Of late I have failed to conduct myself as I should wish; of which the cause has been, in the first place, my removal from the hospital [the infirmary at the University of Kazan], and, in the second place, the company in which I am beginning increasingly to move. Hence I conclude that any change of position ought to lead me very gravely to consider how external circumstances may influence me under new conditions, and how best I can obviate that influence.

If my removal from the hospital could influence me to such an extent, what will be the influence of my removal from the life of a student to the life of a landowner?

Some change in my mode of life must result; yet that change must not come of an external circumstance—rather, of a movement of spirit: wherefore I keep finding myself confronted with the question, "What is the aim of man's life?" and, no matter what result my reflections reach, no matter what I take to be life's source, I invariably arrive at the conclusion that the purpose of our human existence is to afford a maximum of help towards the universal development of everything that exists.

If I meditate as I contemplate nature, I perceive everything in nature to be in constant process of development, and each of nature's constituent portions to be unconsciously contributing towards the development of others. But man is, though a like portion of nature, a portion gifted with consciousness, and therefore bound, like the other portions, to make conscious use of his spiritual faculties in striving for the development of everything existent.

If I meditate as I contemplate history, I perceive the whole human race to be for ever aspiring towards the same end.

If I meditate on reason, if I pass in review man's spiritual faculties, I find the soul of every man to have in it the same unconscious aspiration, the same imperative demand of the spirit.

If I meditate with an eye upon the history of philosophy, I find everywhere, and always, men to have arrived at the conclusion that the aim of human life is the universal development of humanity.

If I meditate with an eye upon theology, I find almost every nation to be cognizant of a perfect existence towards which it is the aim of mankind to aspire.

So I too shall be safe in taking for the aim of my existence a conscious striving for the universal development of everything existent. I should be the unhappiest of mortals if I could not find a purpose for my life, and a purpose at once universal and useful—useful because development will enable my immortal soul to pass naturally into an existence that will be at once superior and akin to this one. Wherefore henceforth all my life must be a constant, active striving for that one purpose.

Next I would ask: of what is my life's purpose to consist during the coming two years in the country? (1) of studying the entire course of juridical science as required for the final examination at the University; (2) of studying practical medicine, with a portion of theoretical; (3) of studying languages—French, Russian, German, English, Italian, and Latin; (4) of studying rural industry, practical as well as theoretical; (5) of studying history, geography, and statistics; (6) of studying mathematics, the gymnasium course; (7) of writing a dissertation; (8) of attaining the highest possible perfection in music and art; (9) of framing a list of rules; (10) of acquiring knowledge of the natural sciences; and (11) of writing treatises on the various subjects which I may be studying.

April 18

I have drawn up a number of rules which I should like to follow in their entirety if my strength be not too weak. However, I will set myself one rule, and add to it another when I shall have grown used to following the first. Rule No. 1 shall be: *Fulfil everything which you have set yourself.*—Hitherto I have failed to keep this.

June 16

Shall I ever reach the point of being dependent upon no extraneous circumstance? That would be, in my opinion, immense perfection, since in the man independent of any extraneous influence the spirit necessarily takes precedence of matter, and he attains his destiny.

I am becoming familiar with my self-appointed rule 1: wherefore to-day I will set myself another rule—as follows: Regard feminine society as an inevitable evil of social life, and, in so far as you can, avoid it. From whom, indeed, do we learn voluptuousness, effeminacy, frivolity in everything, and many another vice, if not from women? Who is responsible for the fact that we lose such feelings inherent in us as courage, fortitude, prudence, equity, and so forth, if not woman? Woman is more receptive than man, and, during the ages of virtue, was better than we were; but now, in this age of corruption and vice, she has become worse.

In June 1853, he had left the [*Hannibal, Missouri*] Journal [*where his brother was editor*] *and said to his mother that he was going to St. Louis to visit his sister Pamela. His purpose from the first, however, had been to try his fortunes in New York. He worked on the* Evening News *in St. Louis merely long enough to make the money to pay his expenses thither* [*where he arrived on August 24*].

Brasher

MARK TWAIN
born Nov. 30, 1835
Florida, Mo.

Age 17

New York, Aug, 31, 1853

My dear Mother:

New York is at present overstocked with printers; and I suppose they are from the South, driven North by yellow fever. I got a permanent situation on Monday morning, in a book and job office, and went to work. The printers here are badly organized, and therefore have to work for various prices. These prices are 23, 25, 28, 30, 32, and 35 cents per 1,000 ems. The price I get is 23 cents; but I did very well to get a place at all, for there are thirty or forty—yes, fifty good printers in the city with no work at all; besides, my situation is permanent, and I shall keep it till I can get a better one. The office I work in is John A. Gray's, 97 Cliff street, and next to Harper's, is the most extensive in the city. In the room in which I work I have forty compositors for company. Taking compositors, press men, stereotypers, and all, there are about two hundred persons employed in the concern. The "Knickerbocker," "New York Recorder," "Choral Advocate," "Jewish Chronicle," "Littell's Living Age," "Irish ———," and half a dozen other papers and periodicals are printed here, besides an immense number of books. They are very particular about spacing, justification, proofs, etc., and even if I do not make much money, I will learn a great deal. I thought Ustick was particular enough, but acknowledge now that he was not old-maidish. Why, you must put exactly the same space between every two words, and *every line must be spaced alike.* They think it dreadful to space one line with three em spaces, and the next one with five ems. However, I expected this, and worked accordingly from the beginning; and out of all the proofs I saw, without boasting, I can say mine was by far the cleanest. In St. Louis, Mr. Baird said my proofs were the cleanest that were ever set in his office. The foreman of the Anzeiger told me the same—foreman of the Watchman the same; and with all this evidence, I believe I *do* set a clean proof.

My boarding house is more than a mile from the office; and I can hear the signal calling the hands to work before I start down; they use a steam whistle for that purpose. I work in the fifth story; and from one window I have a pretty good view of the city, while another commands a view of the shipping beyond the Battery; and the "forest of masts," with all sorts of flags flying, is no mean sight. You have everything in the shape of water craft, from a fishing smack to the steamships and men-of-war; but packed so closely together for miles, that when close to them you can scarcely distinguish one from another.

Of all the commodities, manufactures—or whatever you please to call it—in New York, trundle-bed trash—children I mean—take the lead. Why, from Cliff street, up Frankfort to Nassau street, six or seven squares—my road to dinner—I think I could count two hundred brats. Niggers, mulattoes, quadroons, Chinese, and some the Lord no doubt originally intended to be white, but the dirt on whose faces leaves one uncertain as to that fact, block up the little, narrow street; and to wade through this mass of human vermin, would raise the ire of the most patient person that ever lived. In going to and from my meals, I go by the way of Broadway—and to *cross* Broadway is the rub—but once across, it is *the* rub for two or three squares. My plan—and how could I choose another, when there *is* no other—is to get into the crowd; and when I get in, I am borne, and rubbed, and crowded along, and need scarcely trouble myself about using my own legs; and when I get out, it seems like I had been pulled to pieces and very badly put together again.

Age 15, as a printer's apprentice.

Last night I was in what is known as one of *the* finest fruit saloons in the world. The whole length of the huge, glittering hall is filled with beautiful ornamented marble slab tables, covered with the finest fruit I ever saw in my life. I suppose the fruit could not be mentioned with which they could not supply you. It is a perfect palace. The gas lamps hang in clusters of half a dozen together—representing grapes, I suppose—all over the hall.

P.S. The printers have two libraries in town, entirely free to the craft; and in these I can spend my evenings most pleasantly. If books are not good company, where will I find it?

VINCENT VAN GOGH
born March 30, 1853
Zundert, Brabant
The Netherlands

About age 13.

As a boy Vincent displayed a good deal of charm. Red-haired, freckled, with pale blue eyes that sometimes deepened to green, he was fond of collecting beetles and vacant birds' nests, and had an amiable knack for inventing games. His younger brothers and sisters loved his company; after one particularly pleasant day, they formally made him a present of a rosebush that happened to be growing in their father's garden. But Vincent was also stubborn and hot-tempered, given to strangely contrary behavior. He once modeled a small elephant in clay and made a striking sketch of a cat, but when his parents praised them, he immediately destroyed them. It is likely that the praise embarrassed him.

. . . he was fascinated by books. They appear, with legible titles, in many of his paintings, and he read them with what may at first seem to be a curious lack of discrimination. He admired Shakespeare, but also thought that La Case de l'Oncle Tom (Uncle Tom's Cabin) *was a noble piece of literature. Keats, Voltaire, Homer, the French moralist Ernest Renan and the historian Jules Michelet had Vincent's utmost respect. . . . He once said that he would give ten years of his life for the privilege of being allowed to sit for two weeks with a loaf of bread in front of Rembrandt's magnificent* Jewish Bride. *. . . A common denominator can be found, however, in most of the writers and artists Vincent admired: they dealt with the destitute and downtrodden.*

Wallace

Farm and Wagonshed, age 10 (gift for his father's birthday).

The Milk-Jug, age 9.

These three are attributed to Van Gogh but their authenticity has been challenged by Marc Tralbaut. It has been suggested that Van Gogh may have copied the dog from someone else's painting.

The Dog, age 9.

The Bridge, age 8.

QUEEN VICTORIA
born May 24, 1819
Kensington Palace
London, England

London was awake most of the night before. For days there had been din of hammers, dust of scaffolding and bits falling on people's heads. The town was all mob, the Park all encampment. People were meeting friends up from the country. "We are all mad about the Coronation, raving mad," remarked a Londoner as he welcomed his niece from the country at Charing Cross. At midnight the bells rang in the Coronation and the crowds shouted it in until daybreak. Even those who were not sleeping out rose with the dawn and many ladies in silk and satin, protected only by thin shawls, found themselves at 6 o'clock in the morning shivering in the windy Abbey cloisters until the doors opened at seven.

Longford

Age 19

Thursday, 28th June! [1838, her Coronation Day]

I was awoke at four o'clock by the guns in the Park, and could not get much sleep afterwards on account of the noise of the people, bands, etc. etc. Got up at 7 feeling strong and well. The Park presented a curious spectacle; crowds of people up to Constitution Hill, soldiers, bands, etc. I dressed, having taken a little breakfast before I dressed, and a little after. At 10 I got into the State coach with the Duchess of Sutherland and Lord Albemarle, and we began our Progress. It was a fine day and the crowds of people exceeded what I have ever seen; many as there were the day I went to the City, it was nothing—nothing to the multitudes, the millions of my loyal subjects who were assembled in every spot to witness the Procession. Their good-humour and excessive loyalty was beyond everything, and I really cannot say how proud I feel to be the Queen of such a Nation.

I reached the Abbey amid deafening cheers at a little past ½ p. eleven; I first went into a robing-room quite close to the entrance, where I found my eight Train-bearers, all dressed exactly alike and beautifully, in white satin and silver tissue, with wreaths of silver corn-ears in front, and a small one of pink roses round the plait behind, and pink roses in the trimming of the dresses.

After putting on my Mantle, and the young ladies having properly got hold of it and Lord Conyngham holding the end of it, I left the robing-room and the Procession began. The sight was splendid, the bank of Peeresses quite beautiful, all in their robes, and the Peers on the other side. The Bishop of Durham stood on one side near me, but he was, as Lord Melbourne told me, remarkably maladroit and could never tell me what was to take place. At the beginning of the Anthem where he made a mark, I retired to St Edward's Chapel, a small dark place immediately behind the altar with my Ladies and Train-bearers; took off my crimson robe and kirtle and put on the supertunics of Cloth of Gold, then proceeded bare-headed into the Abbey; I was then seated upon St Edward's chair where the Dalmatic robe was clasped around me by the Lord Great Chamberlain. Then followed all the various things; and last (of those things) the Crown being placed on my head:—which was, I must own, a most beautiful impressive moment; all the Peers and Peeresses put on their Coronets at the same instant.

My excellent Lord Melbourne, who stood very close to me throughout the whole ceremony, was completely overcome at this moment, and very much affected; he gave me such a kind, and I may say fatherly look.

The Enthronization and the Homage of, 1st, all the Bishops, then my Uncles, and lastly of all the Peers, in their respective order, was very fine. Poor old Lord Rolle, who is 82 and dreadfully infirm, in attempting to ascend the steps, fell and rolled quite down, but was not the least hurt. When Lord Melbourne's turn to do Homage came, there was loud cheering; they also cheered Lord Grey and the Duke of Wellington. It's a pretty ceremony: they first all touch the Crown, and then kiss my hand. When my good Lord Melbourne knelt down and kissed my hand, he pressed my hand and I grasped his with all my heart, at which he looked up with his eyes filled with tears and seemed very much touched, as he was, I observed, throughout the whole ceremony. After the Homage was concluded I left the throne, took off my Crown and received the sacrament; I then put on my Crown again, and re-ascended the Throne, leaning on Lord Melbourne's arm; at the commencement of the Anthem I descended from the Throne and went into St Edward's Chapel with my ladies, Train-bearers, and Lord Willoughby, where I took off the Dalmatic robe, supertunics, and put on the Purple Velvet Kirtle and Mantle, and proceeded again to the

Throne, which I ascended leaning on Lord Melbourne's hand. I then again descended from the Throne, and repaired with all the Peers bearing the Regalia, my Ladies and Train-bearers, to St Edward's Chapel, as it is called; but which, as Lord Melbourne said, was more unlike a Chapel than anything he had ever seen; for, what was called an Altar was covered with sandwiches, bottles of wine, etc.

The Archbishop came and ought to have delivered the Orb to me, but I had already got it and he (as usual) was so confused and puzzled and knew nothing, and—went away. There we waited for some minutes. Lord Melbourne took a glass of wine, for he seemed completely tired; the Procession being formed, I replaced my Crown (which I had taken off for a few minutes), took the Orb in my left hand and the Sceptre in my right, and thus loaded, proceeded through the Abbey, which resounded with cheers to the first Robing-room, where I found the Duchess of Gloucester, Mamma, and the Duchess of Cambridge, with their ladies. And here we waited for at least an hour with all my ladies and Train-Bearers. The Archbishop had (most awkwardly) put the ring on the wrong finger, and the consequence was that I had the greatest difficulty to take it off again,—which I at last did with great pain. At about ½ p. 4 I re-entered my carriage, the Crown on my head and Sceptre and Orb in my hand and we proceeded the same way as we came—the crowds if possible having increased, the enthusiasm, affection and loyalty was really touching. I came home at a little after 6, really not feeling tired.

At 8 we dined. Lord Melbourne came up to me and said, 'I must congratulate you on this brilliant day,' and that all had gone off so well. He said he was not tired and was in high spirits. I sat between uncle Ernest and Lord Melbourne. My kind Lord Melbourne was much affected in speaking of the whole ceremony. He asked kindly if I was tired, said the sword he carried (the 1st, the Sword of State) was exceedingly heavy. I said that the Crown hurt me a good deal. We agreed that the whole thing was a very fine sight. He thought the robes, and particularly the Dalmatic, 'looked remarkably well.' "And you did it all so well; excellent!" said he, with the tears in his eyes.

After dinner, we spoke of the numbers of Peers at the Coronation, which Lord Melbourne said, with the tears in his eyes, was unprecedented. I observed that there were very few Viscounts; he said 'There are very few Viscounts,' that they were an odd sort of title and not really English; that Dukes and Barons were the only real English titles; that Marquises were likewise not English; and that they made people Marquises when they did not wish to make them Dukes. I then sat on the sofa for a little while. I said to Lord Melbourne, that I felt a little tired on my feet; 'You must be very tired' he said, spoke of the weight of the robes, etc; the Coronets; and he turned round and said to me so kindly, 'And you did it beautifully, every part of it, with so much taste; it's a thing you can't give persons advice upon; it must be left to a person.' To hear this from this kind impartial friend, gave me great and real pleasure. Mamma and Feodore came back just after he said this. Spoke of these Bishops' Copes, about which he was very funny; of the Pages, who were such a nice set of boys and who were so handy, Lord Melbourne said, that they kept them near them the whole time. Little Lord Stafford and Slane (Lord Mountcharles) were pages to their fathers and looked lovely; Lord Paget (not a fine boy) was Lord Melbourne's Page and remarkably handy, he said. Spoke again of the young ladies' dress about which he was very amusing. He said there was a large breakfast in the Jerusalem Chamber, where they met before all began: he said, laughing that whenever the Clergy or a Dean and Chapter had anything to do with anything, there's sure to be plenty to eat. Spoke of my intending to go to bed; he said 'You may depend upon it, you are more tired than you think you are.'

Self-portrait at age 16.

GORE VIDAL
born Oct. 3, 1925
West Point, N.Y.

The 1939–1940 school year at Los Alamos was unpleasant for Vidal, but in the fall of 1940 he began the three years at Phillips Exeter Academy, Exeter, New Hampshire, which he recalls as "among the happiest of [his] life." At Exeter, the young man was for the first time completely free of the family problems that had soured his childhood. The Exeter years saw the first serious writing by Vidal. . . . In 1943, he adopted his mother's family name as his own first name, and as Gore Vidal he contributed to and helped edit The Phillips Exeter Review.

White

Here is his own choice of the three short stories he published in the Review.

Age 17

MOSTLY ABOUT GEOFFREY

The manuscript of this story was found in the men's room of the Colby Theatre in Colby, Maryland. As the author has never been discovered, we hereby feel safe in printing the following tale for what it is worth.

It was on Thursday, the 8th of August, that my bosom friend Geoffrey told me he was a were-wolf. I must say that I, though surprised, took it rather well. "Were-wolf, you say?" I remarked casually. I made a desperate attempt to sound intelligent, but somehow failed. So I sat there and waited for him to answer.

Geoffrey was a calm, efficient kind of person with a legalistic turn of mind. There was little of the actor about him; if he said he was a were-wolf he was a were-wolf and that was that.

"Yes," said Geoffrey, carefully choosing his words, "I think, in fact I know, I am one. The other day at the Claytons' I was bitten by a wild-looking dog. As it later turned out, the beast was not a dog but a wolf that had strayed into the back garden. According to ancient lore it seems that he who is bitten by a were-wolf becomes one himself. . . ."

"But," I interrupted, "how do you know this . . . this creature was a were-wolf? It didn't change into anyone, did it?"

"I wish," said Geoffrey, petulantly, "you'd let me finish my story. I presume the animal was a were-wolf, because last night when the moon was full I changed into a wolf."

I sat there woodenly for a moment, and looked at him. He was calm; there was a look of oppressive sanity in his eyes, and a feeling of comfortable security in his receding hair line. This was not a mad man, and yet it could not be a were-wolf. I giggled in a hideously strangled voice, and said something like "well, what a funny world it is." I am not at my best in a crisis.

Geoffrey went to the window, and gazed pensively at the nearby woods. I probably should have stated before that we were in his home near the town of Colby, Maryland. Colby is a rustic sort of hamlet set amidst some legend-filled woods. The townspeople are kindly, old-fashioned, and perhaps a little mad.

Standing before the window Geoffrey seemed substantial enough. Without turning around he said, "I think you had better leave here before night fall. The moon will be full again tonight."

I had an insane desire to tell him that I was going to turn into a chipmunk; fortunately I stifled it. At last I said, "I think I had better stay here with you tonight. After all you'll need someone to keep you from eating things like . . . like babies."

Geoffrey wheeled around, his eyes bulging. "Christ, what I'd give for a plump baby!"

Five minutes later I was heading for the most crowded place in Colby, namely the Colby Theatre. I felt safe here, until I discovered that the movie starred Boris Karloff in one of his more vicious roles. I am afraid I was not in the proper mood to enjoy this picture; in fact, I did not stay long enough to find whether I would like it or not.

Just before night fall I decided to return to Geoffrey's house. I suppose I felt it was my duty to be with him.

He was seated quietly in his study when I arrived. He rose when he saw me. "Sorry I bothered you," he said. His voice possessed just the right shade of contrition. Together we sat down before the newly-lit fire.

"The moon will be full in about three hours," he remarked cozily, picking up a book.

"How nice," I said, with studied calm.

We sat there chatting in a desultory fashion for about an hour. Finally I asked him what he planned to do with the rest of his life. "You know you can't go on being both a man and a wolf. People would talk."

He laughed unpleasantly. "What cure would you suggest my taking?" I told him that there was nothing to get nasty about, and added that he did not show the proper spirit. There was an uncomfortable silence.

Geoffrey stood up abruptly, and began to pace the floor. I was becoming intensely nervous. Several times he went to the curtained windows. Each time he halted before them for a moment, and then restlessly moved on. I began to wonder why I had come back. Gloomily I thought of my position should Geoffrey really become a wolf.

Finally he went to the window by his desk; there was determination in his gait. Slowly he pushed back the curtains, and the wind shrieked in. The moon was full in the black sky above the woods.

He gave a cry of delight; and I quickly placed the friendly contours of a large couch between us. Then the incredible happened. Geoffrey began to gasp in the best were-wolf fashion. He seemed to shrink . . . to bunch up. After a moment of what seemed intense pain he turned and faced me. I noticed with horror that he was covered with dark fur.

"How do you feel?" I asked, trying to make conversation.

"Like hell," he replied. I noted that he mumbled a great deal, and had trouble with his diction.

Then a ridiculous thing happened: he stopped changing. I am not acquainted with the various stages of were-wolfdom, but I am quite sure that one does not stop in the middle of the transformation, and remain looking more like a bearded drunk than a wolf. Anyway, that's what happened to Geoffrey.

"I feel an awful fool," he mumbled, and I detected a blush of shame beneath the hirsute growth of his face.

"You look an awful fool," I said, with considerable asperity, for I felt reasonably safe. Anyone as ineffective as Geoffrey looked could not be dangerous. He did look hideous, though, and I felt I should take no liberties with him.

Sadly he huddled himself into a chair; the semi-claws he had for hands beat the air vainly. "It worked last night," he kept repeating.

"Do you think if you tried very hard you could change completely?" I asked curiously.

"Fat chance," he said, but he did grunt a little. It was no use.

"Well, you're not a very effective were-wolf," I said gaily. He looked at me furiously; I had hurt him to the quick. Then to my terror he got out of his chair, and came walking slowly toward me, his semi-tusks slobbering. "So I'm not a very effective were-wolf, am I?" His voice was threatening; he snarled once or twice. Hastily I retreated to the fire-place, and grabbed a poker.

"Come any closer and I'll club you!" I said. He came a great deal closer, and suddenly, when he was about two feet from me, he jumped. There was a brief scuffle in which he bit my arm, and I killed him; the creature turned back into Geoffrey on the floor.

Suddenly I wondered if the police would call me a murderer; it was obvious that they would not believe in my were-wolf story. Panic-stricken I dropped the poker and ran into the town again, leaving a trail of blood behind me. For safety I fled into the men's room of the Colby Theatre.

I have been sitting here for an hour now writing this story on a roll of toilet paper. I can hear the police cars and ambulances outside in the street. But I don't think they will catch me, for I have a feeling that I am going to turn into a wolf. Geoffrey did bite me. Well, I have come . . ."

Here the roll of toilet paper ends. Just as incidental intelligence the "Colby Daily" in an issue dated the 9th of August told a brief story to the effect that a mad dog has emerged from the men's room of the Colby Theatre. It was not caught.

EVELYN WAUGH
born Oct. 28, 1903
Hampstead, London, England

About age 9.

. . . In the first flush of his new religious enthusiasm, however, he conceived a wish to become a person. His mother did not encourage this ambition which was short-lived. She also was a perceptive judge of character.

His new-found enthusiasm led him to his first serious attempt at writing. At the age of seven he had written a five hundred word novel called The Curse of the Horse Race. *Since then he had contributed to a Boy Scoutish amateur publication called* The Pistol Troop Magazine. *He now [at 11], to quote the autobiography, "composed a deplorable poem in the metre of Hiawatha, named* The World to Come, *describing the experiences of the soul, immediately after death. The manuscript was shown to a friend of my father's who had a printing press on which he did much fine work. He conceived the kindly idea of producing some copies on hand-made paper and binding them for my father's birthday. They were distributed within the family. I do not know how many were made or how many survive, but the existence of this work is shameful to me."*

Sykes

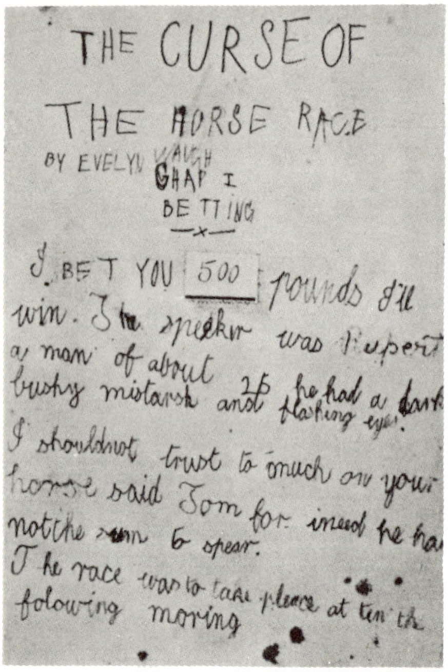

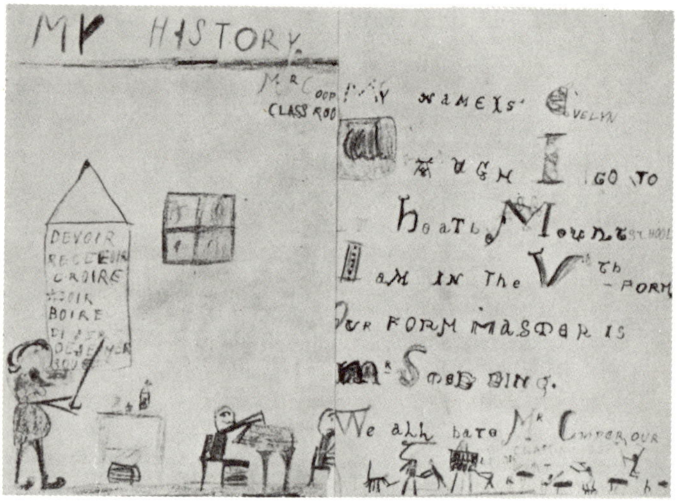

September, 1911; aged 7

MY HISTORY

My name is Evelyn Waugh I go to Heath Mount school I am in the Vth Form, Our Form Master is Mr Stebbing.

We all hate Mr Cooper, our arith master. It is the 7th day of the Winter Term which is my 4th. Today is Sunday so I am not at school. We allways have sausages for breakfast on Sundays I have been waching Lucy fry them they do look funny befor their kooked. Daddy is a Publisher he goes to Chapman and Hall office it looks a offely dull plase. I am just going to Church. Alec, my big brother has just gorn to Sherborne. The wind is blowing dreadfuly I am afraid that when I go up to Church I shall be blown away. I was not blown away after all.

June, 1912; aged 8

. . . Mother read me a article the following morning called 'How To Join the Navy' & I have made up my mind that I am going to be a "Merry Jack tar," if my eyes will pass Mother dous not think they will. If they do not I shall go board a 'Merchantman' for I must go to sea.

I am just go to make my little elaphant a coat.

If I should be a sailor bold
  I'd stand up on the deck
I'd lock my prisoners in the hold
  And make thier ship a wreck

Chap IV

Next morning Mrs Simmons came to see me & showed me some carvings she had done and Max came to tea with me. On the following morning I found I had the appendicitis & had an operation. Mother had a nurse in. This happened VI days ago for I have not been able to write this till now. I have had IX presants since the opeation cheafly soldiers.

This is a list of them

1. Pen 2 Gordon Hilanders 3. Camel corps 4. Mule battery 5. Caesar 6. Puzel 7. French soldier 8. Stories from Iliad 9. Stories of Roland.

A lot of presants have I had
  That makes me very, very glad
The soldiers I like best of all
  They look so very strong and tall.

The end of Vol. 1

About age 19.

June, 1913; aged 9

MY HISTORY
An Diary by E. Waugh

Vollume II

A Poem with Each Chapter

Chapter 1

I do not think that in Voll I I told you I go to Heath Mount school and that I am in Class VB. But even if I did I have told you now so I can go on. One year has past since Voll I and the date is June 21st 1913. I would have been the day of the sports only our cricket field is having a road cut through it.

Haward is on daily reports and got caned because 'Latin Very Poor!!!' was writen on his report.

Poor old Hayward had the cane
Which gave him tremendous pain

Chapter II

The lessons for today were Scripture $^7/_7$ History $^{19}/_{20}$ Spelling $^8/_{20}$ French $^{15}/_{18}$ Latin $^2/_2$. In French we had a ripping row. About Fletcher who we always tell 'My nose is bleeding. It's rude to look up peoples noses' which come from an old joke.

Chapter III

. . . After dinner I fought Geogan. . . .

August 18th 1914; aged 10

Journey

Bath

. . . We would have had a nice journey down if it was not for the presence of a drunk man in our carriage who kept on making wierd signs to his son who answered them with equally wierd gesticalations. When we got out we went to the Roman Baths and had a grand time there was an ass of a guide who showed the others round but Daddy and I did not, prefering our guide book to the repulsive look of that awful guide.

Christmas Term, 1914; aged 11

The miseries of scool

I have come to the conclusion that Heath Mount is the worst managed school in England.

We had 3 classics today which was something awful Mr Hynchcliffe is getting more obnoxious every day and his nose is getting pereceptably longer every day. He spent the greatest part of the first Latin in slobbering over the unfortunate Spenser who has the bad luck to be the favorite of a man like Hynchcliffe.

At Duty's call

Today was Mr Vernon's last day at school. At prayers Edwards gave him the watch we had subscribed to get. When the clapping had died away Mr Grenfell leaned forward 'Boys' he said in a husky sort of voice I had never heard him use before 'Mr Vernon has answered to his country's call. I know you all wish him a happy time and a safe return. Three cheers for him!' By now most of the chaps were blubbing and as the cheers rang out there were many chaps who hid behind each other so as not to be caught blubbing. Brown and I were playing cards in the afternoon in the dining room when the door opened and in came Mr Vernon. 'Goodby V.' cried Brown and then he was gone. That was the last of Mr Vernon that any of the chaps saw. I feel rather sorry now I used to rag him so.

1915; aged 11

Brighton

. . . In the evening we went to church. We struck a horrible low one. I was the only person who crossed myself and bowed to the alter. . . .

Easter Term, 1916; aged 12

My fight with Rostail

It being a wet day and it being above all Heath Mount we had to change our boots like a kindergarten. While engrossed in this exilerating occupation (in the company of a few others) Rostail entered and squatting temptingly on the edge of a basin proceeded to call me 'Wuffles.' I informed him that unless he refrain from using my name in a corupted form I would have to chastise him. He knowing that he was larger than me continued in the name whereupon I fulfiled my promise one hundredfold.

Heath Mount v Street cads

Hooper and I were going home when a kid about 10 yelled out 'Silly old green caps'! We chased him about 300 yards when out came a biger brother who came at us with the usual 'Ere d'you want a fight?' I answered yes and we set to with a mixture of wrestling and boxing ending in my victory.

War Work

On the first day of the holls we went to the Golders Green depot and asked for war work. They received us with open arms and the next day we set to work in cutting out soles for soldiers shoes. All the same I think I shall chuck it soon as it cuts into the holls so frightfully. Dove and Max are of the same opinion. Some of our soles were dreadfully cut out specially Maxwell's.

My shrine

I had started a shrine and mentioned this to the aunts who instantly promised to make me a frontal. Aunt Elsie is going to give me a crucifix when I'm confirmed and Aunt Trissie has given me two sweet brass bowls to fill with flowers.

Summer Term, 1916

Water Rat

We have had the most gorgeous rags with Cameron lately we have ever had with any master. We call him Water Rat to his face and make the desks skweak. One time after they creaked with extra vim he asked the reason. 'Well' said Brown 'You can come and sit here yourself and see if they don't creak.' Then Nobel found a washer and sugested it had come off the desk. It's almost as funny as Mr Vernon.

Finis Vol 2

Westcliffe-on-Sea, Saturday 12 August 1916

Started down with the carriage fairly empty but we soon filled up with vile Southend trippers. The tide was in so as soon as we arrived we left the hotel and went down to the front where I was suddenly struck by an overwhelming desire to bathe. We hurried back and greatly anoyed the domestics who were hard at work getting our room ready by opening our bags and driving them away but I had to change in the bathroom.

Monday 14 August 1916

. . . After dinner we went to the *Happy Valley* not a bad show but not a patch on the *Olympians*. The funny men were as good but the ladies—I mean females—were so aged and so cockney and so dreadfuly painted that they simply spoilt the whole show. They had quite a decent song called *Follow the Sergeant* but their choruses were ragged and out of tune. Still they gave us a happy and amusing evening . . .

Thursday 17 August 1916

We went up to Southend in the morning and spent a small fortune at the slots. Then we took a train to Prittlewell. It is a sweet little village with old houses with wobly roofs. And a mad lovely old church. There is still the little staircase in the wall leading up to where the Rood-Screne ought to be. There is a lovely black oak carved fourteenth century door. After tea I and Girlie then had a single at Babmington and were soon joined by Nora and Jessie and Mrs. Paine. Then Mrs Freeman turned up with an atrocity of about seven and spoilt our game. Whenever he 'no-served' she used to say, 'Never mind darling try again.' . . .

Saturday 19 August 1916

Girlie and I went to the Southend baths as the tide was out and I wanted to get in a bathe before I left but it was not too nice as the towels were filthy and the baths crowded. We had a tremendous rush to get the train and only just bundled into a carriage where there were *three* babies and two females who drank evil-smelling stout to revive themselves the whole time. We had some dificulty with the baggage at Golders Green as there was not a single taxi or cab but we got a tubeman to take them.

[Lancing] Saturday 25 September to Thursday 30th September 1920, aged 16

. . . In the debate on Sunday evening I opposed the motion that 'This House deplores the disrespect for age by modern youth.'

'Anyone, sir, who has toiled through the two volumes of dreaming spires and squalid gutters of *Sinister Street*, will have found on the last page a word of consolation for the time which it has taken him to reach it. Michael is told that there is no tragedy of age. Now this is in part true; I am the first person to agree with the honourable proposer in this statement of the immense gulf between youth and age. Age is of itself a tragedy, the most hideous and ubiquitous tragedy in the world.

'Age, like most virulent poisons, is an excellent stimulant in small doses. Its results are quite satisfactory until a man reaches his prime. Then it begins gradually to undo what it has done, torments, degrades and finally kills him.

'Most people, I suppose, would, like the honourable proposer, fix the prime of a man's life somewhere about thirty or thirty-five. Personally—I am open to conversion and do not hold this out as an essential article in my creed—I should place it at between fifteen and sixteen. It is then, it always seems to me, that his vitality is at its highest; he has greatest sense of the ludicrous and least sense of dignity. After that time, decay begins to set in. Possibly he attains to the "ungainly wisdom" of the Sixth Form and in that languorous atmosphere drinks deep of the opiate of specialization; possibly he attains to some abnormal form of muscular development and in his gyrations upon the football field loses his sense of the ludicrous; possibly he attains to an official position in the school and loses that still greater gift, his sense of humour. After these first steps on the downward path his decadence grows rapidly. Experience leads only to intellectual domesticity. Every day he wakes with his body a little more feeble, his brain a little more haphazard, his soul a little more damned. He becomes narrow and querulous and finally, after the puerility of old age, his jaw drops in the complete imbecility of death.

'And so we come to the one argument that can be urged for this motion. It is the nature of a fool to revere deformity, but it is the nature of a cad to sneer at it. It might be said that the least we can do is to pity these poor phantoms of ourselves. Well, magnanimity is a fine thing towards a beaten people but, as Gladstone found, it is a peculiarly dangerous one to a people who refuse to acknowledge defeat. Too few people follow the precedent of the men of Grantchester and 'up and shoot themselves when they get to feeling old.' They seem positively to glory in their affliction.

'It is easy enough to laugh at the great uncle's 'My-boy-when-I-was-your-age' manner. It is altogether too easy to laugh at terrible things. This pride in their deformity is one of the most hideous symptoms of their horrible disease. These grotesque, decaying old men, with the supreme arrogance of the impotent, take upon themselves to dictate to their youngers and betters how they should paint their pictures and write their sonnets and lay down their lives.

'The old men have just been having a war which the young men have had to fight. The result, to quote a distinguished preacher of a year or so ago, is that his generation is now one of broken and tired men. There are now practically only two generations—the very young and the very old.

'The result is the extraordinary boom of youth, which everyone must have noticed during the last few years. Every boy is writing about his school, every child about her doll's house, every baby about its bottle. The very young have gained an almost complete monopoly of bookshop, press, and picture gallery. Youth is coming into its own.

'Though, I suppose, most members of this house have now passed what I have fixed as the prime of their lives, I think that all can claim a place in the younger generation; and it is to this generation and to themselves that they will be doing a grave wrong if they allow this iniquitous motion to be carried. Respect, if it is to be of any value at all, must include an acknowledgement of superiority. If they pass this motion they will condemn themselves to their own consciences as the inferiors of a generation of narrow, decadent malformities. No generation has ever wreaked such disasters as the last. After numerous small indiscretions it has had its fling of a war which has left the civilized world pauperized, ravaged, shaken to its foundations. By passing this motion they will have registered their complete lack of confidence in themselves to do better, and their profound admiration for the perpetrators of this calamity, and I firmly contend that no man could exist if this was his true estimate of himself.

'I therefore appeal to this house not to let any scruples of maudlin sentimentality outweigh their pride in their own souls. Let them sympathize with the honourable proposer in the quite unjustifiable pessimism with which he appears to regard his own abilities; but let it end there. To vote for this motion would be to betray themselves and their whole generation.'

H. G. WELLS
born Sept. 21, 1866
Bromley, Kent, England

Age 12 and 13

The Desert Daisy . . . appears to be H. G. Wells's earliest surviving narrative of any length . . . [It] is quite typical of other surviving examples of Wellsian juvenilia in its elaborate simulation of all the features of a proper book . . . the several prefaces, the burlesque "Notices of the Press," the analytic table of contents and the concluding notes.

Ray

THE DESERT DAISY

Chapter 1

The King of Clubs was in his Council Chamber

There was with him. The Prince Bishop of Deuceace & the Commander in Chief of the Army & Navy.

They were playing at 'Push Pin.'

(To those who are ignorant I will explain that the game of Push Pin is a very simple game suitable for ordinary children, Idiots or Kings)

The King was striving to win with all his might (& that wasent much), perspiration streamed down his face, He was losing rapidly both temper & cash.

Suddenly an attendant entered & said; "Sire Two 'Eralds from the King of Spades desires to read an a-noucement to you"

Using a very bad word indeed (I am sorry to say.) the King seated himself on a throne hard by. The Commander in Chief (a type of physical power) placed himself on the right of the throne, the Prince Bishop (moral power) put himself on the left. The Heralds then entered.

After blowing his trumpet, the first Herald commenced;

"Whereas & not withstanding, Whereby & therefore! You Egroggetippe King of the once renowned & pussiant, now feeble & helpless Clubs!, You Egroggetippe (not-unjustly called the ace or ass of Clubs), Lord of the Minced Pie (one & indivisible)!

(at this point the King was seen to hand his sceptre to the Prince Bishop, He then gradually removed his crown & royal robes handing them to the same person). Meanwhile the Herald;

"You did send me or a man in the darkness of night into the Laundrey of our Sovereign Lord Methusala the Great! King of Spades &Governor General of the World with intent to do grevious harm unto our Sovereign Lord aforesaid by ripping up the stitches of our Sovereign Lords best britches or breeches (as some hath it) when hung out to dry thereby causing our said Sovereign Lord to imperil the future welfare of his soul by wearing his Everyday Britches (or Breeches as some hath it) on the Lord's day.

"We do demand herewith payment of the sum of twopence halfpenny (being the sum charged for renewing the stitches in the said Britches (or Breeches as some hath it) or we do declare immediately War. against thee & th——

The Herald never finished the sentence for the King (who as I remarked before, had been gradually removing his various incumberances) suddenly sprang at him with the fierceness of a tiger.

The other Herald soon joined in the combat & the Commander in chief followed his Example.

All was confusion for nearly an hour.

Meanwhile where was the Bishop.

Alas! The Crown sceptre & robes had been too much for his honesty.

Wrapping them up in his robe he had fled & was already a good mile away from the Kingdom of Clubs, in the Kingdom of spades.

***

The Combat raged fiercly for more than an hour in the Castle.

The Combatants were then separated & the King asked for his crown.

The Prince Bishop was not to be seen.

They searched high & low.

But they did not find either Prince Bishop or Crown.

What was to be done?

Notes **(at the end of the entire book)**

In the criticisms on the first edition of this great Work it was Remarked that many Glaring defects were to be seen in the illustrations, as on Page 33 where the King has his Crown on when he should not.

To those miserable fault finders I can only reply in the beatiful language of the Author in another of his works:

"The littery man must be emancipated from the chains & superstitious bounds of Criticism from the bonds of metre & from all social restrictions (except Copyright) & he must soar & soar like a captive balloon with the rope broke or a chained eagle on strike or a seagull on the loose or any other thing that conveys the idea of soaring such as a pig or a sewing machine & he'el soar & soar till he can't no more & he'd come down a cropper then in the lands of the (er) Whaddycalls & live happy ever after"

I am &c.
H. G. Wells

& then the end doth come
& joy comes with it
Busses unpublished plays

"Buss" was Wells's fictitious author and co-illustrator. HGW claimed he *was the editor, merely. In the "Editors Preface" he informs us that "He [Buss] after writing the last chapter of this book was seized with a lingering malady & has been obliged to retire to Colney Hatch [London's insane asylum] where he is forbidden to write again."*

Acclaimed as much for her intelligence and charm as for her verse, Phillis Wheatley was probably the best-known black person of her day on both sides of the Atlantic. She was brought to the U.S. on a slave ship [in 1761] and purchased by John Wheatley, a Boston merchant. She soon showed a remarkable aptitude for learning and was encouraged in her studies by Mrs. Wheatley.

Family Encyclopedia of American History

PHILLIS WHEATLEY

born about 1755
West Africa

TO THE UNIVERSITY OF CAMBRIDGE, WROTE IN 1767

While an intrinsic ardor bids me write
The muse doth promise to assist my pen.
'Twas but e'en now I left my native shore
The sable Land of error's darkest night.
There, sacred Nine! for you no place was found.
Parent of mercy, 'twas thy Powerful hand
Brought me in safety from the dark abode.

To you, Bright youths! he points the height of Heav'n.
To you, the knowledge of the depths profound.
Above, contemplate the ethereal space
And glorious Systems of revolving worlds.

Still more, ye sons of Science! you've receiv'd
The pleasing sound by messengers from heav'n,
The saviour's blood, for your redemption flows.
See Him, with hands stretched out upon the Cross!
Divine compassion in his bosom glows.
He hears revilers with oblique regard.
What Condescention in the Son of God!
When the whole human race by Sin had fal'n;
He deign'd to die, that they might rise again,
To live with him beyond the starry sky
Life without death, and Glory without End.———

Improve your privileges while they stay:
Caress, redeem each moment, which with haste
Bears on its rapid wing Eternal bliss.
Let hateful vice so baneful to the Soul,
Be still avoided with becoming care;
Suppress the sable monster in its growth,
Ye blooming plants of human race, divine
An Ethiop tells you, tis your greatest foe
Its transient sweetness turns to endless pain,
And brings eternal ruin on the Soul.

About age 12

As a girl.

To the PUBLICK.

AS it has been repeatedly ſuggeſted to the Publiſher, by Perſons, who have ſeen the Manuſcript, that Numbers would be ready to ſuſpect they were not really the Writings of PHILLIS, he has procured the following Atteſtation, from the moſt reſpectable Characters in *Boſton*, that none might have the leaſt Ground for diſputing their *Original*.

WE whoſe Names are under-written, do aſſure the World, that the POEMS ſpecified in the following Page,* were (as we verily believe) written by PHILLIS, a young Negro Girl, who was but a few Years ſince, brought an uncultivated Barbarian from *Africa*, and has ever ſince been, and now is, under the Diſadvantage of ſerving as a Slave in a Family in this Town. She has been examined by ſome of the beſt Judges, and is thought qualified to write them.[3]

His Excellency THOMAS HUTCHINSON, *Governor*,

The Hon. ANDREW OLIVER, *Lieutenant-Governor*.

The Hon. Thomas Hubbard,	*The Rev.* Charles Chauncy, *D.D.*
The Hon. John Erving,	*The Rev.* Mather Byles, *D.D.*
The Hon. James Pitts,	*The Rev* Ed. Pemberton, *D.D.*
The Hon. Harriſon Gray,	*The Rev.* Andrew Elliot, *D.D.*
The Hon. James Bowdoin,	*The Rev.* Samuel Cooper, *D.D.*
John Hancock, *Eſq*;	*The Rev. Mr.* Samuel Mather,
Joſeph Green, *Eſq*;	*The Rev. Mr.* John Moorhead,
Richard Carey, *Eſq*;	*Mr.* John Wheatley, *her Maſter*.

N. B. The original Atteſtation, ſigned by the above Gentlemen, may be ſeen by applying to *Archibald Bell*, Bookſeller, No. 8, *Aldgate-Street*.

* The Words "*following Page*," allude to the Contents of the Manuſcript Copy, which are wrote at the Back of the above Atteſtation.

JAMES ABBOTT McNEILL WHISTLER
born July 11, 1834
Lowell, Mass.

Sunday, for the young Whistler boys, began on Saturday afternoon, when their Sunday clothes were inspected, their pockets emptied of anything which might distract from the solemnity of the seventh day, their toys put away until Monday, and their heads washed in preparation for church. . . .

Of her son Anna wrote in her journal: "I do not like to make comparisons for Jemie's eagerness to attain all his desires for information and his fearlessness often make him offend us because we love him too tenaciously to be reconciled to his appearing less amiable than he really is. The officers [of the Czar], however, seemed to find amusement in his remarks in French or English. . . ."

Weintraub

Age 10

To My Mother, July 11, 1844

They tell us of an Indian tree,
Which, howsoe'r the sun and sky
May tempt its boughs to wander free
And shoot and blossom, wide and high,
Far better loves to bend its arms
Downward gain, to that dear earth
From which the life that fills and warms
Its grateful being first had birth.
'Tis thus, though wooed by flattering friends
And fed with fame (if fame it be),
This heart, my own dear mother, tends
With Love's true instinct back to thee.

On my tenth birthday, your little James.

Duck drawn at age 4.

Whistler flunked out of West Point. In later life he liked to repeat: "Had silicon been a gas, I would have been a major general."

This somewhat allegorical sketch which appeared in The Rover *[a New York magazine], April 20, 1844, [probably written in 1835], appears to describe Whitman's sisters and some of his brothers. Mary, Louisa, Andrew Jackson, George Washington, and Thomas Jefferson correspond in actual names as well as in relative ages to Whitman's sisters and three of his brothers. . . . The baby girl who died a month after her birth could be the child born to Whitman's parents who died in 1825 a few months after its birth and before it was given a name.*

Bucke

WALT WHITMAN
born May 31, 1819
West Hills (near Huntington)
L.I., N.Y.

MY BOYS AND GIRLS

About age 16

Though a bachelor, I have several girls and boys that I consider my own. Little Louisa, the fairest and most delicate of human blossoms, is a lovely niece—a child that the angels themselves might take to the beautiful land, without tasting death. A fat, hearty, rosy-cheeked youngster, the girl's brother, comes in also for a good share of my affection. Never was there such an imp of mischief! Falls and bumps hath he every hour of the day, which affect him not, however. Incessant work occupies his mornings, noons and nights; and dangerous is it, in the room with him, to leave anything unguarded, which the most persevering activity of a stout pair of dumpy hands can destroy.

What would you say, dear reader, were I to claim the nearest relationship to George Washington, Thomas Jefferson and Andrew Jackson? Yet such is the case, as I aver upon my word. Several times has the immortal Washington sat on my shoulders, his legs dangling down upon my breast, while I trotted for sport down a lane or over the fields. Around the waist of the sagacious Jefferson have I circled one arm, while the fingers of the other have pointed him out words to spell. And though Jackson is (strange paradox!) considerably older than the other two, many a race and tumble have I had with him—and at this moment I question whether, in a wrestle, he would not get the better of me, and put me flat.

One of my children—a child of light and loveliness—sometimes gives me rise to many uneasy feelings. She is a very beautiful girl, in her fourteenth year. Flattery comes too often to her ears. From the depths of her soul I now and then see misty revealings of thought and wish, that are not well. I see them through her eyes and in the expression of her face.

It is a dreary thought to imagine what may happen, in the future years, to a handsome, merry child—to gaze far down the vista, and see the dim phantoms of Evil standing about with nets and temptations—to witness, in the perspective, purity gone, and the freshness of youthful innocence rubbed off, like the wasted bloom of flowers. Who, at twenty-five or thirty years of age, is without many memories of wrongs done, and mean or wicked deeds performed?

As a young man

Right well do I love many more of my children. H. is my "summer child." An affectionate fellow is he—with merits and with faults, as all boys have—and it has come to be that should his voice no more salute my ears, nor his face my eyes, I might not feel as happy as I am. M., too a volatile lively young gentleman, is an acquaintance by no means unpleasant to have by my side. Perhaps M. is a little too rattlesome, but he has qualities which have endeared him to me much during our brief acquaintance. Then there is J.H., a sober, good-natured youth, whom I hope I shall always number among my friends. Another H. has lately come among us—too large, perhaps, and too near manhood, to be called one of my *children.* I know I shall love him well when we become better acquainted—as I hope we are destined to be.

Blessings on the young! And for those whom I have mentioned in the past lines, oh, may the development of their existence be spared any sharp stings of grief or pangs of remorse! Had I any magic or superhuman power, one of the first means of its use would be to insure the brightness and beauty of their lives. Alas! that there should be sin, and pain, and agony so abundantly in the world!—that these young creatures—wild, frolocksome, and fair—so dear to me all of them, those connnected by blood, and those whom I like for themselves alone—alas, that they should merge in manhood and womanhood the fragrance and purity of their youth!

But shall I forget to mention *one* other of my children? For of him I can speak with mingled joy and sadness. For him there is no fear in the future. The clouds shall not darken over his young head—nor the taint of wickedness corrupt his heart—nor any poignant remorse knaw him inwardly for wrongs done. No weary bane of body or soul—no disappointed hope—no unrequited love—no feverish ambition—no revenge, nor hate, nor pride—no struggling with poverty, nor temptation, nor death—may ever trouble him more. He lies low in the grave-yard on the hill. Very beautiful was he—and the promise of an honorable manhood shone brightly in him—and sad was the gloom of his passing away. We buried him in the early summer. The scent of the apple-blossoms was thick in the air—and all animated nature seemed overflowing with delight and motion. But the fragrance and the animation made us feel a deadlier sickness in our souls. Oh, bitter day! I pray God there may come to me but few such!

And there is one again:—and she, too, must be in the Land of Light, so tiny and so frail. A mere month only after she came into the world, a little shroud was prepared, and a little coffin built, and they placed the young infant in her tomb. It was not a sad thing—we wept not, nor were our hearts heavy.

I bless God that he has ordained the beautiful youth and spring time! In all the wondrous harmony of nature, nothing shows more wisdom and benevolence than that necessity which makes us grow up from so weak and helpless a being as a new-born infant, through all the phases of sooner and later childhood, to the neighborhood of maturity, and so to maturity itself. Thus comes the sweetness of the early seasons—the bud and blossom time of life. Thus comes the beauty which we love to look upon—the faces and lithe forms of young children.

May it not be well, as we grow old, to make ourselves often fresh, and childlike, and merry with those who are so fresh and merry? We *must* grow old—for immutable time will have it so. Gray hairs will be sown in our heads, and wrinkles in our faces; but we can yet keep *the within* cheerful and youthful—and that is the great secret of warding off all that is unenviable in old age. The fountain flowing in its sweetness forever, and the bloom undying upon the heart, and the thoughts young, whatever the body may be—we can bid defiance to the assaults of time, and composedly wait for the hour of our taking away.

TENNESSEE WILLIAMS
born March 26, 1911
Columbus, Miss.

One afternoon I heard a child screaming in the alley back of this street. Some young hoods were, for some unknown reason, throwing rocks at a plump little girl. I went to her defense; we took flight into her house and all the way up to the attic. Thus began my closest childhood friendship which ripened into a romantic attachment.

I was then eleven, Hazel was nine. We started spending every afternoon in her attic. Being imaginative children, we invented many games, but the chief diversion that I recall was illustrating stories that we made up. Hazel drew better than I and I made up better stories. . . .

In my adolescence in St. Louis, at the age of sixteen, several important events in my life occurred. It was in the sixteenth year that I wrote "The Vengeance of Nitocris" and received my first publication in a magazine and the magazine was Weird Tales. *The story wasn't published till June of 1928.*

Memoirs

Age 16

THE VENGEANCE OF NITOCRIS

Tennessee as a high school lad.

Hushed were the streets of many-peopled Thebes. Those few who passed through them moved with the shadowy fleetness of bats near dawn, and bent their faces from the sky as if fearful of seeing what in their fancies might be hovering there. Weird, high-noted incantations of a wailing sound were audible through the barred doors. On corners groups of naked and bleeding priests cast themselves repeatedly and with loud cries upon the rough stones of the walks. Even dogs and cats and oxen seemed impressed by some strange menace and foreboding and cowered and slunk dejectedly. All Thebes was in dread. And indeed there was cause for their dread and for their wails of lamentation. A terrible sacrilege had been committed. In all the annals of Egypt none more monstrous was recorded.

Five days had the altar fires of the god of gods, Osiris, been left unburning. Even for one moment to allow darkness upon the altars of the god was considered by the priests to be a great offense against him. . . . It was an unspeakable sacrilege. . . .

But how might it be avenged? That was the question high lords and priests debated. Pharaoh alone had committed the sacrilege. It was he, angered because the bridge, which he had spent five years in constructing so that one day he might cross the Nile in his chariot as he had once boasted that he would do, had been swept away by the rising waters. Raging with anger, he had flogged the priests from the temple. He had barred the temple doors and with his own breath had blown out the sacred candles. He had defiled the hallowed altars with the carcasses of beasts. Even, it was said in low, shocked whispers, in a mock ceremony of worship he had burned the carrion of a hyena, most abhorrent of all beasts of Osiris, upon the holy altar of gold which even the most high of priests forbore to lay naked hands upon!

Surely, even though he be Pharaoh, ruler of all Egypt and holder of the golden eagle, he could not be permitted to commit such violent sacrileges without punishment from man. The god Osiris was waiting for them to inflict that punishment, and if they failed to do it, upon them would come a scourge from heaven.

Standing before the awed assembly of nobles, the high Kha Semblor made a gesture with his hands. A cry broke from those who watched. Sentence had been delivered. Death had been pronounced as doom for the pharaoh. The heavy, barred doors were shoved open. The crowd came out, and within an hour a well-organized mob passed through the streets of Thebes, directed for the palace of the pharaoh. Mob justice was to be done.

Within the resplendent portals of the palace the pharaoh, ruler of all Egypt, watched with tightened brow the orderly but menacing approach of the mob. He divined their intent. But was he not their pharaoh? He could contend with gods, so why should he fear mere dogs of men?

A woman clung to this stiffened arm. She was tall and as majestically handsome as he. A garb of linen, as brilliantly golden as the sun, entwined her body closely and bands of jet were around her throat and forehead. She was the fair and well-loved Nitocris, sister of the pharaoh.

"Brother, brother!" she cried, "light the fires! Pacify the dogs! They come to kill you."

Only more stern grew the look of the pharaoh. He thrust aside his pleading sister, and beckoned to the attendants.

"Open the doors!"

Startled, trembling, the men obeyed.

The haughty lord of Egypt drew his sword from its sheath. He slashed the air with a stroke that would have severed stone. . . .

The mob, led by the black-robed priests and nobles who had arrived at the foot of the steps, now fell back before the stunning, magnificent defiance of their giant ruler. They felt like demons who had assailed the heavens and had been abashed and shamed by the mere sight of that which they had assailed. A hush fell over them. Their upraised arms faltered and sank down. A moment more and they would have fallen to their knees.

What happened then seemed nothing less than a miracle. In his triumph and exultation, the pharaoh had been careless of the crumbling edges of the steps. Centuries old, there were sections of these steps which were falling apart. Upon such a section had the gold-sandaled foot of the pharaoh descended, and it was not strong enough to sustain his great weight. With a scuttling sound it broke loose. A gasp came from the mob—the pharaoh was about to fall. He was palpitating, wavering in the air, fighting to retain his balance. He looked as if he were grappling with some monstrous, invisible snake, coiled about his gleaming body. A hoarse cry burst from his lips; his sword fell; and then his body thudded down the steps in a series of somersaults, and landed at the foot, sprawled out before the gasping mob. For a moment there was breathless silence. And then came the shout of a priest.

"A sign from the god!"

That vibrant cry seemed to restore the mob to all of its wolflike rage. They surged forward. The struggling body of the pharaoh was lifted up and torn to pieces by their clawing hands and weapons. Thus was the god Osiris avenged.

A week later another large assembly of persons confronted the brilliant-pillared palace. This time they were there to acknowledge a ruler, not to slay one. The week before they had rended the pharaoh and now they were proclaiming his sister empress. Priests had declared that it was the will of the gods that she should succeed her brother. She was famously beautiful, pious, and wise. The people were not reluctant to accept her.

When she was borne down the steps of the palace in her rich litter, after the elaborate ceremony of the coronation had been concluded, she responded to the cheers of the multitude with a smile which could not have appeared more amicable and gracious. None might know from that smile upon her beautiful carmined lips that within her heart she was thinking, "These are the people who slew my brother. Ah, god Issus, grant me power to avenge his death upon them!"

Not long after the beauteous Nitocris mounted the golden throne of Egypt, rumors were whispered of some vast, mysterious enterprise being conducted in secret. A large number of slaves were observed each dawn to embark upon barges and to be carried down the river to some unknown point, where they labored through the day, returning after dark. The slaves were Ethiopians, neither able to speak nor to understand the Egyptian language, and therefore no information could be gotten from them by the curious as to the object of their mysterious daily excursions. The general opinion, though, was that the pious queen was having a great temple constructed to the gods and that when it was finished, enormous public banquets would be held within it before its dedication. . . .

It was late in the spring when the excursions of the workmen were finally discontinued. . . . It was a temple to the god Osiris. It had been built by the queen probably that she might partly atone for the sacrilege of her brother and deliver him from some of the torture which he undoubtedly suffered. It was to be dedicated within the month by a great banquet. All the nobles and the high priests of Osiris, of which there were a tremendous number, were to be invited. . . .

The day of the dedication, which was to be followed by the night of banqueting, was a gala holiday. At noon the guests of the empress formed a colorful assembly upon the bank of the river. Gayly draped barges floated at their moorings until preparations should be completed for the transportation of the guests to the temple. . . .

When the queen arrived, clamorous shouts rang deafeningly in her ears. She responded with charming smiles and gracious bows. The most discerning observer could not have detected anything but the greatest cordiality and kindliness reflected in her bearing toward those around her. . . .

When the concluding processional chant had been completed, the queen summoned a number of burly slaves, and by several iron rings attached to its outer edges they lifted up a large slab of the flooring, disclosing to the astonished guests the fact that the scene of the banquet was to be an immense subterranean vault.

Such vaults were decidedly uncommon among the Egyptians. The idea of feasting in one was novel and appealing. Thrilled exclamations came from the eager, excited crowd and they pressed forward to gaze into the depths, now brightly illuminated. They saw a room beneath them almost as vast in size as the amphitheater in which they were standing. It was filled with banquet tables upon which were set the most delectable foods and rich, sparkling wines in an abundance that would satiate the banqueters of Bacchus. . . . Perhaps even if they had known the hideous menace that lurked in those gay-draped walls beneath them, they would still have found the allurement of the banquet scene difficult to resist. . . .

With increasing wildness the banquet continued into the middle of the night. Some of the banqueters, disgustingly gluttonous still gorged themselves at the greasy tables. Others lay in drunken stupor, or lolled amorously with the slave-girls. But most of them, formed in a great, irregular circle, skipped about the room in a barbaric, joy-mad dance, dragging and tripping each other in uncouth merriment and making the hall ring with their ceaseless shouts, laughter and hoarse song.

When the hour had approached near to midnight, the Queen, who had sat like one entranced, arose from the cushioned dais. One last intent survey she gave to the crowded room of banquet. It was a scene which she wished to imprint permanent upon her mind. Much pleasure might she derive in the future by recalling that picture, and then imagining what came afterward—stark, searing terror rushing in upon barbarious joy! . . .

With a motion, she directed them to place the slab of rock in its tight-fitting socket. With a swift noiseless hoist and lowering, they obeyed the command. The Queen bent down. There was no change in the boisterous sounds from below. Nothing was yet suspected. . . .

Slowly, lusting upon every triumph-filled second of this time of ecstasy, she turned her face down again to the formidable bar in her hand. Deliberately she drew it back to its limit. This was the lever that opened the wall in the banquet vault. It gave entrance to death. Only the other bar now intervened between the banqueters, probably still reveling undisturbed, and the dreadful fate which she had prepared for them. Upon this bar now her jeweled fingers clutched. Savagely this time she pulled it; then with the litheness of a tiger she sprang to the edge of the pier. She leaned over it and stared down into the inky rush of the river. A new sound she heard above the steady flow. It was the sound of waters suddenly diverted into a new channel—an eager, plunging sound. Down to the hall of revelry they were rushing—these savage waters—bringing terror and sudden death.

A cry of triumph, wild and terrible enough to make even the hearts of the brutish slaves turn cold, now broke from the lips of the Queen. The pharaoh was avenged.

And even he must have considered his avenging adequate had he been able to witness it. . . .

With the ferocity of a lion springing into the arena of a Roman amphitheater to devour the gladiators set there for its delectation, the black water plunged in. Furiously it surged over the floor of the room, sweeping tables before it and sending its victims, now face to face with their harrowing doom, into a hysteria of terror. In a moment that icy, black water had risen to their knees, although the room was vast. Some fell instantly dead from the shock, or were trampled upon by the desperate rushing of the mob. Tables were clambered upon. Lamps and candles were extinguished. Brilliant light rapidly faded to twilight, and a ghastly dimness fell over the room as only the suspended lanterns remained lit. And what a scene of chaotic and hideous horror might a spectator have beheld! The gorgeous trumpetry of banquet invaded by howling waters of death! Gayly dressed merrymakers caught suddenly in the grip of terror! Gasps and screams of the dying amid tumult and thickening dark!

What more horrible vengeance could Queen Nitocris have conceived than this banquet of death? Not Diablo himself could be capable of anything more fiendishly artistic. Here in the temple of Osiris those nobles and priests who had slain the pharaoh in expiation of his sacrilege against Osiris had now met their deaths. And it was in the waters of the Nile, material symbol of the god Osiris, that they had died. It was magnificent in its irony!

I would be content to end this story here if it were but a story. However, it is not merely a story, as you will have discerned before now if you have been a student of the history of Egypt. Queen Nitocris is not a fictitious personage. In the annals of ancient Egypt she is no inconspicuous figure. Principally responsible for her prominence is her monstrous revenge upon the slayers of her brother, the narration of which I have just concluded. Glad would I be to end this story here; for surely anything following must be in the nature of an anticlimax. However, being not a mere story-teller here, but having upon me also the responsibility of a historian, I feel obligated to continue the account to the point where it was left off by Herodotus, the great Greek historian. And, therefore, I add this postscript, anticlimax though it be.

The morning of the day after the massacre in the temple, the guests of the Queen not having made their return, the citizens of Thebes began to glower with dark suspicions. Rumor came to them through divers channels that something of a most extraordinary and calamitous nature had occurred at the scene of the banquet during the night. Some had it that the temple had collapsed upon the revelers and all had been killed. However, this theory was speedily dispelled when a voyager from down the river reported having passed the temple in a perfectly firm condition but declared that he had seen no signs of life about the place—only the brightly canopied boats, drifting at their moorings.

Uneasiness steadily increased throughout the day. Sage persons recalled the great devotion of the Queen toward her dead brother, and noted that the guests at the banquet of last night had been composed almost entirely of those who had participated in his slaying.

When in the evening the Queen arrived in the city, pale, silent, and obviously nervous, threatening crowds blocked the path of her chariot, demanding roughly an explanation of the disappearance of her guests. Haughtily she ignored them and lashed forward the horses of her chariot, pushing aside the tight mass of people. Well she knew, however, that her life would be doomed as soon as they confirmed their suspicions. She resolved to meet her inevitable death in a way that befitted one of her rank, not at the filthy hands of a mob.

Therefore, upon her entrance into the palace she ordered her slaves to fill instantly her boudoir with hot and smoking ashes. When this had been done, she went to the room, entered it, closed the door and locked it securely, and then flung herself down upon a couch in the center of the room. In a short time the scorching heat and the suffocating thick fumes of the smoke overpowered her. Only her beautiful dead body remained for the hands of the mob.

My third year at the University of Missouri was relatively colorless. My adored Smitty did not return to school at all, and the roommate I had was of no interest to me. In the spring of that year, I had a poignant and innocent little affair with a very charming girl named Anna Jean. My feeling for her was romantic. She was very pretty, she lived just across the street at the Alpha Chi Omega sorority and she had a delightful sense of humor. I wrote a little poem about her, well, I think several. Here's one:

Memoirs

About age 20

Can I forget
the night you waited
beside your door—
could it have been more
plainly stated?—
for something more.

You spoke a rhyme
about young love
while we stood
breathing the rain-sweet
fragrance
of the wood.

I was a fool, not
knowing what
you waited for.
And then you smiled
and quietly
shut the door.

Margaret Edwards, about my own age, was at that time my closest friend in Red Bank. . . . The diary, bound in leather, that she gave me when I was going away, had "My Trip Abroad" stamped on the cover.
I crossed with my family on the North German Line König Albert. *At the dock, I bought a riddle-book, which must have been British. Two of the riddles, because of their badness, have remained in my mind ever since: "Why is a needy pauper like a man getting down a pork pie from the top shelf?" Answer: "Because he is a pore creature." "What is the difference between a beggar and the Tsar of Russia?" Answer: "The Tsar issues manifestoes, and the beggar manifests toes without his shoes." This joke-book is forever embedded in the memory of my first excitement at going to Europe.*
On the boat was William Randolph Hearst, of whose sinister reputation I had been constantly hearing and reading. He resembled the caricatures I had seen of him. Tall and stooping, gray-eyed and gray-faced, he walked the deck by himself.

A Prelude

EDMUND WILSON
born May 8, 1895
Red Bank. N.J.

MY TRIP ABROAD

Age 13

May 8, 1908, The Azore Islands

In the afternoon we passed three of the Azores. First we passed Fayal, then Peko. On Peko is Mount Peko 7613 ft. high, the top of which is in the clouds. After that we saw San Jorge, which was very beautiful. . . .
A lady told us she had three sons who had never seen the Azores, all boys.

May 11th, 1908, Gibraltar

Today we stopped at Gibraltar. The rock looked exactly like the advertisement for the Prudential Life Insurance Company.

May 11th, 1908, Spain, Linea

A guide showed us around. Begging is allowed in Spain and a lot of bogus beggars came around us when we got out of the carriage.

May 15-19, Naples

We arrived at Naples Friday. Naples is a very dirty place, full of howling dagoes. We visited the Aquarium, which, though small, has many interesting fish, including several octopi which we watched a long time. . . . Then we saw the things taken from Pompeii, musical instruments, wall paintings, eggs, grain, olives, latches of doors and other things. The theater tickets were very interesting: there were skulls for dead heads, violins for orchestra seats, pigeons for the gallery and round things for the slaves and ordinary seats. There were also fishes no one knows about. In the next room was Pompeii in miniature, which we did not have time to examine because the guide told us that the museum closed in a few minutes.

May 16, Pompeii

When we first got to Pompeii, we got a very poor guide, but walked until we got to a little post-card store where a man telephoned for a guide. We ate our lunch while waiting for the guide to come and when he came we felt much better.
First he showed us the civil forum and the temple of Mercury, where there was a dining table. In the olden time, when the priests had eaten as much as they could, they leaned over and threw up in a trench where there was running water, and began all over again. We saw the public washing place, in which was the statue of the goddess of washing.
The temple of Isis and the temple of Apollo were very interesting. The temple of Apollo has a statue which was used as an oracle. After the people had paid to hear it speak, a priest would talk through a brass tube which went into the head of the statue and made it look as if it spoke. . . .

After a while we took two chairs which were carried by two men, which we took turns riding in. We finally came back very tired, the only drawback being that the chicken sandwiches were all hide.

Florence

That afternoon Uncle Reuel took us to three moving picture shows [one a film of Dante's *Inferno*]. The next day everything was open, and we went to the galleries. One was all most could stand, but Sandy, Uncle Reuel and myself went to the Pitti gallery principally to see the Titian of the redheaded girl with nothing on but her hair.

Venice

All night the hour is told by electric figures. The square is full of pigeons, which are so tame that they perch on your hands and hat to eat corn. These are the famous pigeons of Saint Mark's. One day we went out in a gondola to the Adriatic Sea, where we bathed. The Adriatic was full of little crabs that you had to be very careful about stepping on or annoying in any way.

Murano

At Murano we went to the glass factory and watched them make glass. They made a goblet and a vase while we watched them and ended up with a bomb which was a large glass bubble burst.

Burano

From Murano we went to Burano, where the lace factories are. The lace there is all made by hand by little girls who at a certain age are all made to work on making lace.

Vienna

Vienna is a very beautiful city, though there is not much to see there.

Karlsbad

When we first came, we stayed at the Grand Hotel Pupp, but after a day we found a "Logis" on the hill called the Villa Victoria, Telegraf and König von England.

Mr. Geller, who owns the place, has a small Heinie dog called "Sleepfer." Karlsbad is full of Heinie dogs. . . .

In Karlsbad they have a cracker about a foot in diameter called Karlsbader Oblaten, they are very good. . . .

There is music all the time in Karlsbad, and at night Mr. Strauss came down and held a concert.

Nuremburg

The great sight in Nuremburg is the tower. . . .

On the first floor of the tower are many torture machines. There are great wooden petticoats for drunkards and gamblers, a confessor's chair full of spikes, masks for scolding women, wooden collars for extravagant women, a ducking machine for bakers who gave short weight, a rack for stretching purposes, a wheel with a knife blade on it which cut the victim up very small and very slowly, a cradle full of spikes in which the victim was rocked to death, a pear which when put in the mouth swells up to four times its ordinary size, thus slowly cracking the victim's head open, and a flute of iron which was fastened to the fingers and mouths of musicians who played badly.

Cologne

There was very little to see in Cologne, and it was very dreary there so we soon left it. Nearly all the cologne is made in Cologne.

I know a lot of poetry and singing. I can't sing but. I sing too far. I can't stop at the end for joy.

Unknown 5 year old
Australian boy

Special thanks to:

Deborah A. Aspen, Frank Brady, Brooklyn College Library, Marie Annick Brown, Mike Brown, City College Library, Columbia University Libraries, Robert Crumb, Dwight Dobbins, Jim Drougas, Jules Feiffer, Allen Ginsberg, Mary Hemingway, Paul Krassner, Gloria Lew, Fanny Mailer, Norman Mailer, J.R. McNeilie, Metropolitan Toronto Public Libraries, Daniel Moshenberg, Malcolm Muggeridge, New York Public Library, Anaïs Nin, Ohio State University Libraries, Lawrence E. Patterson, Aurelia Schober Plath, Rachel Polk, Deborah Robbins, Jeff Rund, Art Spiegelman, James Stern, Tania Stern, I.F. Stone, Robert A. Tibbetts, Helen Thurber, University of Toronto Libraries, Yale University Library.

Credits:

ALEICHEM *List:* Aleichem, S. *The Great Fair.* Trans. by Tamara Kahana. New York: Noonday, 1955.

AUSTEN *Intro:* Pinion, F.B. *A Jane Austen Companion.* London: Macmillan, 1975.

BEATLES *Intro 1:* Fisher, R.B. *Musical Prodigies.* New York: Association Press, 1973. *Lennon's pieces: Mersey Beat.* Drawing by Lennon. *Intro 2 & Letter:* Davies, H. *The Beatles.* New York: McGraw-Hill, 1968.

BEETHOVEN *Intro:* Behrend, W. *Ludwig van Beethoven's Pianoforte Sonatas.* London: Dent, 1927. *Music:* Nottebohm, G. *Thematisches Verzeichniss . . . Ludwig van Beethoven.* Leipzig, 1868. *Letter:* Anderson, E. *Letters of Beethoven.* New York: St. Martins Press, 1965. *Silhouette:* Neesen. *Engraving:* Neidl after Stainhauser.

BEHAN O'Connor, U. *Brendan.* New York: Prentice Hall, 1970.

BLAKE *Intro 1:* Lister, R. *William Blake.* New York: Ungar, 1967. *Poem: Oxford Blake.* 1913. *Afterword:* Bateson, F.W. *Selected Poems of William Blake.* London: Heinemann, 1964. *Intro 2:* Todd, R. *William Blake: the Artist.* London: Studio Vista-Dutton, 1971. & Wright, T. *Life of William Blake,* vol. 1. London: 1929. *Intro 3:* Malkin, B.H. *A Father's Memories of His Child.* (Reprinted in Symons, A. *William Blake.* London: Constable, 1907.) *Afterword:* Lister, *op. cit.*

BRYANT *Intro & Afterword:* Brown, C.H. *William Cullen Bryant.* New York: Scribners, 1971.

BURNS *Poem: Commonplace Book.* Carbondale, Ill.: S. Illinois U. Press, 1966.

CARROLL *Poem:* Reprinted in Hudson, D. *Lewis Carroll.* London: Constable, 1954. *Drawing:* Reprinted in *The Rectory Umbrella and Mischmasch.* New York: Dover, 1971.

CAVETT *Intro & Diary:* Cavett, D., & Porterfield, C. *Cavett.* New York: Harcourt, Brace & Jovanovich, 1974.

CHEKHOV *Letter:* Koteliansky, S.S., & Tomlinson, P. *The Life and Letters of Anton Tchekhov.* London: Cassell, 1925. *Intro 2:* Koteliansky, *op. cit.,* & Simmons, E. *Chekhov.* New York: Little Brown, 1962. *Essay:* Translated for this book by Rachel Polk and Gloria Lew. *Afterword:* Simmons, *op cit.*

CHOPIN *Intro:* Boucourechliev, A. *Chopin.* New York: Studio-Viking, 1963.

CHURCHILL *Intro:* Churchill, W. *My Early Life.* Toronto: Macmillan, 1930.

CLIVE Timbs, J. *School-Days of Eminent Men.* Columbus, Ohio: Follet, Foster & Co., 1860.

COHAN *Intro & Song:* McCabe, J. *George M. Cohan.* New York: Doubleday, 1973.

COLERIDGE *Complete Poetical Works of S.T. Coleridge.* Oxford: Clarendon, 1912.

DICKINSON *Intro 1 & Afterword 1:* Sewall, R.B. *The Life of Emily Dickinson,* vol. 2. New York: Farrar, Straus & Giroux, 1974. *Valentine 1:* Johnson. T.H., ed. *The Complete Poems of Emily Dickinson.* New York: Little Brown, 1960. *Intro 2, Valentine 2, Intro 3 & Afterword 3:* Sewall, *op. cit. Valentine 3:* Johnson, *op. cit.*

DOYLE *Intro:* Pearson, H. *Conan Doyle.* New York: Walker, 1961.

DU BOIS *Intro:* Lester, J., ed. *The Seventh Son,* vol. 1. New York: Vintage, 1971.

DULLES *Story:* Privately published in Washington, D.C., 1902.

DÜRER *Intro:* White, C. *Durer, the Artist and His Drawing.* London: Phaedon, 1971.

EDDY Peel, R. *Mary Baker Eddy. Vol. 1: The Years of Discovery.* New York: Holt, Rinehart & Winston, 1966.

ELIOT Eliot, V., Ed. *Poems Written in Early Youth.* New York: Farrar, Straus & Giroux, 1967.

ELLINGTON *Intro:* Ulanov, B. *Duke Ellington.* New York: Plenum, 1972 (reprint). *Music:* Tempo Music Co., New York.

FISCHER Via Frank Brady.

FLEMING *Intro:* Stephens, L. *Dictionary of National Biography.* 1921 ed.

FOSTER *Intros & Music:* Foster, M. *Biography. Songs and Musical Compositions of Stephen Foster.* Pittsburgh, 1896. *Letters:* Howard, J.T. *Stephen Foster.* New York: Tudor, 1943.

FRANKLIN *Intro:* Fleming, T., ed. *Benjamin Franklin: A Biography in His Own Words.* New York: Newsweek, 1972.

FREUD *Intro:* Jones, E. *The Life and Work of Sigmund Freud,* vol. 1. New York: Basic Books, 1953. *Letter:* Freud, E.L., ed. *Letters of Sigmund Freud, 1873-1939.* Trans. by Tania & James Stern. London: Hogarth, 1970.

GANDHI Bhatia, K. *Indira.* New York: Praeger, 1974.

GINSBERG *Poem: Columbia Jester Review,* May 1944.

GOETHE *Intro:* Duntzer, H. *Life of Goethe,* vol. 1. London: Macmillan, 1883. *Letters:* Bell, E. *Early and Miscellaneous Letters of J.W. Goethe.* London: George Bell, 1884. *Oil painting:* Anton Johann Kern.

GOGOL *Intro & Poem translation:* Troyat, H. *Divided Soul: The Life of Gogol.* New York: Minerva, 1975. *Afterword:* Debreczeny, P. *N. Gogol and His Contemporaneous Critics.* New York: American Philosophical Society, 1966.

GOLDSMITH From her manuscript narrative of Goldsmith's early life. In the British Museum: Percy Papers Add. MS. 42516, ff. 20-26.

HAMILTON *Intros:* Kline, M.-J. *Alexander Hamilton: A Biography in His Own Words.* New York: Newsweek, 1973. *Letter 1:* Reprinted in *The Papers of Alexander Hamilton,* vol. 1. New York: Columbia U. Pr., 1961. *Letter 2: Royal Danish-American Gazette,* Oct. 3, 1772. (Reprinted in Atherton, G. *A Few of Hamilton's Letters.* New York: Macmillan, 1903.)

HEARST Winkler, J.K. *W.R. Hearst: A New Appraisal.* New York: Hastings, 1955.

HEMINGWAY *Intro & Story (reprint):* Montgomery, C. *Hemingway in Michigan.* New York: Fleet, 1966.

HITLER *Intro 1 & Drawing of teacher:* Maser, W. *Hitler's Letters and Notes.* New York: Bantam, 1976. *Intro 2:* Payne, R. *Life and Death of Adolf Hitler.* New York: Praeger, 1973. *Sketches:* Kubitzek, A. *Adolf Hitler, Mein Jugendfreund.* Graz, Stocker, 1953.

POPE JOHN XXIII *Intro:* Johnson, P. *Pope John XXIII.* New York: Little Brown, 1974. *Journal: Pope John XXIII: Journal of a Soul.* London: Geoffrey Chapman, 1965.

KELLER *Intro & Letter:* Keller, H. *The Story of My Life.* New York: Doubleday, 1903.

KEROUAC *Intro:* Charters, A. *Kerouac.* San Francisco: Straight Arrow, 1973. *Story: Horace Mann Quarterly,* Spring 1940.

KIPLING *Intro:* Stewart, J.I.M. *Rudyard Kipling.* New York: Dodd, Mead, 1966. *Poems: School Boy Lyrics.* Lahore, 1881, published by his parents.

LEACOCK *Intro:* Legate, D.M. *Stephen Leacock.* New York: Doubleday, 1970. *Poem: The College Times,* Upper Canada College, Toronto, June 9, 1887.

LOWELL *Intro, Poem & Questionnaire:* Damon, S.F. *Amy Lowell.* New York: Anchor, 1966.

MARIE ANTOINETTE *Intro & Letter:* Van Doren, C. *Letters to Mother.* Great Neck, N.Y.: Channel, 1959.

MARX *Intro 1, Poems & Novel:* From a book of verse dedicated by Marx to his father, Heinrich, on his birthday and written before April 12, 1837. Reprinted in *Karl Marx, Frederick Engels: Collected Works,* vol. 1. New York: International Publishers, 1975. *Intro 2 & Play translation:* Payne, R. *The Unknown Karl Marx.* New York: NYU Press, 1971.

MELVILLE *Intro:* Gilman, W.H. *Melville's Early Life and "Redburn."* New York: NYU Press, 1951. *Letters:* Davis, M.R., ed. *Letters of Herman Melville.* New Haven: Yale U Press, 1960.

MILLAY *Letter:* Macdougall, A.R. *Letters of Edna St. Vincent Millay.* New York: Harper, 1952. *Poem: St. Nicholas Magazine,* Aug. 1907.

MOZART *Intro:* Reprinted from Deutsch, O.E. *Mozart: A Documentary Biography.* Stanford, Cal.: Stanford U. Press, 1966. *Catalog:* Holmes. E. *The Life of Mozart.* London, 1845. *Letters:* Anderson, E., ed. *Letters of Mozart and His Family,* vol. 1. London: Macmillan, 1938.

MUGGERIDGE *Intro:* Muggeridge, M. *The Green Stick.* New York: William Morrow, 1972.

NAPOLEON *Intro & Poem:* Frayling, C. *Napoleon Wrote Fiction.* New York: St. Martins Press, 1972.

NEWTON *Intro 1:* Dr. Stukeley. *Letters to Dr. Richard Mead.* 1727. *Account of youth:* Timbs, J. *School-Days of Eminent Men.* Columbus, Ohio: Follett & Foster, 1860. *Intro 2:* Manuel, F.E. *A Portrait of Isaac Newton.* Cambridge: Harvard U Press, 1968. *Notebook:* "Morgan Notebook," J.P. Morgan Library, New York. (Reprinted in Greenstreet, see below.) *Intro 3 & Inscription:* Greenstreet, W.J., ed. *Isaac Newton 1642-1727, a Memorial Volume.* Chapter by J.A. Holden. London: George Bell, 1927.
NIETZSCHE *Intro:* Frenzel, I. *Friedrich Nietzsche: An Illustrated Biography.* Transl. by J. Neugroschel. New York: Pegasus, 1. *Letter:* Levy, O., ed. *Selected Letters of Friedrich Nietzsche.* New York: Doubleday, 1921.
NIN *Intro:* Stuhlmann, G., ed. *The Diary of Anaïs Nin.* New York: Harcourt, Brace Jovanovitch, 1971. *Diary: Birth 2,* New York, 1959.
NIXON Kornitzer, B. *The Real Nixon.* Chicago: Rand McNally, 1960.
ONASSIS *Intro:* Bouvier (Radziwill), L. *One Special Summer.* New York: Delacorte, 1974. *Anecdote:* Bouvier (Onassis), J. *Ibid.*
ORWELL Intro & Afterword: Stansky, P., & Abrahams, W. *The Unknown Orwell.* New York: Knopf, 1972. *Poem: Henley and South Oxfordshire Standard,* Oct. 2, 1914. Reprinted in Stansky & Abrahams, *op. cit.*
PASCAL *Intro:* Bishop, M. *Pascal.* New York: Greenwood, 1968. *Essay:* Chevalier, J. *Oeuvres Complètes.* Paris: Librairie Gallimard, 1954. Translated for this book by Marie Annick Brown and Dan Moshenberg.
PEACOCK *Intro & Letter:* Wheeler, G.C. *Letters to Mother.* London: Allen & Unwin, 1933.
PICASSO *Intro & Drawings:* Cirlot, J.E. *Picasso: Birth of a Genius.* London: P. Elek, 1972. *Newspaper clipping: NY Post,* June 13, 1972.
PLATH *Intro:* Plath, S. *Letters Home.* Plath, A.S., ed. New York: Harper & Row, 1975. *Story & Afterword: Seventeen,* August, 1950.
POE *Intro 1 & Letters:* Ostrom, J.W., ed. *Letters of E.A. Poe.* Cambridge: Harvard U Press, 1949. *Intro 2:* Quinn, A.H. *E.A. Poe: A Critical Biography.* New York: Appleton Century, 1941. *Intro 3:* Bittner, W. *Poe, a biography.* Boston: Little Brown-Atlantic Press Monthly, 1962.
POLLOCK *Intro & Letters.* Friedman, B.H. *Jackson Pollock.* New York: McGraw-Hill, 1972.
POPE *Poem 1:* Boynton, H.W., ed. *The Complete Poetical Works,* Cambridge Edition. Cambridge: Houghton, Mifflin, 1903, 31. *Intro 2:* Sherburn, G., ed. *Correspondence of Alexander Pope.* Oxford: Oxford U Press, 1956. *Poem 2:* Sherburn, G. *The Early Career of Alexander Pope.* Oxford: Clarendon Press, 1934.
ROCKEFELLER *Intro & Letter:* Morris, J.A. *Nelson Rockefeller: A Biography.* New York: Harper, 1960.
ROOSEVELT, E. *Intro & Story:* Lash, J.P. *Eleanor and Franklin.* New York: Norton, 1971.
ROOSEVELT, F.D. *Intro:* Davis, K.S. *F.D. Roosevelt.* New York: Putnams, 1971. *Story: Harvard Advocate,* February, 1903.
ROOSEVELT, T. *Intro 1 & Diary:* Hagedorn, H. *The Boys Life of T. Roosevelt.* New York: Harper, 1919. *Intro 2 & Story:* Robinson, C.R. *My Brother Theodore Roosevelt.* New York: Scribners, 1921.
RUSSELL *Intro & Diary: The Autobiography of Bertrand Russell.* New York: Little Brown, 1967.
SALINGER *Intro, Song & Afterword:* Grunwald, H.A., ed. *Salinger.* New York: Harper & Row, 1962.
SCHUBERT *Intros:* Fisher, R.B. *Musical Prodigies.* New York: Association Press, 1973. *Letter:* Reprinted in Wheeler, O., & Deutscher, S. *Franz Schubert.* New York: Dutton, 1939. *Songs: Schubert's Complete Works.* Dover reprint of 19th century Breitkopf & Hartel edition. *Illustration:* Edward Ardizzone.
SHAW *Intro & Letter 1:* Shaw, B. *Collected Letters.* Laurence, D.H., ed. New York: Dodd, Mead, 1965. *Intro 2:* Weintraub, S., ed. *Shaw: An Autobiography, 1856-1898.* New York: Weybright & Talley, 1969. *Letter 2: Public Opinion,* April 3, 1875.
SHELLEY *Intro:* Medwin, T. *The Life of P.B. Shelley.* London: Oxford U Press, 1913. *Chapters:* London: G. Wilkie & J. Robinson, 1810. *Afterword:* Holmes, R. *Shelley: The Pursuit.* London: Weidenfeld & Nicolson, 1974.
SOUTHEY *Intro:* Haller, W. *The Early Life of Robert Southey.* New York: Columbia U Press, 1975. *Article: The Flagellant,* March 29, 1792. Via Beinecke Library, Yale University Libraries.
STEVENSON *Letter & Afterword:* Wheeler, G.C., ed. *Letters to Mother.* London: Allen & Unwin, 1933.
THOMAS *Intro & Afterward:* Sinclair, A. *Dylan Thomas: No Man More Magical.* New York: Holt, Rinehart & Winston, 1975. *Letter:* Fitzgibbon, C., ed. *Selected Letters of Dylan Thomas.* New York: New Directions, 1965.
THURBER *Intro:* Bernstein, B. *Thurber.* New York: Dodd Mead, 1975. *Prophecy:* From typescript in Thurber Archives, Ohio State University, Columbus, Ohio.
TOLSTOY *Intro:* Simmons, E.J. *Leo Tolstoy,* vol. 1. New York: Little Brown-Atlantic Monthly Press, 1945-6. *Diary: Diaries of Leo Tolstoy. Trans. by C.J. Hogarth & A. Sirmis. New York: Dutton, 1917.*
TWAIN *Intro & Letter:* Brashear, M.M. *Mark Twain: Son of Missouri.* Chapel Hill: U. North Carolina Press, 1934.
VAN GOGH *Intro:* Wallace, R. *The World of V. Van Gogh.* New York: Time-Life, 1969. *Drawings:* Reprinted by Tralbaut, M.E., & Lausanne, E. *Vincent Van Gogh.* New York: Viking, 1960.
QUEEN VICTORIA *Intro:* Longford, E. *Queen Victoria.* New York: Harper & Row, 1964. *Journal:* Queen Victoria's Private Journal, The Royal Archives. Reprinted in Barton, J. *The Hollow Crown.* London: Hamish, 1962.
VIDAL *Intro:* White, R.L. *Gore Vidal.* New York: Twayne, 1968. *Story: Phillips Exeter Review,* Fall, 1942.
WAUGH *Intro:* Sykes, C. *Evelyn Waugh.* New York: Little Brown, 1975. *Diary:* Davie, M., ed. *The Diaries of Evelyn Waugh.* London: Weidenfeld & Nicolson, 1976.
WELLS *Intro & Story:* Ray, G.N., ed. *The Desert Daisy* (facsimile edition with illustrations). Carbondale, Ill. S. Illinois U. Press: 1957.
WHEATLEY *Poem:* Renfro, H., ed. *The Life and Works of Phillis Wheatley.* Washington: (no publisher given), 1916. Reprint of 1773 London edition. *Attestation:* Mason, J.D., Jr., ed. *The Poems of Phillis Wheatley.* Chapel Hill: U. North Carolina Press, 1966.
WHISTLER *Intro:* Weintraub, S. *Whistler.* London: Weybright & Talley, 1974. *Poem:* Elbogen, R. *Dearest Mother.* New York: L.B. Fischer, 1942.
WHITMAN *Intro:* Bucke, R.M. *The Complete Writings of Walt Whitman.* New York: NYU Press, 1963.
WILLIAMS *Intros & Poems:* Williams, T. *Memoirs.* New York: Doubleday, 1975. *Story:* Reprinted in *The Pulps.* New York: Chelsea, 1976.
WILSON *Intro & Diary:* Wilson, E. *A Prelude.* New York: Farrar, Straus & Giroux, 1967.